The Rise of Management
Consulting in Britain

T0331457

Modern Economic and Social History Series

General Editor: Derek H. Aldcroft

Titles in this series include:

The Rise of Management Consulting in Britain

MICHAEL FERGUSON

Routledge
Taylor & Francis Group

LONDON AND NEW YORK

First published 2002 by Ashgate Publishing

Reissued 2019 by Routledge
2 Park Square, Milton Park, Abingdon, Oxon, OX14 4RN
52 Vanderbilt Avenue, New York, NY 10017

Routledge is an imprint of the Taylor & Francis Group, an informa business

Publisher's Note
The publisher has gone to great lengths to ensure the quality of this reprint but points out that some imperfections in the original copies may be apparent.

Disclaimer
The publisher has made every effort to trace copyright holders and welcomes correspondence from those they have been unable to contact.

A Library of Congress record exists under LC control number:

ISBN 13: 978-1-138-74039-6 (hbk)
ISBN 13: 978-1-138-74037-2 (pbk)
ISBN 13: 978-1-315-18353-4 (ebk)

Contents

List of Tables

Preface

The profession of management consultancy service in Britain has a long background history of valuable contribution to the betterment and progressive advancement of operational and managerial performance in the industrial and commercial sectors, and as well in the financial domain, in local authority services and administration and in later periods even among Government Departments. Broadly, however, there has been during all the decades inadequate public understanding of the realities of that service and of the profession. The latter has recurrently been the butt of comedy, or parody and of derision, that last utterly not deserved.

Dr Michael Ferguson has rendered to our nation a significant and valuable presentation of the long evolution of that service and of its gestation into the level of profession, emerging from very small beginnings. This study is the outcome of long and in-depth research, comprehensive in its scope, for which the author very deservedly gained award of the Doctorate of Philosophy in Management History, his thesis absorbed into the earlier chapters of the volume. The study extends and improves upon the earlier classics from Stanley Hyman, Laura Tatham and Patricia Tisdall, forming a valuable and significant addendum to the literature in management studies, contributing as well to according to the management consultancy profession its due recognition.

E.F.L. Brech
Doctor of Philosophy in Management History

Acknowledgements

It is inevitable that when compiling a history of this nature that many individuals and organisations will have provided support in some form or another, both in the course of the research and in the compilation of the final text. This history was complicated because it was subject to two pieces of research, initially for the period 1869 to 1965 as a focus for my PhD, and the remainder of the period to the present day in order to bring the account up to date. Whilst it would not be possible to acknowledge all that have helped throughout – these are too numerous to mention here but all are recognised in this dedication – I can acknowledge the support I have received directly in both phases of my research.

I am especially grateful to Professor Andrew Thomson who guided me through the PhD programme at the Business School of The Open University. His steady and thorough approach to research was undoubtedly a crucial factor in my ultimate success. I would also like to acknowledge the help and guidance that I received from John Wilson, both in the submission of my thesis and in reviewing many of the chapters that appear in this volume. Outside of academia a large number of individuals and organisations have played a significant role in supplying me with the information and data that underpins this history. Consultants past and present all deserve a mention, especially those who served in INBUCON, Harold Whitehead and Partners, Urwick, Orr and Partners, Production Engineering Limited, PA Consulting Group and PricewaterhouseCoopers. I would also like to acknowledge the help I have received from the Management Consultancies Association, the Institute of Management Consultancy, the Institute of Management and FEACO.

I would like to make a special mention of Edward Brech who throughout the whole of my research and the compilation of both texts, my thesis and this history, has always been there when I needed assistance and advice. His knowledge of business and management history is unparalleled. He tirelessly waded through numerous versions of this text, providing both editorial support and historical context whenever it was needed.

Finally, none of this would have been possible without the support of my wife Glenda, whose never-ending patience and encouragement provided me with the inspiration to complete the task. It is to Glenda that I dedicate this book.

Mike Ferguson

Modern Economic and Social History Series
General Editors Preface

Economic and social history has been a flourishing subject of scholarly study during recent decades. Not only has the volume of literature increased enormously but the range of interest in time, space and subject matter has broadened considerably so that today there are many sub-branches of the subject which have developed considerable status in their own right.

One of the aims of this series is to encourage the publication of scholarly monographs on any aspect of modern economic and social history. The geographical coverage is worldwide and contributions on non-British themes will be especially welcome. While emphasis will be placed on works embodying original research, it is also intended that the series should provide the opportunity to publish studies of a more general and thematic nature which offer a reappraisal or critical analysis of major issues of debate.

Derek H. Aldcroft

Manchester Metropolitan University

To Glenda, without whose support this history would not have been possible

CHAPTER 1

The Background to Management Consulting

Bringing together the various threads in order to map the history of management consulting in Britain has been a similar exercise to that of completing a jigsaw puzzle in which a number of the important pieces are missing. One major piece of this particular puzzle, and the one that has proved the most elusive, is identifying that point in time when management consulting first became established as a form of service in Britain. Potentially, it could have coincided with the inception of management itself, the dating of which has proven to be equally problematic because the act of management has existed ever since human activities have involved organisation and co-operation in some form or another (Urwick and Brech 1946b).[1]

The one primary reason why it has been difficult to identify when management consultants first offered their services in Britain is because records have not been discovered to make identification possible. In the early days of management consulting individuals engaged in this field tended to be either sole practitioners or they worked in small partnerships and records have simply not survived. In fact, the first management consulting company was not established in Britain until 1926 and it is really from that point onwards that information has become available.[2] This may also partly explain why the activities of early consultant pioneers have escaped the notice of business historians and other interested parties. To complicate identification further, in the early days the practice of advertising services was simply not carried out, that is with very few exceptions. Clients generally became aware of the existence of such men either through direct contact by the consultant himself, the more usual method, or via some form of recommendation, possibly from other satisfied clients.[3] Other avenues of recognition included articles written by these men in journals and other publications, or through the papers delivered by them at professional and other forms of meeting.

This opening chapter is concerned with setting the scene for a review of the history of management consulting in Britain for the period from the 1860s to the present day; to help achieve this there are three distinct aims. Firstly, no historical review could be carried out without a clear focus. The history of management consulting is no exception and, therefore, the first section is concerned with the development of a definition of management consulting. Secondly, it is necessary to provide a summary account of Britain's business history in the period leading up to and during the period when management consulting services first commenced in this country. This helps to provide an explanation both as to why consulting services were first provided and of the form that those services took. Finally, no history of management consulting would be complete without some knowledge of the theoretical concepts and practical application that underpinned the development and trends within business and management. Such factors also helped shape the form of services provided by the consultants.

Consulting and Consultants

Britain's position as world leader in technological development, manufacturing and trade seemed secure during the early period of the Industrial Revolution. Britain was the first industrialising nation and, consequently, enjoyed a dominant position in the global marketplace at that time. By the mid-nineteenth century the picture was changing. The newly industrialising nations, exemplified by the United States and Germany, effectively challenged this position and Britain had lost its dominance in both overseas and domestic markets. From the perspective of the history of management consulting in Britain it is probably no accident that the first identified instance of a management consultant service occurred in the second half of the nineteenth century. Nonetheless it would be a mistake to conclude that Britain's waning industrial might brought with it a new phoenix to boost its industrial position. The early management consultants were not giants in the mythological sense, providing new vigour to a declining industrial base. Their numbers were too few. But from those small beginnings in the nineteenth century, management consultancy was eventually established and through the process of time, as their numbers increased and the range of services they provided widened, management consulting's position as a sought-after source of advice and assistance to business and governments became established.

At the outset one important question needs addressing; what is a management consultant? Robert Townsend (1970), in his sometimes humorous examination of business practice, suggests that management consultants are '…people who borrow your watch and tell you what time it is and then walk off with it'. This rather cynical view of the American consultancy market thirty years ago suggests that relationships between clients and consultants were and are not always positive. One reason for this might be that services provided by some consultants failed to meet the expectations of their clients. Part of the reason may be that not all those who describe themselves as management consultants actually are; many individuals and organisations advertise themselves as consultants and consultancies without providing a service of a full consultancy nature.[4] Other explanations may centre on the competence of individuals or the provision of unrealistic expectations. Whatever the reason, there is a need to explicitly describe the role of a management consultant, if only to separate out those for whom management consulting is a business title only.

Successful management consultants were and are involved in improvements to the process of management within client firms. In the pioneering days of management consulting (covered in Chapters 2 and 3) consultants were engaged in activities in support of management across a range of operational areas in manufacturing and related industries. In other words, they were concerned with the day-to-day operations of the business rather than the strategic decision-making processes. Initially, assignments were concerned with the management of production processes, both at the shop-floor level and within the administrative set-up of the businesses. In the early days of consultancy outside interference in those areas associated with strategic decision-making was considered taboo, the role being the sole preserve of those born to the task. Attitudes reflected the situation that '…managers are born, not made' (Wilson 1995). This attitudinal stance only slowly changed, with changing attitudes becoming more noticeable in the post Second World War period, and this was reflected in the form of services provided by management consultants. Today involvement in areas associated with production management is but one aspect of management consultancy and delving into the strategic areas of business is as common as improving operational performance.

The range of services provided by consultants did not stand still; they evolved and widened over time to take account of the changing circumstances found within the various industrial and commercial settings. Later, in the period after the Second World War and onwards, consultants were found operating within Government Departments. From a definitional perspective, this meant that the role of the consultant also evolved over time; it still continues to evolve even today as the boundaries of management consulting are pushed even wider. Nevertheless, it is possible to provide an outline definition of a management consultant, identifying the core elements of the role through an acceptance of the evolving service base and the levels within the firm to which it is applied.

The consultant is a specialist provider of services in support of management in exchange for a fee. Initially, definitions of consultants identified their independent nature in not being direct employees of the firm. Such definitions have changed over time to bring them in line with the view that internal consultants can also exercise a level of independence in carrying out their tasks.[5] Nevertheless, any definition of a consultant must identify their impartiality, to the extent that he or she is free from the internal political wranglings of the firm. Their advice should have no preconceptions; it should be objective and honest. Such advice is concerned with all the elements of management and would fit within the broad areas of strategy, policy, markets, organisation, and procedures and methods at the various levels within the firm (Boakes 1999).

From a historical perspective, the areas identified above are those that apply now and these have not always been present within the portfolio of services provided by management consultants throughout their history. Similarly, the categorisation of services has also changed, with the current categories differing from those that applied in the early period of the consultants' history.[6] For example, information technology lies at the heart of consulting today, both as a distinctive service area and as an aid to consulting. In the early years some individuals and companies did not follow the general trend of providing services in production management as a core focus. Some of the early consultants were concerned with the marketing and sales aspects of a client's business, although instances of work in these areas were relatively rare. This was because management consultants, by and large, either came from an engineering or accountancy background, at least during the first half of the twentieth century. Regardless of background, however, all consultants require knowledge of the particular operational environment in which they are involved, as well as an interest and experience in management.

As a consequence of their involvement in an organisation consultants develop a plan determined through some form of analysis, and having made recommendations are at the point in the series of events for which those engaged in a purely advisory capacity would have completed their task. This is the point, in definitional terms, which separates management consultants from those providing services of an advisory nature whose responsibility ends with the presentation of their recommendations. From here on, to be a consultant, part of the role is to provide assistance in the execution of the recommended plans where such assistance is required. The management consultant is, therefore, more than a provider of advice on payment of a fee. The consultant is responsible for ensuring that solutions are fully effective, only handing over the remaining portion of responsibility to the client at the conclusion of the assignment. In this way, solutions that have to be modified as a consequence of their practical application, or those that require further translation in the operational setting, are carried out under the supervision of the consultant. In succinct terms, the consultant is employed to identify and correct deficiencies and weaknesses in the firm, as well as to search, identify and define opportunities for improvement where that is appropriate.

The definition is complicated because traditionally management consultants have also played their part in the continuing development of managers. Chapter 7 specifically deals with this aspect of consultancy work, although instances of consultant involvement in the broad fields of management education and training can be found throughout this book. In parallel with this and throughout the history of management consulting, less formalised methods have also resulted from the involvement in consultants in client firms. For example, Kubr (1977) points toward the consequential development of client personnel through observation and involvement with the consultant when problem solving is taking place during an assignment. Therefore consultants also have a role to play in the continuing development of managers and client personnel as part of the consulting function.

Today, management consulting is an accepted and commonplace form of service, but this has not always been the case. Management consulting has been labelled in many different ways at different times and some labels have engendered fear amongst the working population, for example in the early years the title 'efficiency engineer' was linked to the activities of those providing consultancy services. Many of the early consultants were engineers by profession and improvements to manufacturing efficiency were the hallmark of their service. Consultants were known as 'industrial engineers', 'consulting engineers' or 'field engineers', amongst other titles. 'Management consultant', as a job title or as a descriptive label, is the more recent form of terminology dating from the post 1930s setting within Britain. The first instance of the usage of the term 'consulting' in a business title occurred in 1919 with the formation of the partnership of Brindley and Elbourne (see Chapter 2). For the purpose of this history management consulting and management consultants, as generic norms, are applied in all instances, unless some other form of terminology has specific relevance to the particular setting being described.

An Outline History of Britain's Business Environment

There appears to be little doubt, and this history supports this contention, that the growth of management consulting in Britain has in part been influenced by wider trends in Britain's economic and business environments. A pocket history in but a few pages cannot possibly hope to provide a comprehensive account of the changing nature of Britain's businesses. In any event there are a number of volumes in existence that perform this role very well.[7] The purpose of this part of the chapter is to provide an outline sketch of some of the main events that occurred within Britain in the period leading up to and during the commencement of management consultancy services.

During the Industrial Revolution, particularly during the period of the latter part of the eighteenth and the beginning of the nineteenth centuries, production in industries such as textiles, engineering, timber and mining within Britain tended to be widespread; generally the size of enterprises was relatively small, although there were exceptions. These enterprises, workshops and domestic arrangements, were predominantly family owned and controlled, and after the 1770s many of them were located near to cheaper sources of labour and water (More 1989). During the nineteenth century, industry began to concentrate in urban areas where economies of scale and the use of steam power helped facilitate change. By the mid-1880s there was an increasing number of consulting engineers who acted as salesmen abroad; this was made possible because of seminal events such as the birth of railways. These consulting engineers working in countries outside of Britain, as well as within it, sold railway installations, factories, harbours, and a whole host of major structures and other forms of installation. Orders for specifications to fulfil their clients' requirements were passed on to a multiplicity of workshops and factories specialising in individual areas of manufacturing. This was a complex process of ordering, manufacture and eventual passage of goods for assembly and installation under the control of the consulting engineers themselves.

In the textile industry from the late eighteenth century onwards, a plethora of textile manufacturers, specialising in their own particular areas of production, produced only what was asked of them. In support of this structure, and intimate to the overall process, were merchants, particularly for colonial markets servicing a growing export trade. These merchants initially operated in Liverpool and Manchester, and later in London, acting as the sales managers for the myriad numbers of small firms that tended to concentrate on only one process within the whole scope of textile production. The situation in textiles was similar to that of engineering, concerning a complex series of orders being fed into a range of manufacturers for eventual transmission to fulfil client requirements. Other industries were similarly affected, for example within furnishings and in household goods. During this overall period of expansion, the general population of Britain was also growing, for example between 1855 and 1900 the population increased by more than 50 per cent (Feinstein 1976). Civic services (such as they were) and other services were expanding to cope with the needs of a growing population, also being serviced by this myriad number of predominantly small-scale manufacturing units.[8] This is emphasised through the situation in which output in industrial production and manufacturing had almost tripled during the same period, even though Britain's share of world production fell (Pollard 1965).

Expansion was brought about, in some measure, through the realisation of some within industry that they were in a position to start up on their own account. Many became journeymen in the first instance working for other employers, eventually moving on to setting up their own workshops. Some of these businesses, albeit largely small-scale, grew from workshops into company formations, especially during the latter part of the nineteenth century. This provided those companies with the opportunity to bring in outside money to stimulate further expansion, although family ownership and self-investment meant that little outside money was ever raised, at least until the early-twentieth century (Wilson 1995).

More generally in Britain there was a growing realisation of inefficiencies in the production process. This failing situation came to a head in the late 1860s and was a subject of discussion about the Paris Exposition of 1867 which demonstrated that Britain had lost its primacy in some of the major manufacturing industries and it was significantly losing trade to competitors abroad. Jeremy (1998) highlighted this situation and pointed towards the erosion of the UK share of world manufacturing exports during the twentieth century, stressing inefficient management, poor productivity and non-competitive wage rates as major factors. It was inevitable that much larger economies caught up and overtook Britain as the major producer in the world marketplace. More specifically these inefficiencies were highlighted by concerns expressed within the engineering industry, echoed through the media of the day. For example, two editorial articles in *The Engineer* in 1867 and 1869 pointed to some of the deficiencies in the British industrial environment of the nineteenth century.[9] Both of these articles focused on the fact that consulting engineers were not very conscious about costing or even the processes from which the costings were derived. Part of the reason for this was that the consulting engineers did not carry out costing exercises themselves but passed this responsibility on to others, namely the manufacturers, and this generally resulted in sloppy estimates. Consequently, the form of services provided by the early consultants were initially concerned with the development and implementation of methodologies in relation to costing; this enabled estimating and pricing to be carried out more effectively. Additionally, the technical press of the day acknowledged that there were problems within the manufacturing sector concerning the meeting of deadlines, but they did not appear to emphasise it as a negative aspect of business; nowhere did they highlight the underlying cause that was a deficiency in the planning and control of operations. This was particularly the case concerning the smaller manufacturing units that were feeding in the component parts that were to be brought together to create, for example, a factory and all its equipment for the consulting engineers.

Such concerns were expressed in Frederic Smith's (1878) 'Workshop Management: A Manual for Masters and Men'. Smith was recognising that there was a management process and it could be learnt by others.[10] By the end of the nineteenth century, services in management consulting had expanded and were equally concerned with production efficiency, emphasising the central role of production planning and control. Such needs were emphasised through wider trends in mechanisation throughout industry and this was also an influencing factor in the need for greater efficiency within the workplace. Mechanisation had been predominantly found within the textile industry of the early-1800s, but as time progressed it also spread throughout Britain's industrial base (More 1989). This added complexities to the workplace and facilitated growth, both in terms of enterprises and in the speed of production. As organisations grew and mechanisation took hold the need for processes in support of production planning and control was further emphasised. In spite of criticisms in relation to industry at the time, commentators did not emphasise managerial deficiency as being a cause but instead pointed towards lack of education.[11] Whilst some improvements to occupational and general education had been occurring, it did not occur to anyone to highlight the relevance of it to industrial management in the manufacturing setting (Brech 2002e).[12] Frederic Smith, mentioned previously, referred to systematic methods within aspects of management, and several other writers also pointed out that management is a subject that can be learnt. What they were not saying was that management as a theory, a profession, a process, or a philosophy could be learnt, but rather it was managing in the manufacturing context that was being emphasised.[13]

By the turn of the century significant changes had taken place in the structure of manufacturing through the emergence of a greater number of larger-scale enterprises facilitated by waves of merger activity in the period after 1890 (Hannah 1976; Jeremy 1998; Wilson 1995). The first merger wave (1890-1906) was marked specifically by the pattern of industrial concentration, in that the majority of mergers involved the combination of firms within the same industry (Jeremy 1998). These larger-scale businesses, some of which were very large compared with the situation previously within individual industries, had to be systematic in their approach to conducting operations to make them more effective. For example, the Calico Printers' merger of 1899 involved the combination of 46 individual firms (Jeremy 1998). By 1907 it was the nineteenth largest employer in the United Kingdom with 20,500 employees (Wardley 1999).[14] As a historical note, the majority of companies ranked above the Calico Printers in terms of size of personnel employed were railway companies.

In terms of education and training, formal training for management or, for that matter, training for engineers in management techniques, was non-existent at that time, other than possibly some on-the-job or in-house schemes within the larger individual firms. During the nineteenth century and beyond Britain lagged behind competitor countries that were beginning to utilise educational establishments to train their engineers in business practices (Keeble 1992). This may be partly explained by the pervasive general belief that 'managers are born, not made' (Wilson 1995). Owners and managers of firms did not see the need for background knowledge, but instead believed that practical experience was the all-important factor. Within this general setting, the period of the nineteenth and early twentieth centuries, when Britain's industries were performing less well than their competitors abroad, there was sufficient justification to warrant the formation of services directed towards the support of management, both conceptually and operationally.

Management Theory and Practice

The practice of management is underpinned by theoretical knowledge (Wren 1994). That knowledge base and the practice of management itself, in a similar fashion to the business trends identified in the previous section, are directly related to the form of services provided by management consultants. Where such knowledge appears to move through phases of development, then the development and application of consultant services have also evolved similarly. General knowledge of the practice of management and the evolution of management thought in Britain will bring with it a greater understanding of the evolutionary trends in management consulting.

Management as a functional role, regardless of setting or position within an organisation, has been historically a controversial issue in terms of definitional content, and remains so to the present day. The reason for this may be partly related to the view that the role of the manager is different among different operational and functional settings. Many commentators have struggled with the notion that it is possible to analyse the job of a manager and present a coherent breakdown of the various elements contained within the role; that is the aspects of the managerial function as distinct from the technical requirements needed to fulfil a particular job. Early writers on management, for example Joseph Slater Lewis (1896), attempted to describe the principles and develop the application of management in practical settings. Taking definition a stage further, Henri Fayol, working from the top downwards, developed a definition of management in which its function was broken down into a series of elements: planning, organising, command, co-ordination and control (Storrs 1954).

One definition that has stood the test of time, primarily because credible challenge has been absent, is that presented by E.F.L. Brech (1953) in his publication 'The Principles and Practice of Management'.[15] This was at least until the development of 'National Management Standards' produced by the Management Charter Initiative (1991) more recently and, in any event, these largely supported Brech's treatise. The model developed by Brech is still relevant and a review of the services provided by management consultants confirms their association with it.

Within Brech's model there are four elements: planning, motivation, co-ordination and control. He further suggested that management is a process of exercising responsibility for planning, arranging and conducting the activities of an enterprise. This includes its people and its other aspects, both tangible and intangible. Management can be found at all levels within the firm where, ideally, they all work towards a common task or known objective. Within the process of exercising responsibility can be found each of the elements. Whilst it is possible to describe each separately, in reality they are interlinked. The emphasis of each element within any particular setting will vary but is, nonetheless, always present.

Planning The first element 'planning' is concerned with determining the broad lines of approach; its strategy, the time-frame within which the strategy fits, the plan of action, the budget and the structure of the organisation. It concerns effecting the appropriate methods to facilitate positive action, which itself includes determining the working environment and the setting of standards under which the various assets operate. Planning involves the setting of targets and, by its very nature, determining the costs and the viewed outcome of them. In real terms, planning can be associated with the strategic as well as the operational aspects of the business. The part played by individuals in the planning process can depend

THE BACKGROUND TO MANAGEMENT CONSULTING

upon their position within the organisation, with strategic decision-making (e.g. high level planning) being the preserve of those who have responsibility for the overall direction of the organisation. This element of management was an increasing concern of management consultants in the post-Second World War period. However, planning at this level is largely to do with policy and the development of the organisational structure of the firm. Within the various operational and administrative areas of the firm the planning function is more to do with supporting strategy rather than with influencing it. These lower-order planning tasks and techniques were a key focus of management consultants in their early years; these included production planning and control, and methods and time study. Today, project management and various computer modelling techniques are examples of modern day equivalents.

Control A parallel activity to that of planning, 'control' is to do with ensuring that performance is directed at, and kept within, the pre-determined plans and changing the operational aspects of those plans in the light of varying circumstances. In real terms, the elements of planning and control are seamlessly linked into a single process. These are often supported through the overt application of information directed towards the development and application of metrics to ensure that targets are met and expectations are realised. For example, utilisation of management accounting techniques can provide the level of assurance that targets and actual performance become and remain one and the same thing. Management consultants have developed, and continue to develop, methodologies linked with the element of control. Both planning and controlling are partly achieved through the third element, co-ordination.

Co-ordination The penultimate element 'co-ordination' is the bringing together of the apparently disparate activities and resources of an organisation towards the common aim. It is the pivotal mechanism for ensuring that effort is optimised and directed towards the determined goal under the umbrella of the 'team', ensuring where possible a harmonious approach to effect positive action. The activities of planning and control should naturally contribute and strengthen co-ordination. By and large, it is the skill of the manager that is responsible for enabling co-ordination to be achieved. In much the same way that skill has a role to play in co-ordination, the final element, motivation, is the all-important human aspect.

Motivation Promoted by the positive intervention of supervision, 'motivation' is concerned with concepts such as morale, loyalty, pride, team working, and so on. These human relations aspects of the management function are at the heart of many of the consultants' services. Some of these services are extremely specialised, but in the main the human element was and is a natural factor in the success of consultancy assignments and in the change process generally.

All of these elements have a role to play and are rarely considered in isolation. The success or failure of any management task will depend on the skills of the individual and each element should be exercised to full advantage within whatever setting is appropriate at the particular time, changing in emphasis in relation to one another dependent upon the particular setting in which they are being employed. Each can be described individually, but in practice they inter-link and support one another. For example, the business of management can be found in the areas of marketing and sales, and within production and manufacturing. It is also concerned with the personnel function and human activity, and has a role within financial administration and control, as well as being found within the supporting services of the business. Management is not just to do with the overall control of the business. It can be found at all levels and within all environments.

Management theory (thought) underpins the practice of management. In the British context management thought has been described as the formalisation of that body of knowledge, in recorded form, utilised to effect improvement to management practice (Child 1969). This has, historically, been through the efforts of a range of individuals for the perceived common good. These individuals have included practising managers and consultants, and in the post Second World War period social scientists, who at different times have contributed to that body of knowledge. Historically, that collective was described as the 'management movement'. More recently, individuals associated with the development of the theory of management have simply been described as gurus, many of whom are themselves practising consultants. Child suggested that management thought was largely the concern of only a minority of individuals, collectively attracting little attention in terms of the academic community.[16] A review of the historical situation confirms this contention.

In the second half of the nineteenth century Britain was dominated by laissez-faire and self-help economics, both in terms of industrial philosophy and industrial practice. This was reflected in a concept of 'father knows best' in terms of employer/labour relations; unions were regarded as unwelcome in terms of interference in the running of the firm. It is within this period that the control of labour as an economic commodity was seen as key to the success of many enterprises. Industrial welfare policies, present within some firms at that time, did not feature strongly as a model for improved worker performance. Little wonder that in the period of the late-ninteenth century, consultancy services were concerned with developing costing methodologies for clients and improving productive performance.

Just before the First World War a few notable employers were challenging the notion of laissez-faire as a working model; some of these were Quakers and others included progressive businessmen such as Hans Renold (Child 1969). Before that in the nineteenth century other pioneers such as Charles Babbage had concentrated on more 'scientific' methods of management. Babbage was a mathematician, but in his book (1832) 'On the Economy of Machinery and Manufactures' he did not concern himself with the design and construction of machines, rather he was concerned with their use and the organisation of labour (Urwick and Brech 1946a). Scientific, in this sense, included the division of labour and efficiencies within the workplace. In effect, Babbage emphasised the use of mathematics in determining operations of various kinds, including the timing of work, the layout of machinery in factories and the importance of the human factor in engendering worker co-operation. Consequently, some regarded Babbage as one of the principal originators of modern management theory. Notable, therefore, at the end of the nineteenth century there were theories and practices associated with scientific management. These were largely formalised by management pioneers in the United States, with 'scientific' principles and practices originating through reactions to the growing size of firms and the increasing complexities of new technology. In the vanguard of the development of these theories was Frederick Winslow Taylor and the concepts of models for raising industrial productivity (Child 1969; Wren 1994).[17] Critics of scientific management accused it of speeding up the production process at the expense of workers, viewing them merely as tools to be employed in order to raise profits.

In parallel with these developments within Britain there existed a movement that emphasised the importance of elements within the production process. These elements included costing, production planning and control, stock control and various administrative techniques to aid improvements to efficiency and the raising of productivity overall. Leading exponents of this movement included Joseph Slater Lewis (1896), Edward Tregaskis Elbourne (1914), and Dempster Smith and Philip Pickworth (1914) who compiled milestone publications on these subjects.[18] The concentration on consultancy services associated with the production function and the general scientific management movement became a feature of the first few decades of the twentieth century in Britain.

In the post-First World War period, and to a lesser extent before that, recognition of the managerial function as a separate entity from that of ownership of the enterprise was beginning to emerge, albeit in a minority of instances. Such recognition was emphasised through the formation of the Institute of Industrial Administration in 1919-1920 (Rose 1954). In parallel with these conceptual developments a number of early textbooks and important publications appeared highlighting and explaining management techniques that supported the concept of industrial efficiency. Also during that period there was the early stirring of movements towards the application of policies that subsumed human relations into its core. This was partly as a reaction to the perceived negatives of scientific management and techniques to improve industrial efficiency at the expense of the worker. Following on from the immediate post-First World War period, management thought progressed to subsume concepts such as management as a profession, echoed through Sheldon's (1924) publication 'Philosophy of Management'. Also during that period a number of other textbooks and papers appeared that were written by manufacturing managers and the early, consultants, forming a growing base of literature that tended to be disregarded by the academic community at large. At the same time that some of these operational managers were turning their thoughts to print there was a growing movement in Britain towards seeking worker co-operation' in the workplace. This co-operation was echoed through the formation of worker committees and the emphasis on supervision to bring the workforce along in order to improve productive output (Child 1969). Overarching all this, the general fields that encompassed industrial efficiency witnessed the arrival in Britain of techniques such as work measurement and the involvement of industrial psychologists. These concerned themselves with studying fatigue, monotony, and the impact on the worker of the effects of the physical environment and payment incentive schemes, and so on. Just the techniques that had been developed and employed by Charles Eugene Bedaux for use in Britain from 1923 onwards (see Chapters 2, 3 and 4). These techniques, in one form and another, became the mainstay of consultancy services to the mid-1960s in Britain.

Two events occurred in the 1920s that brought the attention of management to the wider community. The first of these, the Liberal Party *Yellow Book* of 1927, called for the formation of an institute of management for the dissemination of knowledge in the management function. The second event, the World Economic Conference in Geneva in 1927, used the term 'rationalisation' to describe systematic management and Urwick (1929) was invited by the CIOS International Committee to write 'The Meaning of Rationalisation'.[19] During the latter part of the 1920s and the early 1930s a number of background events changed the context within which management was viewed. These events included the formation of the Management Research Groups (MRGs) for the exchange and experience of information. In addition, MRGs sponsored a proposed draft constitution for a British institution of management, even though nothing was done about it at that time.[20] During the 1930s Britain went into depression, causing the state of the economy to become the central focus at that time in terms of Britain's industrial well-being. Also during the 1930s the formation of two professional bodies (The Works Management Association in 1931 and The Office Management Association in 1932) reflected the first practical and serious efforts to form management associations in the UK. All of these events, together with the formation of The Confederation of Management Associations in 1934 as a co-ordinating framework, the re-commencement of the Oxford Management Conferences in 1935 and the International Management Congress of 1935 in London (the first time it had been held in this country) attracted a good deal of public attention to the role of management.

The period of the Second World War and thereafter witnessed the influence of the human relations movement and the increasing significance of management principles (Child 1969).[21] The period commenced with considerable public criticism of managerial inefficiencies (see Chapters 5 and 6). This public criticism centred on ineffective performance and the treatment of the worker. Occurring at the same time was the formation of the British Institute of Management in 1947; set up as a non-profit-making, non-political central management organisation. At a governmental level the post-war period was emphasised through reconstruction and the need to improve industrial and commercial productivity.[22] It is within such an environment that consultant services were deployed in support of such initiatives, both centrally and at the level of the firm (specifically, see Chapter 6). Criticisms of the human relations approach and some of the developments of the principles of management were echoed within a growing body of social science research (Child 1969). Such research indicated that problems existed within the then traditional approach to management theory. This criticism largely stemmed from the fact that management theory was based on generalisms rather than the specific problems associated with individual firms. Social scientists suggested that enterprises should be viewed individually and not subjected to generalised theories that may or may not have relevance within their particular settings.

The development of general theories of management continues to the present day. These theories included those relating to the decentralisation of enterprises (multidivisional organisational structures), Management by Objectives, just-in-time production methods, Business Process Reengineering and 'e' business systems. One thing is certain, the process of management thought will continue and new theories will replace old as long as management itself has a role to play in the organisation and operation of businesses.[23] What is certain is that whenever new concepts are developed management consultants will always be found at their heart, either through innovation or delivery, or both.

This outline review of the practice of management and gallop through the history of British management thought provides an appropriate introduction into the history of management consulting in Britain. The chapters that follow are concerned with providing a historical review of management consultancy in Britain and are structured in three parts. Chapters 2 to 5 review the history of management consulting through a series of time frames from the late-1860s to the cessation of hostilities in 1945. During that period, management consulting was largely concerned with improvements to efficiency within organisations, especially in manufacturing. Chapters 6 to 10 each have a theme, concentrating on an aspect of management consulting. In the post-war period, management consulting witnessed a significant change in the form of services provided and the way in which consultancies were organised. Finally, Chapter 11 reviews the overall history of management consulting in Britain, to bring together the various threads into a single coherent summary account.

Notes

1. The second volume in a series of three entitled *The Making of Scientific Management*: Vol I Thirteen Pioneers, Vol II Management in British Industry and Vol III The Hawthorne Investigations.
2. Whilst Robert Stelling set up a company in his name c1920s prior to 1926, it is believed that this was a one-man operation with the company title used simply as a means of formalising his operation.
3. There are no recorded instances of British women involved in management consulting in this country until the period of the late-1930s.
4. If everyone that described himself/herself as a management consultant actually was, and this is simply not the case, then management consultancy would be one of the largest service sectors in the British economy.
5. The Institute of Management Consultancy, when it was formed in 1962, only admitted external consultants as members. Over time, this restriction was lifted and internal consultants are now fully entitled to apply for membership.
6. The 'President's Statement and Annual Report' of the Management Consultancies Association in 1999 identified a number of broad categories, or service areas, in which management consultant companies are involved. These categories are IT consultancy, IT systems development, corporate strategy, financial and administrative systems, production management, human resources, project management, marketing, and economic and environmental management.
7. For comprehensive accounts of Britain's business history, see J.F. Wilson's (1995) 'British Business History, 1720-1994', and D.J. Jeremy's (1998) 'A Business History of Britain, 1900-1990s'.

8. The general structure of the economy was partly confirmed by the Census of Production of 1907, indicating the continuing prominence of small-scale units. The Factories and Workshop Act of 1901 required businesses to register all those enterprises that employed ten or more workers and had female labour included within the establishment. This meant that enterprises of fewer than ten workers, or those that employed more than ten that did not include female labour, were not registered. In 1907, there were approximately 18.5 million people employed in Britain (Feinstein 1976). Included within the Census were 7 million workers, spread amongst 160,000 enterprises. Therefore, the average employee size of those enterprises surveyed was 44. However, with less than half the employed population included within the survey this tends to support the contention that most people were employed in small-scale units. What this further indicates is that the owner/managers of these smaller enterprises had less of a need to understand the principles of management than knowledge of the technical requirements of the business. Recent studies have indicated that many of the larger British firms were of a comparable size to their competitors in the United States and Germany where management practice tended to be more systematic (Wardley 1999; Wilson 1995). In addition, of the top 130 firms in terms of employee numbers in Britain at the time of the Census, they ranged in scale from approximately 200,000 employees at one end to 4,000+ at the other. This meant that many British firms were very large, even when compared with today. These firms at the very least had a need for more systematic methods of management, even though it is highly unlikely that those listed in Wardley's (1999) top 130 firms in Britain circa 1907 were clients of British management consultants at that time.

9. The two editorial articles were titled 'Prime Cost', 8 November 1867, pp.405-406 and 'The Estimates of Consulting Engineers', 3 September 1869, p.166.

10. Other publications offered similar advice, for example Garcke and Fells' (1887) 'Factory Accounts: Their Principles and Practice', Joseph Slater Lewis's (1896) 'Commercial Organisation of Factories', and Smith and Pickworth's (1914) 'Engineers' Costs and Economical Workshop Production'.

11. Prince Albert, at a conference of 'The Society for the Encouragement of Arts, Manufactures and Commerce' in the 1850s (later to become known as the Royal Society of Arts), emphasised this situation. He stated that hardly more than eighteen to twenty per cent of the nation's children had any education at all. According to Brech (2002e), what was going on in industry was a situation in which men were attempting to establish their own education through 'mechanics institutions' in cities up and down the country. A survey carried out in 1841 on these institutions found that they were providing the basic education upon which these men could build up their own competence and efficiency. By the middle of the 1850s there were known to be 350 of these mechanics institutions across the country and it is at this point in time that the Society began to guide them. Therefore, occupational education began to be addressed (but it was some time before it was fully established in this country).

12. E.F.L. Brech, researching the history of management over many years, has produced a five volume series entitled 'The Evolution of Modern Management' to be published in April 2002 by the Thoemmes Press. Within this account of the history of management consulting, the series is referenced in line with their volume numbers, e.g. 2002a-e representing Volumes One-Five.

13. Later, in the twentieth century other authors such as E.T. Elbourne (1914) also provided practitioner's step-by-step guides of good practice for others to copy and apply. Within Elbourne's book he partly focused on the accounts of a business, but the bulk of the book was about administration, his word for production planning and control as the essential foundation for managerial control in manufacturing.

14. Identifying the need to adopt a more systematic approach to the management of an organisation is one thing, acting upon it is another. The Calico Printers' merger resulted in a board of directors that was 84 strong. This was because the merged companies simply joined their boards together (Horn 1983). This particular mode of higher management reorganisation following a merger was fairly common at that time (Wilson 1995).

15. Brech's book ran through a number of editions and was widely read with nearly 100,000 copies sold worldwide.

16. Child also suggested that poor regard had been paid to the development of educational courses in business and management subjects. This contention is supported by a review of the educational and training environment depicted within a series of booklets produced by the British Institute of Management for the period 1953-1968, generally referred to as 'A Conspectus of Management Courses'. It is only at the beginning of the 1960s that it is possible to detect business and management beginning to feature as a serious academic subject. This may go some way to explain why the management consultant companies devoted so much time in the post-war period to the development and training of client personnel (Brech 2002e).

17. Taylor was dubbed 'The Father of Scientific Management' and was the most prominent of the early pioneers in this field. For an account of his life and work, see L. Urwick and E.F.L. Brech's 'The Making of Scientific Management, Volume I: Thirteen Pioneers' and 'Vol II: Management in British Industry'.

18. Both Lewis and Elbourne operated in a consulting capacity at various times during their working lives.

19. The impact of the 'Rationalisation Movement' in Britain has been the subject of many debates. Exponents would argue that it was successful because it was at the forefront of innovating techniques within firms (Hannah 1976). Those against it suggested that it was used as an excuse to force factory closures and was associated with general industrial depression (Wilson 1995).

20. That proposition was made and a memorandum was drafted by Lyndall Fownes Urwick who later became a prominent figure in the British 'Management Movement', and the founder and chairman of Urwick, Orr and Partners Limited, one of the 'Big Four' consultancies in Britain until the 1980s.

21. Human relations maintained its central focus within management thought until at least the period of the mid-1950s.

22. In the twenty or so years that productivity was at the forefront of government policies, output in Britain experienced fairly consistent growth. However, when compared with some competitor nations, Britain failed to keep its progress at a comparable level. For example, in export trade Britain had been losing ground to competitors for all of that twenty-year period (Brech 2002b).

23. For a graphical review of the theories and practices of management see the *Harvard Business Review* (September-October 1997), '75 Years of Management Ideas & Practice'.

CHAPTER 2

The Pioneers, 1869-1925

General opinion tends to date the commencement of management consulting services in Britain as being sometime during the 1920s. With respect to the operation of consulting companies that opinion would be correct. However, the concept and practice of management consulting have much earlier antecedents. That was in the form of services that attracted such labels as efficiency engineering, industrial consulting, and so on (see Chapter 1). This general situation was not unique because the practice of management consulting occurred in other countries, equally without reference to that descriptive title. For example, in the United States the efficiency movement in the late-nineteenth and early-twentieth centuries centred upon a group of individuals that provided services of a consultancy nature. Regardless of this similarity, the history of management consulting in Britain appears unique in the sense that it has not been possible to identify any other country that followed a similar pattern of growth or development at that time. The foundation and growth of management consulting in Britain was intimately related to the evolution of business and the theoretical trends and practical application of management within British companies, the subject of review of the first chapter.

The period of 1869-1925 in industrial and economic history lay in the wake of Britain's loss of position as the 'workshop of the world'. During the early part of this period, as outlined in the previous chapter, the economy was largely made up of a multiplicity of workshops and factories, specialising in individual areas of production. Larger-scale businesses were also operating at that time, but they only increased in proportion as the period progressed. By the turn of the century, recent research has indicated, many of these large-scale businesses were very large indeed and the top 100 companies in Britain collectively employed over eight per cent of the population (Wardley 1999). Furthermore, the same research has also indicated that there was very little difference between the relative size of Britain's largest firms in terms of personnel employed and those of the United States and Germany. Therefore, size on its own cannot be the dominant factor in the acceptance of consultancy services generally because management consultancy in both the United States and Germany took off with more vigour than here in Britain. Nevertheless, there appeared in Britain a small number of individuals offering services in support of the management of businesses. These individuals were largely engineers or accountants, each applying their own personal experiences and self-developed methods to varying situations and problems within the operational areas of firms. In order to review this period, and some of the early pioneers and the types of services that they provided, a structured approach is used, through two time-frames (1869-1914 and 1914-1925), to break down the first fifty or so years into logical manageable chunks.

Before commencing this review, this second chapter travels further back in time before the birth of consultancy. It was at that time that advisory services were established by individuals that were external to the manufacturing or operating firm itself; specifically as a consequence of the development of specialised equipment, for example in spinning and weaving, or through the invention of water and steam power. The inventors of these equipments were the early development engineers, some of whom provided services in addition to direct installation. Such services included giving guidance and assistance to clients with regards to the proper and effective method of their use. In addition to these development engineers, others also became specialists in specific forms of equipment and provided a similar range of services, for example within the collieries where steam power increased the volume of materials extracted and was used to pump out water from the mines. Some within the first group, however, also provided services in relation to techniques for the efficient operation of the business. For example, advising on factory layout, definitive modes of operation (forms of work-study), costing methodologies, and so on. These were just the forms of service that were subsequently provided by the early management consultants. It is important to identify the work of some of these individuals, if only from the perspective of dispelling the myth that the early management consultants were solely responsible for developing the underlying principles that resulted in the creation of techniques for the efficient operation of businesses.

The Forerunners of the Pioneers

The bleak scenario described in Chapter 1 with regard to Britain's engineering and manufacturing sectors in the nineteenth century could give the impression that very little was going on in an attempt to improve productivity and efficiency within some firms. However, there are references within the annals of literature to incidents of individuals engaged in activities, employing techniques which later fitted within the arsenal of tools that were used by management consultants from the second half of the nineteenth century onwards. These individuals were not consultants, but they utilised the various techniques of consultancy in embryonic form as a means of improving the processes associated with their daily working lives (Ferguson 1999). The purpose of citing some of these examples is to highlight the fact that 'scientific' methods within business did not simply appear as a consequence of the work carried out by the early consultants during the first half of their history in Britain, or indeed elsewhere in the world. The pioneers of consultancy improved on and formalised techniques that had been utilised by others before them. Two groups of men exemplify the situation and provide useful working examples of where the use of efficiency methods was put to good effect. Neither of the groups were consultants, and the provision of advice and assistance were incidental to their primary roles.

The first group was the 'coal viewers' and 'captains' of mines, originating in the North East of England and Cornwall respectively in the late-eighteenth century (Pollard 1965). The coal viewer's role was initially that of an agent for the colliery owners, primarily ensuring that standards were maintained across the range of collieries for which the viewer had responsibility. The captains provided a similar service, although not on such a wide scale, during the same period within the tin and copper mines of Cornwall and the lead mines of Derbyshire and the North. Specifically, the viewers utilised their technical skills in the general management setting, but their role widened through time to encompass those softer skills associated with other aspects of management. Through this evolutionary process these softer skills came to include the development of contracts, human resource management, the development of basic wage systems and stock control management. In addition, the viewers also developed basic costing methodologies associated with colliery production. In real terms, they were consulting engineers in addition to being early management specialists. For example, the viewers involvement with the Newcomen engine used in mining for water pumping not only included its use but also extended to manufacture. That is in addition to them having been heavily involved in the construction of rail systems, including tunnelling and bridging.

Fortunately, the viewers were prolific writers of their own biographies and numerous volumes exist through which to judge their work. One such example was the work of John Curr who, in the late-eighteenth century, wrote a practical guide for the coal viewer and engine builder (Curr 1970).[1] Curr's account is a detailed record of the development of a cast iron railway and the associated equipment needed for its operation. The book is also concerned with the manufacture of the Newcomen steam engine. The importance of the book with regards to this history of management consulting, however, relates to the detail contained within it in the areas of costing (estimating) and the carriage of coal and ores. In effect, what is witnessed is a form of detailed work-study, down to the level of size of carriages, to enable an optimum selection for the movement of materials dependent upon output. This indicates the relatively advanced nature of the use of techniques that became associated with the work of management consultants in the latter-nineteenth and twentieth centuries.

There is a link between the viewers and captains and the second group of men of interest within this pre-history. The viewers and captains working in the mining industry were not alone in providing external advisory services to management. Other men, manufacturing and designing engineers by profession, were providing a similar role in the factories and workshops of the late eighteenth century in Britain. Within this setting, some of these men specialised mainly in the design and development of equipment and machinery for use within the manufacturing environment and in other productive areas, which included mining through the deployment of equipment; here a second link can be found. In addition, some of the manufacturing and designing engineers concerned themselves with the various processes relating to the installation and implementation of the equipment, sometimes made, or partially made, within their own workshops.[2] The label 'development engineers' could quite comfortably be applied to these individuals. Their roles included the planning and supervision of manufacture and all aspects of the installation and operating processes. In addition, in some instances, it was also to do with the development of processes and techniques to aid efficient operational performance.

This group of men is exemplified through the work and formation of the company of Boulton and Watt (Roll 1930). Specifically in the context of the techniques associated with consultancy, in this example it is more to do with the sons of the founders, Mathew Robinson Boulton and James Watt Jr, than with the founders themselves. Such techniques included employing methodologies associated with costing, factory layout, the sub-division and specialisation of labour, the standardisation of products, improvements to labour processes, remuneration packages, and so on. This prompted Roll (1930) to suggest that some of the techniques employed by Frederick Winslow Taylor and the other early scientific managers of the late nineteenth and early twentieth centuries in the United States were not new but merely formalised by them for application in a consultancy capacity.

It is clear that this digression was necessary to highlight the fact that many of the early techniques of consultancy were not the direct result of innovation on the part of consultants themselves. However, it does partly help to explain why it is difficult to identify that point in time when consultant services first commenced in this country because some of the 'tools of the trade' predated the 'trade' itself.

The Gestation and Birth of Management Consulting

Two editorial articles in *The Engineer* in 1867 and 1869 (referred to in Chapter 1) highlighted the fact that engineers were not particularly effective in carrying out the financial aspects of their business. Many of them may well have turned to the traditional accountants of the day, some of whom had written books on their recommended accounting methods. This was specifically in relation to the implementation of financial systems in support of their operations. However, those traditional accounting systems were concerned with recording and reviewing financial information and were not concerned with costing and cost review. Traditional methods of accounting enabled accountants to determine costs based only on past occurrences. In other words, it was retrospective information and not forward looking in the sense that it enabled firms to use it to determine precise methods for future conduct in the operational setting (Chatfield 1977). Costing, or more precisely cost recording, review and control, enabled an assessment of both the present and a prediction of the future. This provided information that was fundamental to the efficient operation of the business. Equally, costing was related to the operational aspects of production and provided timely information on the deployment and usage of resources, including labour. All of this was in addition to providing financial information to assist in pricing and profit allocation calculations. Costing systems were, nevertheless, in use within some firms but what was lacking was literature on the subject and specific professionals that could implement such systems.

The emphasis on the financial aspects of businesses at that time causes problems in identifying early pioneers of management consultancy because both professional accountants and management consultants offered services in relation to the financial dealings of firms. This is emphasised by examples of some accountants that appeared to conduct advisory services in support of management. These services were provided by accountants in, what would appear to be, less prosperous times within their own profession; some of these accountants used the term 'consultant' to describe their roles (Kettle 1957; Holmes and Green 1986). It is within such an environment that the first identified occurrence of an activity that fits within the definition of management consulting occurred in the period 1869-1870. The individual concerned was Montague Whitmore, a chartered accountant, of Clerkenwell Green, London, who employed techniques in costing and management accounting. The main difference between Whitmore and his accountant colleagues was that even though some of the additional services provided by accountants could possibly have been described as consulting, they were ad hoc in nature. Whitmore was a full-time consultant with a background in accountancy; having developed a service specifically concerned with consulting in respect of cost recording and review.

Attention was drawn to Whitmore through an advertisement that he placed in *The Engineer* during 1869, simply entitled 'Avoid Losses and Failures', in relation to a cost management system for installation into factories and engineering workshops. Real interest into the activities of this man occurred as a consequence of a series of letters to the editor in the same publication during the latter two months of 1870. It would appear, according to the content of these letters, that systems producing 'accurate results' in relation to systematic cost recording, review and control were not universally available at this time. There were, nevertheless, individuals with experience and expertise available that had developed their own systems for employment on the payment of a fee, Whitmore being one such individual. Unfortunately, the precise nature of the service is unknown. But, a letter in *The Engineer* in December 1870 by an engineer using the pseudonym Alpha, in response to an enquiry by a reader in relation to the service provided by Whitmore, indicated that he had by this time served numerous other engineers and manufacturers in a similar capacity. According to the letter, Whitmore provided a service for the installation of what was regarded as a reliable system for costing and cost review. The fee for his services was 10 guineas and 10 pounds for the necessary ledgers and associated paperwork. What this letter indicates is that Whitmore did not simply provide advice, he conducted a complete analytical review of the requirements. As a consequence of that review, he installed his system, provided training on its usage and maintained links with the client.

Within this same period as Whitmore another accountant, Edwin Waterhouse, provided services outside of what was generally considered normal practice for the auditors of the day.[3] Such services were provided during the 'quiet periods' when auditing activities were less in demand. It was during these periods that there appeared to be opportunities for accountants to widen their service base in order to bring in additional income. This has prompted some to comment that this was the beginning of the development of management consultancy services within accountancy firms (Jones 1995). One example of the way in which this form of service was provided can be found in the 1870 assignment at Fox, Head and Company, a Middlesborough rolling mill company. The assignment consisted of an investigation into determining methods for calculating profits in order that bonus payments could be allocated to workpeople (Jones 1988). Clearly, in order to make a profit, calculations involving the use of costing techniques would be unavoidable in order to prevent arbitrary methods being employed. This particular assignment was conducted partially to avoid a conflict arising between the management of the firm and the labour force. The relative success is unknown, but the system put into place was short-lived for reasons that were not stated, possibly because it had served its initial purpose.

A similar assignment was conducted in 1877 at the Consett Iron Company where wage levels were determined by the selling price of the iron at any particular time (Jones 1988). Accurate cost information would have been a prerequisite for the determination of those wage levels in order to prevent wide-ranging fluctuations in profit margins. Therefore, the use of traditional accountancy methods would have been inappropriate in such an environment. Assignments such as these were conducted within an era where little formal knowledge had been documented to aid the employment of such techniques, because processes and techniques employed by these accountants would, in all probability, have been of their own devising. Equally, such services were more likely to do with the provision of advice rather than the implementation of solutions.

Nevertheless, if one ignores the technicalities associated with definitions relating to the exact make-up of assignments, there is little doubt that the work of Whitmore and other accountants at that time was important from the perspective of the birth of consultancy. It is probably no accident, however, that both of these men, and others providing similar services, had a history entrenched within the accountancy profession. This would have provided them with knowledge of the working practices prevalent within businesses at that time, especially in those firms where they had personally carried out accounting activities previously. From the perspective of acceptance, accountants had already been accepted by the owners and managers of firms as an external agent and it was only a short hop between auditing accounts and conducting cost analysis. The difference between these two men, Whitmore and Waterhouse, and the form of services provided by them lay in the fact that they were carried out in completely different circumstances. Whitmore had specifically developed a consultancy service based on his own methods and there are indications that he retained ownership of the solutions he had derived for clients until the new system was up and running within the firm. Waterhouse, on the other hand, only provided consultancy-type services when things were not going particularly well within his own area of professional expertise and he was, therefore, more opportunistic in approach than established as a management consultant.

Early Evolutionary Processes and Pioneers

The available evidence has suggested that management consulting services were first provided to give financial information on the operational aspects of the business through the development of costing methods tailored to meet the clients' needs. Some owners and managers did not consider this form of external involvement in the firm as unwelcome because of the link between costing and traditional accountancy methods. Although there is a direct relationship between the application of costing techniques and factors involved in the production process, there is little evidence to suggest that the first management consultants provided services in relation to improvements to productivity and the control of labour. That is until the end of the nineteenth century with the consulting service provided by Alexander Hamilton Church (1866-1936).

Church was an engineer by qualification and was probably the most prominent of the early pioneers during the latter years of the nineteenth century in Britain. According to Urwick (1956), Church gained a reputation as a pioneer in cost and works accounting, as well as an author of one of the early textbooks on scientific management, written and published after he had emigrated to the United States in 1905, 'The Science and Practice of Management'. The work carried out by Church in the field of costing has been praised because of the way in which it encouraged others to use the techniques and take costing forward as a subject for study. Church's primary importance in terms of consulting relates to the way in which he associated costing with production planning and control. He was undoubtedly influenced by Joseph Slater Lewis (Vangermeersch 1988), with whom he worked for a period in the last decade of the nineteenth century, and who had a profound impact on Church's later work. Church was an associate of Lewis's at P.R. Jackson and Company, an engineering manufacturing company in Manchester. Lewis paid compliments to Church in his important publication on business efficiency in which he highlighted Church's contributions to the chapter relating to 'Establishment Charges' (Lewis 1896).

The first consulting assignment attributed to Church occurred at B. and S. Massey in Manchester where he was primarily involved in the re-organisation of the costing and financial accounting methods of the

Company. In addition, Church was also responsible for effecting improvements to the management methods employed within the office environment of the firm. It was a tribute to Church's work that the systems developed by him remained in place during the period 1900-1960 (Vangermeersch 1988). Church had created his management accounting and consulting service in 1898 when he pioneered the concepts of production centres as a methodology for controlling the allocation of overheads and establishment charges to products and processes. In addition to that, he also developed the machine hour rate for the allocation of overhead expenses, as well as the utilisation of budgets as a controlling mechanism within the production process (Cheadle 1995). The concept of production centres, an important innovatory approach to costing, was based on the principle that a factory should be divided into a number of smaller shops, or groups of machines. The overhead costs of each were calculated. These costs were then associated within each group or shop and charged to the work moving through individual areas at a pre-determined hourly rate (Chatfield 1977). This process enabled more accurate cost determination and information than had previously been available through the overall 'averaged' methods generally employed at that time. The machine hour rate, a charge for machine usage on an hourly basis used in conjunction with the production centre approach, provided a method of determining costs based on individual machines or groups of machines. This provided a more reliable assessment of overhead costs in an environment where a diverse range of equipment was used on the factory floor. Equally, it highlighted areas where efficiencies and improvements could be made within the production process.

Following on from his work at Massey's, Church moved to the Renold company in 1900 where, in conjunction with Hans Renold, he developed costing processes for employment in the firm. These processes were based on a system of monthly cost control returns that covered manufacturing activities and stock movements in addition to financial information. This prompted Urwick (1956) to remark that Church's work formed the basis for the development of scientific methods within the whole field of costing. However, costing aside, Church had by then also developed an interest in management. He recognised the volume of changes that had occurred within British industry since the late-eighteenth century (Litterer 1961). He considered that three particular aspects of change were fundamental to highlighting the need for improvements to the basic requirements of greater managerial skill and competence in industry (Church 1900). These aspects were the technological advances made in the manufacturing environment, specifically in machine tools, the resultant new specialised skills required to support these advances and the growth in the number of employees generally within firms. His approach to the analysis of and subsequent corrective action to any inefficient areas that he found was based on a 'functional approach'. His solutions were concentrated on the identified problems and to the removal of inefficiencies through some form of direct remedial action in those areas where they were found (Church 1901 and 1910). Church has been described as having developed ideas that were more important and more co-ordinated than F.W. Taylor. He advanced the notion of control and, as a consequence, his systems provided accurate information in support of the management decision-making process (Jelinek 1980). In effect, he took over from where Taylor left off.

Church emigrated to the United States, the birthplace of his parents, in the first decade of the twentieth century. There he carried out the majority of his consultancy work and developed the ideas that remain associated with his name to the present day. Church was not alone in supplying services within the production environment; a number of other individuals were known to be active during this period. One engineer involved in applying principles for the application of efficiency services within the operational setting was G.C. Allingham. Assignments were conducted within the production environment, but again the lack of records detailing the activities of this man prevents an understanding of the exact nature of the processes employed by him. As Brech (2002b) points out, this is not surprising because, in retrospect, wider knowledge of the work of individuals providing services of a consultancy nature within industrial settings would have been obtained mainly through the contributions made by them in the journals of the day. However, generally one glaring omission within these articles was the names of the individual authors. This may have been because the direct advertising of services was not the general method of obtaining work and journal articles were not used with that intention in mind. The more likely reason for this was that by-lines were not customary at that time and, therefore, contributors of journal articles rarely found their names in print. Where they were, it is possible to identify some individuals that were providing services of a consultancy nature.

One such consultant, Percy Martin, in a similar vein to Church, advocated a systematic approach to the allocation of manufacturing overhead costs and establishment charges. Like his contemporaries, he aired his ideas through the medium of professional and technical journals and through the presentation of papers at professional venues. For example, in 1907 Martin addressed the Institution of Automobile Engineers, reproduced as a paper entitled 'Works Organisation'. This paper benefited from even wider circulation when it was reproduced in serial form (four parts) in *The Mechanical World* in April of that year. Martin emphasised the relationship between manufacturing planning with estimating and costing, advocating that costs should be known in advance of estimating. In effect, this was the embryonic beginnings of an approach to 'standard costing', albeit not known by that name during this period. At the time of that address to the Institution of Automobile Engineers, Martin was carrying out work for the Mercedes Benz motor company in Britain. The content of his paper, and the detailed knowledge of high level strategy that he demonstrated, indicated that he had wide-ranging experience, gained through work in a diverse range of areas. Also in 1907 another pioneer and chartered accountant by profession, Harvey Preen, published a book that he entitled 'Reorganisation and Costings'. Whilst this volume was insubstantial in terms of size, its value was immense in that it contained advice on how to make use of a budget framework as an approach to managerial control. This concept was at least a generation ahead of its time (Brech 2002b). A second edition of this book, almost double in size to the original, appeared in 1913. Within this volume, Preen expanded upon the information contained within the original publication, providing detailed descriptions of his methods together with specimen documents.

Preen specialised in providing services to smaller firms and urged his fellow accountants to do likewise. In 1908 a pamphlet entitled 'Falling Sales, Yet Increased Profits' written by Preen provided summary accounts of the assignments conducted by him in the period leading up to the publication. He was critical of contemporary industrial managers with respect to their intransigent attitudes towards change. He also advocated combining sales with production planning. This was fairly radical advice for its day and generally would not have been accepted by his peers. Preen was proved wrong only on one point by the passing of time. This concerned his prophesy that within a few years of his 1913 publication professional accountants would find themselves forced into managerial advisory roles to undertake re-organisation of manufacturing firms; it was more than fifty years before that actually occurred to any significant extent.

There was during this period a realisation that competition from abroad (a point noted in Chapter 1) in both domestic and export markets necessitated change to enable firms to face up to this threat on a more even footing. During the period 1911-1914 H.W. Allingham, whose relationship to G.C. is unknown, is credited with having provided assistance to Hans Renold during his experiments in 'scientific management'. This was the only serious application of scientific management in Britain. Allingham had previously been an employee of Renold at the turn of the century and had gained managerial experience of the methods employed by F.W. Taylor (Brech 2002b), concerning himself with improvements to operational performance through the application of practices relating to planning, organisation and control. Renold employed Allingham during the period 1900-1902. He gained subsequent experience of scientific management methods whilst working in the United States and then later for an American company based in London. Another individual who worked with Allingham at Renold's was A.D. McKillop who later produced a book on 'Efficiency Methods' (1917). Not surprising, therefore, the content of the book was heavily slanted towards the methods employed by the American scientific managers in relation to production planning, costing, progress control, methods improvement and payment incentive schemes. Renold presented a review of it in October 1913, entitled 'Engineering Workshop Organisation', including documents and charts, to the Manchester Association of Engineers. During the same period another engineer, J.W. Stannard, performed the role of advisor in methods improvement. Stannard's approach was one of standardisation in relation to the specification of the design of components within the production process.[4] His work came under critical review within an editorial article in *Engineering* in June 1913. Stannard was an advocate of scientific management methods and critical of contemporaries whom he felt failed to understand the central principles that underpinned much of Taylor's work (Brech 2002b).[5]

The existence of these individuals acting in a freelance consultancy capacity in Britain at that time suggests that there was an underlying demand for their services. The relatively small number engaged in this service area suggests that the level of demand was relatively small. There may be a number of reasons for this; one compelling reason could be that knowledge of activities of these men was not widespread. This was, in all probability, associated with the fact that much of the work carried out by them was in small and medium sized businesses and, therefore, improvements to those businesses would have been less visible in the wider economy than had they occurred in much larger firms. Another likely explanation is that there still remained an entrenched attitude at that time with regards to the non-acceptance of outside interference in a firm. Before turning to the work of consultants during the period of the First World War and beyond, one area not yet covered in terms of advisory and consultancy services was that which related to salesmanship, sales promotion, advertising and publicity.

Whilst largely concerned with the home market rather than overseas trading, numerous firms and individuals had established themselves as 'agents'. These initially served their clients in the placement of advertising copy in the national and regional newspapers and in various periodicals, both commercial and general. Even in the late nineteenth century agents were increasingly serving their manufacturing and trading (merchant) clients in the content and layout of advertising materials. This was in addition to advising them on areas of sales promotion (for example gifts, coupons, discounts, free samples, and so on) and the general approach to salesmanship. As the advertising specialists established and maintained their own active circles for interchange of experience (notably through the 'publicity clubs'), they became extensively knowledgeable about the home market for a wide range of consumer commodities, both durable and consumable. Therefore, they were well placed to serve their clients on marketing policies, product development, trading channels, sales techniques and promotion. Another support service in marketing and selling for industrial and trading firms, though not in the advisory mode, lay in the training of salesmen, partly through evening classes and partly through specialist correspondence schools, several of which were started in the first decade of the twentieth century. A focus for all those activities was created when both the Association of Advertising Consultants and the (incorporated) Sales Managers' Association (ISMA) were formed in 1911. The latter initiated programmes of lunchtime sessions for the presentation and discussion of topics in sales policy, management and methods.

Items such as those discussed in the lunchtime sessions were often reported in the commercial journals as well as in the ISMA publication (*Sales Promotion* founded in September 1910). The journals also carried contributed feature articles on similar or related topics: the contemporary convention favoured anonymous contributions rather than by-lines, therefore the identities of authors were mostly not disclosed. Yet content and treatment suggested that at least some of them were 'salesmanship or sales consultants' and occasionally there were attributed articles by such practitioners; they were then not bold enough to style themselves 'sales management consultants'. At that time, the concept of 'marketing' as the policy link between product (manufacturer) and market (customer) had not been developed. The outbreak of war inevitably brought curtailment of the scale of these activities in the home market and correspondingly in the usage of commercial advisory services. However, Government Departments, for public promotion of war-related needs and issues, took up some of those services. At the same time the services of the consulting engineers and cost consultants were taken up by companies for war-related production problems and developments.

The Outbreak of War and Beyond

In 1914 an important book by E.T. Elbourne was published, 'Factory Administration and Accounts'; he was later to become a management consultant. This was a 600 page compendium containing in-depth information on works management, organisation and methods (Rose 1954). According to Brown (1977), the book was well received because it took account of the peculiarities of Britain's industrial scene. The book was widely read, more so than any previous publication of its type, which was reflected in the volume of its sales. In particular, this publication was recognised within the Ministry of Munitions as being an important contribution to the standardisation of processes. For the Ministry, this was important because it was being serviced at that time by a large number of contracting firms and factories, generally employing methodologies that were considered to be less than efficient. Consequently, through the encouragement of individuals within the Ministry there were over 10,000 copies sold during the period of the War. However, the importance of this book relates partly to its time-specifics in that it was published five months before the outbreak of the First World War. From 1915 onwards there was a massive increase in production output within industries that supported the war effort.

During the period of the War, and beyond, the work of Herbert Newton Casson, though not a consultant in the full definitional sense, provided some assistance to management and consultants alike. This was through the medium of his *Efficiency Magazine*, founded in 1915, and through his books and training courses.[6] According to Brech (2002b) he provided a distinctive approach and contribution to the promotion of efficiency within both industry and commerce. Casson's input into the field of training was also significant within this scenario, largely through correspondence courses, direct tuition and the development of in-house company training programmes.[7] All this was made possible through his previously gained practical experience under the tutelage of Harrington Emerson in the United States in the period before his arrival in this country.[8] As a point of inspiration and as a source of reference, primarily within the supporting role, Casson was undoubtedly influential in the efficiency processes employed by the consultants of the day. He was, according to his own account, engaged in management advisory activities, largely for those companies wishing to employ efficiency measures in order to improve their operational performance. It was just such a role that he offered to provide in response to a campaign conducted by the *Evening News* through services directed at inefficiencies within the telephone service of the General Post Office. Not surprisingly the offer of assistance was refused; nevertheless he forwarded his recommendations to a House of Commons Committee charged with reviewing the situation.

In addition, again according to his own account, during the period of the First World War he was engaged in activities relating to the training of foremen and of raising productive output in no less than sixty establishments.[9] His role as an advisor, if his account is correct, was clearly a significant one. However, the sheer volume of this work would have prevented him from engaging in activities of a full consultancy nature. Unusually at this time, unlike the majority of his contemporaries, Casson was in a position, through his having had a sound financial background, to advertise his services in technical publications.[10] These were largely the publications that were personally associated with him, for example the *Efficiency Magazine* mentioned previously, although he did use the other technical publications of the day. Nevertheless, his involvement in providing advisory services directly to clients was limited in the period following on from the War because much personal effort was expended in publishing his thoughts and work. Reportedly, Casson by 1931 had written 70 books and booklets, the majority of which could be linked to his work in the area of efficiency (Brech 2002b). Therefore, the importance of this man in terms of consultancy related not to the advisory services that he provided directly to clients, but to the literature and supporting services that would have been a source of inspiration to the consultants of the day.

The persistence of production problems and the many endeavours made within firms to overcome them did, however, serve to bring the broad question of 'industrial efficiency' actively into the forefront of public discussion after the cessation of hostilities in 1918. This led to the formation of a number of national propaganda campaigns dedicated to seeking modes of improvement. The consulting engineers and other advisory specialists were able to make important contributions to those campaigns, but inevitable post-war boom for industrial and commercial activity in making good the deficiencies of the war years was short lived. By the autumn of 1920 the signs of a severe downturn and serious decline were evident and 1921 witnessed depression, shutdown and unemployment in virtually every sector across Britain. The need for efficiency improvement and cost reduction as the means of regeneration thus became as important as it had been for war production purposes, if not even more so. The opportunity was there for every kind of specialist service and system to offer and provide a contribution, but there was no such dearth of provision on offer. That was neither from consultant service nor through books or articles, the latter frequently coming from the former, largely because previous demand had not justified wide-ranging services.

In the six years following on from 1920-1921 there was increasingly more activity involving Britain's management consultants. This is more easily understood in outline by sub-dividing activities into sections or aspects, of which a number can be identified worthy of record: production efficiency, costing and works accounting, administration in the office, human relations, salesmanship and sales promotion, management information and general business services. Another category cut across several of these, though it was not involved with specialist advisory services. That category was the inception of serious attention towards the improvement of managerial knowledge, the foundation being laid in the immediate post-war years 1919-1920. Such an inception can be identified in the post-war period through the work of E.T. Elbourne.

Having been engaged at the Ponders End National Shell Factory as Assistant General Manager under Mr (later Sir) Harry Brindley, E.T. Elbourne formed a consulting partnership with Brindley at the cessation of hostilities (Messrs Brindley and Elbourne, Consulting Engineers of 110 Victoria Street, London, S.W.1.). This is the first recorded instance of the usage of the term 'consulting' within the title of a management consulting organisation in this country.[11] Elbourne had already made his mark through his book 'Factory Administration and Accounts', cited earlier, raising the profile of the notion that management was a subject that could be studied and, therefore, taught. This was a movement away from the idea that the manager's job was made up of a series of ill-defined responsibilities and functions. The driving force behind the partnership undoubtedly came from Brindley but, because of his untimely death in 1920, Elbourne had to continue in the capacity of a sole practitioner, revising his portfolio of services to enable a concentration on the administrative aspects of his clients' activities.

Because of Brindley's death, and because Elbourne invested much of his time towards the formation of a professional body for management as well as expending energy on his many writing and educational activities, it is unlikely that Elbourne was able to devote much effort towards his consulting practice. The educational aspects of Elbourne's work are covered in more detail in Chapter 7. During this same period, H. McFarland Davis, a chartered accountant and an associate of Elbourne's in the formation of the Institute of Industrial Administration, offered a free-lance service as a cost consultant. The services provided and the lectures given by this man were clearly within the Elbourne tradition. Another chartered accountant also offering similar services, unusually using the title cost consultant, was E. Miles Taylor. These men were not alone within the accountancy profession at that time providing consultancy services; some of the early members of the newly formed Institute of Cost and Works Accountants (ICWA) were clearly consultants offering services in that general field. Another accountant, John Manger Fells, was responsible for providing services in costing and cost accounting. Chapter 1 noted that a book written by this man in collaboration with Emile Garcke (1887) concerned itself with estimating and costing. Fells had a general management background; he was not an accountant by profession. Articles written by him in the post-war period emphasised cost and cost accounting as a specific discipline in its own right; a position that had been rejected by many within professional accountancy circles.

In addition to the accountants, others were also providing services of a consultancy nature at that time. A number of these individuals were providing services in relation to productivity and efficiency within manufacturing and engineering firms during the period of the War and thereafter. One such individual was Francis Malcolm Lawson who specialised in services directed at planning and control within manufacturing establishments. The hallmark of his approach was a system that he described as 'exposed records', in effect a progress system based on using a planning board to chart the progression of work (Lawson 1920). One of the purposes behind this approach was to inform the workforce of progress, thereby acting as a psychological stimulus for worker performance. The main purpose, however, was to provide co-ordination of output through visible means, indicating the direction of movement of materials through control points. Lawson suggested that there were three basic advantages of his system. Firstly, it reduced inventory stock levels, thus reducing investment in that area. Secondly, it enabled staff reductions, specifically in the area of shop floor control. And, finally, it reduced the need for workers to be switched from one job to another simply because the visibility of operations helped with the decision-making process. In other words, less time was wasted through inappropriate decisions that had to be reversed causing disruption to the manufacturing process.

These were not just bold statements, a number of companies that employed the Lawson system testified to its effectiveness. For example, the managing director of Hans Renold Limited confirmed Lawson's claim that less capital was tied up in inventory stock, similarly the managing director of the Chatwood Safe Company stated that the decision-making process was enhanced through visible and accurate information (Lawson 1920). A hallmark of the Lawson approach was consultation with the workforce and the engendering of worker co-operation through reward mechanisms to encourage operative performance. J.E. Powell was another consultant during this period specialising in production planning. In support of that objective, he also concerned himself with designing and applying bonus incentive schemes in general support of industry's pre-occupation at that time with the control of labour; the one management tool that seemed to offer a consensus of approach across the major industrial firms of the day.

In addition to these men there were a number of production consultants individually advertising their services in the Journal of the Industrial League and Council during the period 1920-1922; these consultants included J.F. Butterworth, H. Atkinson and Robert Stelling (Brech 2002b). All three were contributors to the League's educational programmes and journal. What they all appeared to offer, albeit in different forms, was advice and assistance in improving production efficiency. For example, Butterworth was a motion study specialist who also included a service in relation to improvements in the office as part of his portfolio.[12] One article written by Butterworth pointed to the efficiencies that could be gained through applying a sound standard method in routine tasks within the office environment (Butterworth 1920). The article was heavily slanted towards describing methods within those firms where large quantities of circulars and mail were despatched as a normal part of office routine. Robert Stelling, of the three, was probably the most important contributor to the spread of knowledge in his writings in the League's journal and other publications, through his public speaking at professional and other venues, and in his contributions to the League's educational programme. His distinctive style emphasised the supervisory role within a systematic approach to management, highlighting the need for the training of foremen (Brech 2002b). His approach subsumed the elements of organisation, technical standardisation, work and progress flow, and costing within an environment that utilised planning boards for effective overall control. What was absent in his approach, surprisingly, was the use of techniques within the personnel field, for example the setting of time standards and bonus incentive schemes, aspects of management that his contemporaries employed. Also unusual was the fact that Stelling had set up a company in his own name, although the detail and make-up remain unknown. In all likelihood the company formation was simply a title through which Stelling carried out his operations and was not an organised affair in the traditional sense.

Other consultants were also regular contributors to the Journal of the Industrial League and Council. These included A. Cathles, W.J. Hiscox, F.W. Lawrence and J.E. Powell. They all specialised in aspects of production management, some of them covering the whole range of manufacturing organisation and managerial practice. Of these, Hiscox was the most prolific contributor through his publications on the general subject of factory operations. Four books that were written by Hiscox in the period of the 1920s (1921, 1923, 1924, 1926) all emphasised different aspects of the production process. His concern in the name of efficiency covered the whole spectrum of factory production, including design and layout, purchasing of raw materials, effective throughput (emphasised through production planning and control), payment regimes and administrative operations. The one area he did not cover, however, was that of marketing.

At about the same time (1920s) in the Birmingham area there appeared to be a co-operative grouping of production consultants operating under the name of 'The Institute of Industrial Efficiency'. This group advertised their services, for example, in a series of five advertisements in *Works Management* in the period 1919-1920. Each advertisement emphasised a different theme and was sequentially numbered. For example, number four in the January 1920 edition was concerned with factory and office layout, emphasising the importance of work flow for efficient operation, and the reduction in time and costs that resulted from a non-interrupted movement of materials. The advertisements included a photograph of an area of a firm for which services had been applied, in the case of number four the Motor Department of Charles Purden Limited of Birmingham was displayed. The precise nature of the work of the co-operative remains largely unknown, but the range of services they appeared to offer included production planning and control, methods improvement, administrative operations, cost modelling and payment incentive schemes. Their prominence, through advertising, waned in the period to the mid-1920s. The reasons for this are unknown but there may be some relationship between their disappearance and the poor state of firms operating in the economy at that time. This would have been just the sort of scenario that would have warranted the involvement of consultants if it were not for that the fact that many firms make decisions on their future activities based on their current economic conditions.

One fundamental area that is related to the production process that appears to have 'escaped the net' cast by what could be described as the conventional consultants during this period was sales and marketing. In the immediate aftermath of the First World War, one individual providing this form of specialist service was Wallace Attwood. As a consultant Attwood was the pioneer of this form of service. In a similar vein to the majority of other consultants, Attwood refrained from overtly advertising his services, especially those relating to aspects of sales management because the climate of opinion was not yet ready to accept such assistance at the managerial level. Nevertheless, he did provide services at the operational level in salesmanship, sales promotion and publicity, with a full sales management package following later in the mid-1920s. He was a regular contributor to articles in *Sales Management*, a periodical produced by the Cassier Company. As an additional service, together with other 'experts', Attwood formed an advisory panel within this magazine for the provision of advice, free of charge, on a whole range of topics related to selling. Some of these topics were undoubtedly within the sales management field. Also by that time he was well known for his correspondence courses in salesmanship. Attwood included market research in his range of activities, a specialisation on which his attention focused increasingly through the passage of time.

Finally with regards to this period, in 1925/26 another consultant, T.G. Rose, who subsequently gained high office in the Institute of Industrial Administration, commenced a freelance consultancy practice. Rose was concerned primarily with medium-sized manufacturing enterprises, concentrating on the consolidation of financial and operational information of the firm with the view to enhancing overall management control. Rose's procedures were formalised in a number of textbooks: 'Business Charts' (1930), 'The Management Audit' (1932) and 'Higher Control in Management' (1934). The major consulting companies operating in this country (see Chapters 4 and 5) from the mid-1930s onwards mirrored the form of service provided by Rose. His ideas, therefore, pioneered the concept of 'management information' as a tool in the manager's decision-making process. However, very much in line with the situation in the first half of this period, the activities of all these individuals were confined to largely piecemeal operations at the operational level of the firm. In the period of the mid-1920s the worth of consultancy services and their importance to industry was beginning to be recognised. For example, in a speech at Bradford in 1922, Sir Eric Geddes, the then President of the Federation of British Industries, mentioned the work of consultants and suggested that their value had been understated. He highlighted the importance of efficiency to the wellbeing of industrial enterprises and suggested that it would be advantageous to firms to utilise the services of consultants in the achievement of this objective (Brech 2002b).

Towards the Future

The examples of consultant activity cited in the previous sections provide only an indication of the volume of work carried out in the field of management consulting during this whole period; much of the work went unnoticed. Each of the consultants tended to specialise in a particular form of service, although within some areas (for example production) the breadth of service provision could have been fairly wide. Overall, examples of management consulting activities have indicated that the consultancy environment was fragmented to the extent that organised consulting practices had not been established in Britain by the end of this period. This was a feature of the next period of the history of management consulting in Britain, the roots of which lay further afield across the other side of the Atlantic, in the United States. There, the development and delivery of management consulting was progressing at a faster pace. This may have been because, unlike Britain, there was more general acceptance of scientific methods and less resistance to outside intervention on the part of the employers. Therefore, businesses sought the assistance of outside consultants in developing the complex structures and processes necessary within their organisations.

To help cope with these challenges, consulting adopted parallel streams of development. Within one stream could be found the efficiency engineers such as Taylor, Emerson and the Gilbreths. They had formed their own companies for the development and delivery of efficiency services, primarily within production-centred organisations. Within the other stream, a body of organisations and individuals developed and deployed services in the structural and managerial aspects of the business. This group was largely made up of engineers, accountants and lawyers who thrived as a consequence of the growth of organisations within the United States during the period at the turn of the century and beyond (McKenna 1995). Within this burgeoning consultancy environment, the work of Charles Eugene Bedaux and his company provided services in the general field of efficiency, concentrating on improvements to productivity and the deployment of payment incentive schemes. Consultants of the Company, known at that time as 'field engineers', arrived in Britain in 1923 to conduct an assignment at the British subsidiary of an American company, the Eastman Kodak Company. This heralded the way forward for the Company to set up offices in Britain in 1926. The first of the 'Big Battalions' had arrived, irreversibly changing the shape of the British consultancy environment from one made up of a number of sole practitioners to that which was dominated into the future by major consultancies.

Notes

1. Reproduced from the original (1797).
2. Other manufacturers, on a contracting basis, carried out the majority of the manufacturing work.
3. Edwin Waterhouse was a founder of the firm Price Waterhouse in 1865, now re-named PricewaterhouseCoopers following a merger with Coopers and Lybrand in 1999. The work of this man highlights the difficulty of differentiating between some of the services provided by accountants and management consultants.
4. Stannard was invited to give the inaugural lecture to the newly formed Production Managers Association at Bradford in February 1913 where the subject of his lecture was the principles of scientific management. Confirmation of his activities can be found in Volume 1, 'Factory Organisation and Management', in the Harmsworth Business Library (1911), where a number of examples were cited for the improvement of systems, methods and documentation.

5. Criticism of Stannard's support for scientific management principles can be found in an editorial article in *Engineering*, June 1913. Stannard's response appeared in the July issue in which he countered with the argument that ignorance was responsible for the negatives associated with contemporary attitudes.

6. Casson was the founder, owner, editor and primary contributor to the magazine that reached a monthly circulation rate of 100,000 by the late-1930s and was, according to Casson, the most influential magazine in the British Empire (Brech 2002c). In the early years of production, the orientation of articles was clearly towards the manufacturing and industrial sectors, but during the 1920s and 1930s commercial and other business interests occupied its pages.

7. This work was largely centred on the London offices of the Sheldon Training School. The School, founded in Chicago in 1902 for the purpose of delivering training through correspondence courses, had been purchased by Casson prior to his arrival in Britain.

8. Harrington Emerson was one of the prominent pioneers of scientific management in the United States and the founder of a consulting service in his name.

9. One example of work in this area was the lecture series arranged for the foremen of Mather and Platt (Manchester) in 1917.

10. Prior to his residency in Britain, Casson's financial position was secured through his previous involvement with H.K. McCann in the founding of a successful advertising agency in the United States.

11. Born in Hampshire in 1875, Elbourne had a background firmly entrenched within the engineering industry. In 1915 Elbourne, then approaching middle-age, took up the appointment of Assistant General Manager, under Mr (later Sir) Harry Brindley, at the Ponders End National Shell Factory. Brindley was a like-minded soul, with a deep commitment to developing better methods of management. In 1919, with the assistance of Brindley, Elbourne formed the Institute of Industrial Administration in an attempt to professionalise industrial management (Brech 2002a). The Institute got off to a poor start, was moribund by 1924 and was later revived in 1931-1932. Also in 1919, Elbourne was awarded the MBE for his contributions at Ponders End.

12. Butterworth was the British representative of the Gilbreths (Frank and Lillian) for motion and method study assignments. They were the husband and wife team who were best remembered for their work in those fields.

CHAPTER 3

The Beginning of Organised Consultancy, 1926-1933

The arrival in Britain of the Bedaux company in 1926, setting up a permanent operation, coincided with a turbulent period in Britain's industrial history. The industrial milieu in the post-war years, especially between 1920 and 1925, was complex and confused. The first part of the period was over-shadowed by heavy unemployment and recurrent labour disputes, occurring mainly in coal mining and in the traditional heavy engineering sectors (shipbuilding, locomotives, machine tools and plant) and textiles. These industries had already experienced considerable unrest in the pre-war decade arising from disputes over piecework prices, rate-fixing and premium bonus systems. It was from those sources that the 'General Strike' of 1926 was to stem and, sparked by the coal miners' dispute, 162 million worker-days were lost through industrial action.[1] Those industrial sectors disrupted by industrial disputes were also the ones that (together with textiles) had been most strongly affected by losses of export trade through competition from other supplying countries.

From 1922 onwards the newer industries (vehicles, electrical appliances and equipment, radio, domestic equipments and utensils, and a number of others) were beginning to expand rapidly. It was in these industries that many of the new methods of managerial techniques were being applied, either from in-house inauguration or through the assistance of the early management consultants. The balance between the newer and older industries was unequal, with employment opportunities in the newer industries failing to compensate for the losses in the others (Horn 1983). This was apart from the geographical disparities and the non-transferable skill-sets of the workers that prevented the free movement of personnel between one form of industry and another.

The business environment in the inter-war period witnessed a fall in output in industrial production. Gross profits fell specifically from the mid-point of the period and unemployment had risen to 1.8 million of the employed population, the highest level for four years (Feinstein 1976). Throughout this period, there had been much criticism of management, even within public enterprises, prompting comments such as management was backward in its approach, failing to rationalise both production and marketing within businesses (Hannah 1976). Despite of all this, the 1920s also witnessed a period of extensive merger activity. This caused some commentators to remark that what was being witnessed was concentration on a scale previously unprecedented in Britain's industrial milieu (Wilson 1995). Some of these firms created through merger activity, for example ICI, became important clients of the management consulting companies that were formed during the 1920s and beyond. Therefore, the turbulence of the mid-1920s appeared to be a less than ideal time for the commencement of consultancy services in Britain. Exponents of consultancy practices would argue that such periods were precisely the right moments to employ external aid. That is because a successfully applied consultancy assignment can turn around the fortunes of a company when competitor businesses are not doing particularly well (Hyman 1970).

Nevertheless, managers require a more convincing line of argument during periods when falling profits constrain the level of flexibility enjoyed by individual companies. The expense of paying for consultancy services at a time when the financial health of a business is at a low ebb can only be justified if there are obvious benefits to the firm. Such benefits in a time of depression are not immediately apparent and individuals require a lot of persuasion before they are willing to commit scarce resources to a promise that things will improve in the future. 'The Beginning of Organised Consultancy' was that period in time (1926-1933) when the structure of the management consulting environment in Britain irreversibly changed from one made up of a disparate band of sole practitioners to that of one dominated by a handful of emerging companies. This period witnessed the first stage of a wider set of changes that took place within management consulting in the 1930s and beyond (see Chapters 4 and 5). However, the initial concern of this chapter is 1926 when Britain saw the arrival of the first organised consultancy practice, one that bore the name of its founder, Charles E. Bedaux.

Because the period of the mid-1920s is critical to understanding the factors that affected the evolution and growth of management consulting in Britain, this chapter has one primary aim. That aim is to describe the principles and practices that underpinned the whole concept of the efficiency model that was practised by management consultants in Britain, both at that time and for the next 40 years. To achieve that aim, the chapter reviews the formation of the Bedaux company and the philosophy that underpinned its practices. To turn that philosophy into reality, the chapter will also review some of the early applications of the Bedaux company and the range of services that it provided. In addition, the chapter is also concerned with the views of some of the commentators at the time, and will provide a balanced account of these, as well as identifying the circumstances that forced irreversible changes to the Bedaux company's modus operandi.

Historical Foundations

Charles Eugene Bedaux, a naturalised American citizen of French origin, opened an office at Bush House, Aldwych in London in 1926 (Charles E. Bedaux and Company). This was an offshoot of an international operation that formally commenced in about 1918 in Cleveland, Ohio (Ferguson 1996a; Flanner 1945a).[2] It was not chance circumstances that brought Bedaux to Britain in the first place because, as the previous chapter highlighted, Bedaux consultants had previously conducted an assignment in Britain in 1923. This was at a subsidiary of an American company for which the Bedaux company had already provided services in the United States (Eastman Kodak Company). The most likely explanation why Bedaux went to the expense and took the risk of setting up a new business venture in an alien land was that he was a shrewd businessman and recognised the potential in Britain, as well as elsewhere in Europe, for the application of his efficiency methods.[3]

The first assignment in Britain in 1926 was in a similar vein to that of Eastman Kodak; namely for a subsidiary of an American company (British Goodrich Rubber Company Limited). Both the assignments were largely extensions of those conducted in the United States. In real terms, Bedaux had taken the opportunity to expand his operations into Britain on the back of work previously conducted. This begs the question, were there others in the wing waiting for similar opportunities? The simple answer is both yes and no. Yes, because within the United States at that time there was a significant volume of work being carried out in the name of 'efficiency' by engineers subsumed within the 'scientific management' tradition. Some of those engineers had made visits to Europe earlier in the century.[4] In fact, on one or two of these a young Charles Bedaux had accompanied those engineers as an interpreter (Kreis 1992).[5] The scientific management movement was burgeoning in France at that time and, hence, this was reflected in the growth of the number of individual practitioners in that country. Similarly within Germany there was a growing consultancy industry, with more than one hundred consultant practitioners operating there by the mid-1920s (Kipping 1997). In Britain there were no such firm foundations as resistance to change came from two broad areas, employers and employees.

There still remained during this period a broad continuation of the paternalistic approach adopted by employers and a rejection of outside intervention in the firm, specifically with regards to the strategic decision-making process. Within the employed population there was a general distrust of 'scientific' methods, especially within the trade unions. Negative reports had reached these shores of the work of efficiency engineers in the United States; even as early as the beginning of the century the trade unions had developed a network of contacts with trade unionists in America. The main differences between British trade unionists and their American peers was that in Britain trade unionism was more organised and militant. Therefore, trade unionists in Britain were more resistant to change, protectionist in their attitudes and taken more seriously as a force to be reckoned with by the employers. This may partly explain why in Britain the growth rate of management consultants was significantly less than in the United States.

Regardless of that overall situation, Bedaux had spotted an opening and commenced operations in the turbulent industrial environment of the 1920s. He was not alone. The next chapter will indicate that at least one other American consultancy company had opened an office in Britain by the end of the decade. This was, however, only on a small scale. Therefore, those American consultants who concerned themselves with efficiency at the shop floor level did not use Britain as a new base of operations at that time. The other group of consultants within the United States, those who developed services at the board room level of the firm, were not at that time in sufficient numbers to mount an assault on British businesses, this became a feature of later periods.[6]

A New Era in Consulting

The British Bedaux company was formed with a board of directors that was made up largely of American citizens. The one exception was Sir Francis Rose Price, a non-executive director, of native British origin.[7] The chairman of the company was Charles Bedaux, having appointed as managing director Frank R. Mead, the only American to take up residence in this country at that time. In practice, Mead was the chief, and one and only operating consultant, senior sales executive and director of operations. The other two Americans on the board were D.S. Keogh and R.B. Mudge. Both these men remained in the United States where they were senior executives in Bedaux's American operation. They visited Britain only on those occasions when the need demanded it.

The new Bedaux company, regardless of its geographical headquarters in the heart of London, and its British-based managing director, came under the direct control of its chairman residing, predominantly at that time, in the United States. Very little autonomy was afforded to the British operation in those early days, apart from its responsibility for generating its own business. The reason for this was that the working practices of the Company had been developed and documented through the experiences gained in the industrial environment of the United States under the direction of Bedaux himself and they were not open to negotiation or change. Bedaux firmly retained control of his global empire and all its international business activities. Any proposed changes first had to be authorised by him and these required the force of considerable persuasion before he considered any changes to his 'tried and tested' methods (Ferguson 1996a). In spite of this, it was the sales abilities and personal qualities of Frank Mead, together with the social and business connections of Sir Francis Rose Price, that were to play no small part in the initial success of the Company.

Mead was a professional consultant with a background in engineering, very determined and with a charming personality. He was experienced in matters relating to sales, and this combined with his professional expertise, enabled him to build a consultancy practice that grew from those initial modest beginnings. He developed a system of identifying potential client companies and corresponding with them in the form of a standard letter. The letter simply stated that he would be in the area between certain dates and that he would like the opportunity to discuss the Bedaux system with a view to commencing its application at the firm (Brownlow 1972). Sir Francis Rose Price assisted Mead in this marketing venture. Price's appointment to the board was probably no accident; in all likelihood Bedaux selected him for his business contacts and social position. Price advertised for an engineer and that attracted the attention of Norman Pleming, a professional engineer with a railway engineering and management background.[8] Following an interview with Price, Pleming accepted the post of Bedaux engineer and became the second operating consultant of the company in the latter months of 1926.

Training for a new consultant in the Company in 1926, and indeed up until the beginning of the 1930s, consisted of receiving a copy of the 1921 reprint of Bedaux's (1917) book, 'Industrial Management: The Bedaux Efficiency Course for Industrial Application'.[9] This was accompanied by a period of 'on-the-job' training in the company of an experienced consultant. In Pleming's case that was Mead. Training was relatively short because new recruits were chosen for their professional background and experience of management practice. The purpose of the training, therefore, was to learn the techniques associated with the Bedaux philosophy. It is the development and application of this system that remains Bedaux's legacy through to the present day. Terminology has changed, although the underlying principles have remained largely unaltered.

The Eight Principles of Industrial Efficiency

Bedaux suggested that his consultant service was capable of revolutionising the operation and output of a business through the implementation of methods aimed at improving the efficiency of operations at the shop floor level. The substance of that service had been committed to print in the form of a book (Bedaux 1917). The book was unusual in that it was a step-by-step guide for the improvement of operational efficiency based on the lessons learnt through the example of a fictional company that was badly managed and run. Each chapter in the book related to a lesson, or part of a lesson, and there were 18 in total. The stated audience for this publication were students of management, operational managers, businessmen and trainee consultants. Throughout its pages, Bedaux developed eight principles of 'Industrial Efficiency'. He suggested that each principle should not be viewed in isolation, but should be considered as a package of measures. From the British perspective, the importance of these principles lay in the fact that they formed the basis for subsequent techniques applied by other consultant companies following in Bedaux's wake within Britain. Because of the fundamental nature of this model in terms of the history of management consulting, it is important to understand in outline their application.

Principle 1: Keeping of Records

As much a reference to the formalisation of processes as to identifying the establishment of channels of responsibility. In Bedaux's view, records were pivotal to the efficient operation of the business and they underpinned all the other principles within his efficiency model. Records were responsible for describing particular aspects of the production process and, from that perspective, provided an audit trail in the event of subsequent review and/or amendment to those processes. Bedaux pointed out the importance of ensuring that duplicate records did not exist, thus preventing misunderstandings in the future. Ultimately, he hoped that his emphasis on providing this audit trail for subsequent review and amendment partly forced clients into an intellectual process of analysis, thereby creating a barrier for rash decisions based on pure intuition.[10]

Principle 2: Establishment of Standards

Linked to the 'Keeping of Records' through their formalisation in written form, 'standards', according to Bedaux, supported the determination of costs and provided the necessary information for establishing appropriate remuneration packages for the workforce. It was the determination of standards that lay at the heart of the Bedaux efficiency model.

From a practical perspective, three analytical techniques were associated with the principle of standards: waste, time and motion studies. The waste study was employed as the preparatory review for both the time and motion studies. It was an examination of the actions performed by individuals and/or groups of workers over the period of a working day. This would, according to Bedaux, provide a general idea of the percentage of wasted effort that resulted from the consequence of the 'current' working practices and methods. In effect, it was a visual review, noting the obvious wasted actions involved within a particular process. The second technique, the time study, was a determination of the time taken to complete an individual operation, or of a series of operations that were inter-linked. Once again, this could be carried out through an analysis of an individual's work or that of a group performing the same task. Bedaux viewed the total reliance on time study, which he suggested was a methodology employed by many consultants of his day, as being ineffective and inexact as it merely recorded existing operations without leading to any improvements. He believed that the setting of time standards, apart from its relationship with the other two forms of analysis, should also be positively linked with the standardisation of facilities (see principle six below). In effect, the development of time standards at this stage of the process provided consultants with a baseline upon which subsequent changes to methodologies could be compared, thus indicating the level of improvement.

The timing of operations was intimately associated with the third technique, motion study. Bedaux's definition of motion study related simply to the decomposition of operations with a view to creating improvements through either removing inefficient operations or implanting new improved ones. Motion study would lead, invariably, to recommendations for changes in methods. It was the new methods, when timed, with all elements of waste removed that formed the new standard. For each different operation or series of operations, a fresh analysis was conducted; this resulted in multiple 'standards' being set within each working environment. It was, therefore, through the application of all three analyses that best practice was recorded (standards) and timed. However, Bedaux suggested that there were real dangers associated with the overt timing of operations. These, in his view, resulted in either the speeding up or slowing down of operations simply because operatives were being observed and they were putting on a 'show'. This provided false readings of true attainment that would not be maintained. He argued that times should only be recorded when operatives had become used to the consultant's presence and a return to normal routine had taken place.

Bedaux further suggested that when setting formal standards, the average worker should be used as an exemplar (other prominent efficiency engineers at the time used the fastest and most efficient worker). In addition, allowances should be made for rest and potential delays to the process outside of the control of the operative. Bedaux further suggested that greater productivity would be achieved through the sub-division of labour, resulting in the specialisation of functions within the overall production process. The consequential outcome of this aspect of his model prompted others to argue that what was occurring was a form of deskilling and job fragmentation (Littler 1982). Bedaux's position was that specialisation enabled an increase in the level of individual expertise, albeit only in one area of the production process, and this resulted in output to improve overall. Consequently, this negated the need for employing expert labour because compliance with the standards set was achievable by all operatives that had received training in the specific skills associated with their individual operations.

Principle 3: Planning

'Planning' reflected the standards set and the formal records kept. Planning could take a number of forms, but was essentially determined by the type of operations being conducted. Bedaux suggested that the depth to which planning should take place was inversely related to the amount of detail and complexity within the manufacturing process. In other words, a complex multi-functional environment would require more detailed planning than a simple one product manufacturing process.

Principle 4: Compilation of Schedules

Each schedule indicates all the operations required to complete a task; this included information on when tasks were to be completed and the standards that were to be applied.

Principle 5: Routing and Despatching of Work

The 'routing and despatching of work' was a method of ensuring that the extraneous factors associated with direct operator performance were taken into consideration in order to avoid losses in time within the production process. Such factors included the layout of machinery, the movement of raw materials, workflow, and so on; these were optimised to reduce the risk of poor performance.

Principle 6: Standardisation

The concept of standardisation within Bedaux's model was wide-ranging and encompassed three sub-principles: the development of standard operations, the maintenance of standard conditions and the manufacture of a standard product range.

Standard Operations, a reference to the improved methods and processes for which defined time standards had been applied (principle 2).

Standard Conditions, this resulted from an investigation into three broad areas: the mechanical, the physical and the psychological. From the perspective of the mechanical, this was a reference to the building and its contents in which it was proposed that various studies take place to determine machinery location, stores control and general factory layout. Consequently, an environment was created that was free from obstructions and excessive movement of raw materials and finished products. In addition, the importance of utilisation of like machinery was stressed because this minimised the requirement for wide ranging skills within the maintenance department and negated the need for holding a large number of spare parts for a variety of different machines. Analyses within factories that utilised conveyor belt technology considered layout from the objective of simplifying the workflow process. The physical environment was analysed from the perspective of improving the general working conditions on the shop floor. This was an early example of taking into consideration health and safety aspects, coupled with recognition of the effects of fatigue associated with the intensity of effort required within some settings. Bedaux understood that whilst it may be possible to generate conditions in which the speed of processes were greatly improved, they could only be sustained through improvements to conditions that were aimed at enabling minimisation of effort. It is the combination of effort, rest and contingencies that provided the components that made up the timed standard. Bedaux suggested that an allowance for fatigue (rest) was so fundamental to the achievement of maximisation of output that a physical law existed:

> For a muscular effort of a given power, the duration of work and rest periods is inversely proportioned to the rapidity of the motion.

This was a crude attempt at suggesting that mathematical calculations could be made without real regard to the physiological differences between operatives. It, nevertheless, indicated a progressive attitude towards recognising what was possible with regards to the sustainable output of operators. The physical was linked to the psychological through the notion that creating appropriate conditions generated co-operation and self-discipline within the workforce; a happy worker was an effective worker.

Standard Product Range, an emphasis on the benefits associated with economies of scale. These were gained through a movement away from small-batch production, based on a wide variety of products, to long production runs based on a narrow product range. It was Bedaux's contention that this was made possible through a clear identification and understanding of the customer's needs. In essence, this was a reference to linking production to market demand in a disciplined environment of limiting ranges of products to a sustainable level.

Overall, therefore, the principle of standardisation was concerned with the setting of definitive operational standards, based on the sub-division of labour, in an environment that had been created through careful analysis to ensure optimum performance at least cost. This was then directed towards the production of a narrow range of goods, determined through market analysis, in order to achieve greater profits through economies of scale.

Principle 7: Graded Remuneration According to Individual Production

This principle generated the most hostility towards the application of Bedaux methods. However, it is sufficient to state at this juncture that graded remuneration was the principle of applying wage incentives based on the productivity of the operative. Unlike piecework and other incentive methods, its calculation was not initially given a monetary value, thereby ensuring its durability in fluctuating financial circumstances. Remuneration was based on a unit of production known as the 'Bedaux Unit', or simply the 'B Unit'. Each unit equated to one minute of time, or one sixtieth of a working hour at a pre-determined standard rate. Great emphasis is placed within Bedaux's book on the concept of quality being intimately linked with the level of output. In other words, production levels alone did not determine monetary reward; payment for productive output was based on both the quality and quantity of production. Thus, this ensured that standards were being maintained and that output was not artificially increased through the production of sub-standard products.

Principle 8: Standard Practice Instructions

'Standard practice instructions' were the all-encompassing written expression of the constraints of the operational process together with the desired outcome. For each process, standard practice instruction sheets were compiled where the level of supervision was such that no guarantee of the precise outcome of the operation could be given. This was with regard to efficiency and the level of optimum performance required of the operatives. Standard practice instruction sheets were compiled in such a way that clearly defined steps and procedures were annotated together with the expected outcome in terms of the standard. It was yet another level of administrative control aimed at ensuring optimum performance and typified the complex web of documentary practices that surround Bedaux applications.

In addition to his eight principles, Bedaux emphasised the importance of social welfare with regards to the workforce. It is, however, the efficiency model described above for which Bedaux is remembered best. His eight principles formed the core focus of the activities of his consultancy work within a package of measures that became known as work-study. The overall Bedaux model was modified and improved upon by other consultant companies and remained at the heart of service delivery applications in Britain whenever productive efficiency was the principle concern of the assignment. In essence, Bedaux's philosophy was simple: apply each principle in the spirit that it was developed, ensure compliance with each and the rewards would naturally follow. However, key to ensuring compliance with this process at the level of the shop floor was the complex reward package (principle 7) that was linked to the output of each individual operative.

The Bedaux 'B'

The period leading up to the Bedaux era, described in the previous chapter, witnessed the delivery of consultancy services that were based on the techniques that were developed by the individual consultants. What Bedaux achieved was the introduction of a system, based on systematic analysis, which was universally applied across the whole of management consultancy for at least the next 40 years, albeit with some modifications. His package also included operator training, the training of supervisors and functional managers, appreciation courses for senior management and the training of selected individuals in order to carry the application forward long after the consultants had completed their assignment. These aspects will be reviewed in later chapters. At the core of the package of measures, and pivotal to them, lay a financial reward system based on the productivity of operatives, the 'direct' workers of the business. This package became known as the 'Bedaux Premium Points Plan'.

The Plan was based on a non-monetary indicator known as the 'Bedaux Unit', or simply the 'B Unit'.[11] Reward systems such as those devised by Bedaux were controversial, receiving both support and criticism. Where support was evident, the virtues that were highlighted included the potential for providing high average productivity per employee, greater employee rewards, self imposed penalties for those individuals who were less industrious, the provision of information on which to base operator training regimes and better management information (Sellie 1982). If not properly employed, such a methodology would have the opposite effect. At the heart of the Bedaux model, the 'B', as it shall henceforward be known, was the pivotal mechanism that linked the standard, determined by analysis, with the wage level, determined by output. The previous section highlighted that Bedaux considered it a mistake simply to time existing operations without applying improvements and to ensure that momentum could be maintained and that an allowance should be applied for operator fatigue and contingencies.

One should not get confused with jargon that gives the appearance of scientific legitimacy. Whilst the recognition of rest as an important factor in the maintenance of output was clearly a step forward, its calculations cannot be considered scientific because they were never open to any formal process of critical review. They were ad hoc in nature, reflecting the contingency requirements of the client's business, including possible constraints imposed by the local labour market, together with an element of pure guesswork. They were, however, in the main, remarkably accurate for all that (Littler 1982). Because the time standards developed by the Bedaux approach were based on the output of the average worker, this afforded opportunities for increased output through exertion above the norm. It was to this time standard, together with its allowances for rest and contingencies, that the concept of the B was applied which marked the main difference between the Bedaux system and others that appeared outwardly similar.

The B was more than a calculation of effort and rest, it was a statement of the working environment pertaining to the expected output of the operative. For output to be achieved at the expected level consistently, conditions had to be standardised and free from distractions, such as delays in raw material flows, which would prevent output being maintained at the declared standard. Therefore, reduced levels of output resulted when the working rhythm was adversely affected, but would then rise when effort was increased and rest not taken. As an explanation of the benefits of the Bedaux system, Carney (undated) suggested that it was reasonable to expect: a 40 per cent increase in worker productivity, a reduction of 20 per cent in unit labour costs and a rise of 12½ per cent in the hourly earnings rate of workers. Consequently, employers expected a greater increase in output at proportionately lower labour costs or to maintain 'current' levels at lower costs. For 'current' output to be maintained at proportionately lower costs, then, all aspects of the production process had to be operating at maximum efficiency. However, generally for such cost reductions to be achieved, fewer employed operatives performed at a higher rate of productivity.

Operatives were guaranteed payment for output at a level of 60 Bs per hour, regardless of whether or not they actually attained it.[12] To help achieve the standard Bedaux insisted that before moving over to the new payment system the standard was put on trial for a period of at least one-month. In his view, that would provide operatives with the time necessary to gain confidence in the new methods and raise output to the required level. During that trial period and beyond, the Bedaux consultant assisted in the training of operatives. There was, for all that, a 'sting in the tail'. It was Bedaux's philosophy, at least during these early years of application of his methods in this country, that direct operatives (those intimately engaged in the production process) should only receive 75 per cent of the bonus attributed to raising the level of output above the standard. It was Bedaux's contention that the standard rate of 60 Bs per hour could only be achieved through the efforts of the whole workforce, not just the direct operatives. The maintenance of the standard, and increases to it, were perceived to be the direct consequence of the effort of all workers, at various levels in the firm – direct, indirect and supervisory, these included personnel such as machine setters, inspectors and maintenance men, as well as supervisors and office staff. If direct workers were paid 100 per cent of the bonus, there would be no incentive for the remainder of the production 'team' to create the conditions to enable output to rise. It was, therefore, Bedaux's view that because all workers had a stake in the process of raising levels of productivity then all workers should receive a reward as an incentive to ensure that that the so-called 'normal' working conditions were maintained.

Consequently, only 75 per cent of the bonus was paid to the direct operatives and the remaining 25 per cent were distributed to those not intimately involved in direct production (Brownlow 1972). Of that 25 per cent:

- a quarter went to foremen as an incentive to ensure that disruptions were kept to a minimum;
- a quarter went to those individuals in direct support of the operatives (indirect workers);
- a half went to cover clerical costs and to production control staff.

The Bedaux system was maligned and received extensive critical review, both in the contemporary press and by some prominent individuals concerned with management processes and the welfare of the working man (see below). Other criticisms centred around the complex web of administrative processes and documentation associated with the Bedaux system, not least of which related to documentation which was designed to compare the results of output levels of individual operatives and departments. Such documentation, reflecting the performance of operatives, was open to review through 'Posting Sheets' that recorded output on a daily basis in relation to operational sections or groups, and were displayed prominently for all to see within the factory. These documents, and others, enabled managers to view individual performance and enabled the operative to see the amount of bonus payment that was owed to them. From these 'Posting Sheets', 'Weekly Analysis Sheets' were produced comparing the performance of individual sections within the workshop.

In large multi-factory companies, these documents enabled comparisons to be made between plants. Importantly, criticism centred on the fact that performance under standard was laid bare for all to see. The concern was that this public display engendered fear for the security of employment on the part of the poorly performing operatives. Nevertheless, in those early days, as a result of practical applications in the United States, the Bedaux system received some qualified support. That support centred on the notion that if the Bedaux system was applied in an objective and fair manner, and that the welfare of the worker was taken into consideration, it would receive the support of both management and the employees alike (Lytle 1929).[13] However, theory is one thing, practical application was somewhat different.

Theory into Reality

Two operating consultants (one the managing director, the other the trainee), a non-executive director and a single client were the foundations upon which Charles E. Bedaux Limited became established in Britain. The early assignments of the company were centred in and on the manufacturing and engineering sectors, and were confined to the practical aspects of the production process and payment incentive schemes. As mentioned above, the first client of the company, a British offshoot of an American concern, was the British Goodrich Rubber Company Limited. This was an extension of an application that had commenced in the United States with the parent company. The operating consultant was Mead, assisted after a short period by the trainee Norman Pleming. The assignment commenced on 27 September 1926 with a visit to the company by Sir Francis Rose Price and Frank Mead. The latter conducting what can only be described as a preliminary investigation. The original series of reports survived in part (Mead 1926), and much can be learnt from them in terms of the assignment and the Bedaux approach in general. Within the reports there are indications that, even at that time, compromises had to be made due to the inappropriateness of employing the American model within the British environment. Goodrich, therefore, provides an example of the extent to which theory had to be adjusted to suit the practical realities of the operational setting.

Goodrich (situated at Leyland in Lancashire) was a large manufacturing company for its day. Apart from managerial, clerical and other support staff, 450 operatives were employed at the premises. The payment structure for workers engaged in direct production was split between piecework and daywork. From the preliminary investigation report, three important points are noted. Firstly, the Tube Department was identified as the appropriate starting point for the Bedaux application because, from the perspective of Goodrich's management, this would provide the most dramatic impact in terms of efficiency and savings. This was important from the general perspective of acceptance and as a demonstration of the justification for bringing in the Bedaux consultants. Secondly, initial studies conducted on the first day, a form of limited 'waste study', indicated that savings of between 16 and 44 per cent could be made. Finally, the need for an appropriately selected representative of the firm to be trained in Bedaux methods for continuance of the application in the post-assignment period was highlighted.[14]

The assignment was largely a success with improvements to productivity justifying the consultants' involvement, but a number of negative features emerged that were replicated in some subsequent assignments conducted by the Bedaux company. There was a lack of consultation between the consultants and the workforce, and management was relied upon to keep the workers informed of the progress of the assignment (this was a criticism that haunted many of the early Bedaux assignments). Consequently, there was a lack of understanding on the part of the workforce of the overall objectives of the assignment; this was clearly a failure of the principle of consultation at all levels. It was probably not surprising, therefore, that this lack of understanding was reflected in a general belief that the 'normal' rate of 60 'Bs' was impossible to attain. This psychological barrier may have been one of the root causes for output levels remaining below the level of expectation; in fact they fluctuated between 27 and 65½ Bs, with the scale skewing towards the lower end of the range. Because of these negative features there was a break up in relations between the consultants and the workforce and their immediate supervisors; this led to modifications being made to the remuneration package to make it more acceptable on the shopfloor. Therefore, the B did not reflect the analysis conducted and productivity targets were below expectations.

There was clearly a failure on the part of the Bedaux consultants to implement all the elements of the Bedaux approach. Failure to implement aspects of that approach would have, and did have, the effect of watering down the impact of the assignment in terms of productivity improvements. It is not surprising, therefore, that in those early days that some applications of the Bedaux approach were not always wholly welcome, especially on the part of the workers and some sections of the supervisory team responsible for the operational sections of the direct workers. It is also not surprising that in the period following on from the application of such assignments, some firms made modifications and on a number of occasions Bedaux practices were ceased altogether (Wilson 1995). However, more significant is that the outcome of some of these early assignments, especially in the period at the end of the decade, resulted in industrial action (this is covered in the later sections of this chapter).

Initial Growth

Using the analogy of a military operation, the Bedaux company had established a 'beachhead' in Britain and the assignment at Goodrich provided it with the opportunity to 'breakout' (expand its operations). It set the scene for growth, both in terms of the number of assignments conducted and in the numbers of consultants employed by the Company in the first eight years of its existence. On 13 December 1926 the second assignment for the Bedaux company commenced at the British-American Tobacco Company Limited (BAT) at Liverpool. The consultant in charge of this assignment was Norman Pleming, fresh from his experiences at Goodrich. This assignment, the same as the one carried out at Leyland, consisted of time study operations in parallel with the development of a staff remuneration package based on the B Unit.

The methods employed at BAT mirrored precisely those used at Goodrich. A partial survey was conducted on the first day when an initial assessment of the situation was made. Such a pattern of activity continued to exist until the methods of conducting survey analysis improved through the process of time. These improvements centred on the separation of the survey from the main assignment, being conducted as an important first stage and prior to it. The survey highlighted, among other things, whether or not the assignment lent itself to consultant intervention, what the parameters of the task should be, what the potential areas were where improvements could be made and the development of a set of terms of reference. Necessarily, therefore, there should be a gap between the initial investigation and the assignment to permit suitable preparation and review to take place.

By the end of 1926 the Bedaux company recognised the need for expansion. A second British engineer, John Leslie Orr, responded to an advertisement that had been placed in a number of leading newspapers by Sir Francis Rose Price. Orr had a different background from Pleming in that he had no previous experience of scientific management methods in its definitive sense, but he was, nevertheless, well accustomed to analytical review of management practices, having had experience abroad in a consultant capacity. He was a Scotsman by birth and had returned to Britain having had spent a number of years working in South Africa, New Zealand and Australia.[15] Orr was successful in his application and joined Pleming in the early months of 1927 on a very important assignment, as it later turned out, at Messrs. J. Lyons and Company Limited (bakery supplies). At Lyons the time study operations, which had included motion study analysis, drew attention to the considerable potential for efficiency savings. A re-distribution of manpower had the effect of enabling greater output without an increase in the number of operatives engaged within the various processes (Pleming 1927). These savings resulted from the erosion of idle time and improvements to processes connected with the flow of resources; worker productivity, based on new methods and a re-distribution of staff, increased considerably.

What the assignment highlighted was the importance of continuance in terms of the consultant remaining on the client's premises and assisting with the introduction of the new methods.[16] As a consequence of a knock-on effect in later stages of the production process, problems resulted from the initial application of the recommended course of action that highlighted the need for changes to working practices elsewhere within the factory. In outline, efficiencies in one area – the swiss roll rolling area – resulted in increased production with reduced worker input. Increased production consequently caused bottlenecks in other departments because those departments had not received the benefits of consultant review and the improved methods. Subsequent studies, and the resultant improvements to those other areas, had the effect of removing these bottlenecks and increasing production overall within the division. Without a flexible approach, facilitated through the continuing involvement of the consultant within the assignment process, savings would not have been realised in this instance. In all likelihood, without Pleming's intervention the improvements would have been discontinued. As a direct consequence of the work carried out by Pleming (Pleming 1968), there were a number of extensions to the original assignment within the Lyons company. These extensions included work in provincial bakeries, Hayes Laundry, Strand Hotels, Lyons Tea Shops and the Lyons factories producing tea, coffee and confectionery.

An extremely important facet of this assignment was the keen interest taken by the management of the Lyons company in the progress made. This was especially in those areas that involved staff training for facilitating the continuance and maintenance of the Bedaux methods at the conclusion of the assignment. The management were clearly impressed with the work of the consultants, being reflected in the extensions that were authorised to the original assignment. From small beginnings, the Lyons assignment generated increased business for the Bedaux company and spread the delivery of its methods across a range of locations within the food industry. Without doubt, this was an important turning point. As a consequence of the assignment, the directors of Lyons agreed to provide recommendations of the work of Bedaux consultants to prospective clients (Brownlow 1972). Because of these recommendations, a lot of additional work was gained.

The first eight years of the Bedaux company's history (1926-1933) bore witness to steady growth. In terms of staff numbers, this was from a consultant strength of two in 1926 to 40 by 1931. The majority of these men were engineers; all were professionally qualified within their own discipline areas and experienced managers. Their collective experience and antecedence enabled the company to increase its range of services; from an initial concentration on time study and associated premium payment systems to assignments that had an orientation towards production planning and control, costing, operator training, factory layout and organisation structure review. By the end of the period the client list included within it many firms that would comfortably fit within a 'Who's Who of Business'. Amongst these firms, and in addition to those previously mentioned, were Imperial Chemical Industries; Peak, Frean and Company Limited; Huntley and Palmers Limited; Avon Tyre Company; Wolsey Limited; Joseph Lucas Limited; Mander Brothers Limited; James Hayes and Company Limited; Enfield Cable Works Limited; to name but a few. Therefore, accumulated client numbers had risen from one in 1926 to 50 in 1931. Charles E. Bedaux Limited had made its mark; it had broken out of the 'Beachhead' and was expanding its involvement in Britain's industrial and commercial milieu.[17]

Concern and Critique

Concern had been expressed over the relative merits and usefulness of the techniques employed by the Bedaux company as well as other scientific management methods in Britain. This continued to be the case with Bedaux long after his name ceased to be specifically associated with such methods.[18] Inevitably, where concern is expressed some form of critique will follow. Examples of critical review can be found within numerous sources up to and including the present day. For a balanced perspective, and one in which the effects of the period co-locate themselves with the review itself, the following four contemporary accounts provide an insight into the perceived merits and usefulness of Bedaux methods.

Dr C.H. Northcott

In the May 1932 issue of *Unity* Dr. C.H. Northcott wrote an article entitled 'The Bedaux System: A Critical Appraisal'. Northcott was the Labour Manager of Rowntree's of York and a highly regarded figure in industrial circles.[19] The Rowntree company had no links with the Bedaux company or its techniques, therefore this important appraisal was based on an independent analysis of the Bedaux methods. The article contained an outline examination of the various techniques found within the Bedaux system and a summarisation of the main points with regards to the author's impressions and criticisms. At the outset Northcott levelled criticism of all such methods that had been developed outside of this country, specifically those that had not been adapted to serve the needs of the British industrial environment. This was a direct criticism of Bedaux and a reference to the industrial action taking place at that time in a number of establishments where Bedaux's methods had been employed. Northcott's appraisal highlighted nine individual points, some of which can be viewed positively and others less so. A general comment, however, indicated that some companies were forced to modify the Bedaux applications in order to make them more acceptable to their individual labour force. This was precisely what happened at Goodrich in order to prevent industrial action. The nine individual points made by Northcott can be grouped into four broader areas:

- There was little evidence to support contentions that speeding up resulted as a consequence of Bedaux applications. Quite the reverse; he felt that generally the standard (60 Bs) was set lower than could reasonably be expected. Therefore, in his view, the Bedaux consultants had not gone far enough in raising the levels of efficiency overall.
- Of all the incentive schemes available to industrial enterprises at that time, Northcott indicated that operatives faired less well under the Bedaux system in terms of remuneration. This is partly a reference to only 75 per cent of the potential bonus being paid to operatives (see the final point below). However, in terms of the employer, the Bedaux system provided the greatest return on unit labour costs.
- There was a general pre-occupation on the part of Bedaux consultants with obtaining time values for operations at the expense of efficiency improvements. By this, Northcott meant that existing operations were timed, thus providing definitive time data, but there was a general failure to remove the elements of waste from the operations through the introduction of new methods. This is a damning criticism because it indicates that the emphasis was on introducing a new payment regime at the expense of more wide-ranging improvements to operational efficiency.
- The allocation of 25 per cent of the bonus payments to indirect workers was considered a disincentive to the direct workers. Furthermore, Northcott felt that the practice should cease in order to make Bedaux applications more acceptable to workforces in general.

Northcott's account was an important contribution, primarily because of its independent and objective nature, and may have prompted, at the time, a realisation that improvements to the Bedaux system were a prerequisite for maximising its incentive value. His comments relating to lost efficiencies are an indication of the debate over the relative importance of time study versus methods study. In Bedaux's view there was no debate as each method was important in its own right, with timing representing the formalisation of standards following methods improvement, a point clearly made by Bedaux (1917) in his book. Therefore, a failure to maximise on the available efficiencies provides an indication, once again, that the

Bedaux philosophy was not always practised with vigour by some consultants of the Company during those early assignments.

Trades Union Congress

At about the same time (1932), and precisely because its members felt that the Bedaux methods were unwelcome, the Trades Union Congress presented a report on the findings of an inquiry over the deployment of the Bedaux system in British industry. The stated purpose of the report was to provide an objective assessment of Bedaux methods. Included within the report was a presentation of the experiences of a number of trade unions in their efforts to either defeat or modify some of the effects of Bedaux (Trades Union Congress 1932). One would expect that a report by such a body, some of whose members were at that time openly engaged in tactics to ensure the discontinuance of Bedaux methods, would present a damning argument in favour of its removal from the workplace. This was not entirely the case as the report had the face validity of a balanced and objective assessment, primarily because it canvassed and took note of a range of opinion. Not only opinion from its members, but also from the National Institute of Industrial Psychology and from the Bedaux company in the person of John Leslie Orr.

One hundred and four unions affiliated to the Trades Union Congress replied to the questionnaire that was sent out to seek their views. Of these, five unions had successfully resisted attempts to impose the application of Bedaux methods. Two were engaged in the process of their introduction and six had experience of its usage. The remainder (91) had no direct experience of the operation of the system. This was not entirely surprising because a number of firms where Bedaux methods were employed had no formal union representation. Regardless of the limitations concerning the TUC's direct involvement with Bedaux applications, a number of important criticisms manifested themselves within the report. There was a general view within the report that straightforward piece-rate payment systems were preferred because it was felt all other reward systems, especially Bedaux, resulted in an increase of effort for proportionately less reward. This again highlighted the Bedaux practice of transferring 25 per cent of the bonus payments to indirect workers. In any event, the TUC suggested that the calculations used to determine bonus payments were too complex to be easily understood by the operatives. Workers were unable to calculate their likely bonus payments or confirm in retrospect that the bonus paid was correct. In addition to these issues, the TUC was also concerned with the psychological effects of Bedaux applications on two accounts.

The TUC felt that workers were being de-humanised to the extent that there was a general perception on their part that Bedaux consultants treated them simply as a factor in the production process. In other words, the consultants were mechanising their human operations. This led, it was believed, to a loss of pride on the part of the workers through their inability to demonstrate effectively the quality of their work. Equally important was the feeling of insecurity, resulting in the notion that as a consequence of the enactment of new efficiency processes labour was vulnerable to displacement. In other words, it was inevitable that redundancies always followed the application of Bedaux methods. The report went on to state that, in the opinion of the TUC, the benefits to management were overshadowed by high installation costs. Consequently, some employers urged consultants to come to a speedy conclusion. This, it was argued, resulted in a less than accurate assessment.

Having said this, the report concluded that of all the payment by results systems available at that time, the Bedaux system facilitated timely management information and was less harmful to the workforce than the other systems.[20] The essential ingredient, as far as the TUC was concerned, was that the consultation process, a pivotal mechanism, should always be followed with vigour. This was to prevent actions that may result in speeding up of the work process to the disadvantage of the ordinary workers. On balance, the report, based on the experience of just over ten per cent of the corporate membership that replied to the questionnaire, accepted the inevitability of the introduction of such methods. However, they remained cautious of the outcome of applications without prior consultation and some form of modification.

A Correspondent

In the following year (1933), and at the end of this chapter in terms of time-span, an article appeared in *The Manchester Guardian Commercial* on 10 June. It was simply titled 'The Bedaux System in Britain: Eliminating Wastage in Works', written by 'a correspondent'. The report had the outward appearance of an independent account, but sought to provide responses to some of the criticisms levelled against the application of Bedaux methods. The whole of the article portrayed the Bedaux company as the saviour of industrial enterprises through a focus of attention on eliminating those aspects of the operational setting that produced waste in terms of effort and practices. It attempted to describe the method of application and the reasoning behind the reward system for indirect input to the outcome of production – the 25 per cent bonus payment to indirect operatives. The usage of the article as a propaganda instrument was not lost on the Bedaux company who reproduced it as a marketing aid for potential clients.

P.K. Standring

An address given by P.K. Standring (1934), a works manager at Imperial Chemical Industries, to the Manchester Branch of the British Works Management Association was reproduced in written form within the May/June issue of *Industry Illustrated*. Both ICI and Standring had had experience of Bedaux applications since 1929 and Standring was clearly a supporter of their outcome. Notwithstanding, this is an important contribution in that it portrays the perspective of management in the light of criticisms levelled by the unions. Standring pointed out that craft production methods were no longer appropriate in large industrial operations and that the division of labour, based on specialism of work, was more effective in the workshops of industrial enterprises. He believed that the application of methods directed at improving productive processes had a part to play in ensuring an effective and efficient outcome. Standring offered a note of caution, and agreed with the position of the unions, that the consultation process should be applied in all instances in order to ensure a more consensual outcome – a lesson no doubt learned through the bitter experience of industrial conflict within ICI itself.

All four accounts, when taken in concert, generally provide a balanced examination of the real effects of employing techniques that radically changed the workings of the operational environment, at least within settings involving physical productive output. Each account examined the Bedaux methodology from different viewpoints. However, collectively they provide a series of recommendations that were largely heeded in the light of the experience gained through industrial action in the period of the early 1930s.

Clandestine Operations

The work of Bedaux consultants, principally in the first three years of the 1930s, was constrained partly through criticisms of their modus operandi. This was in addition to the effects of protective practices deployed by both unions and non-unionised workforces in the businesses to which their methods were directed (see the next section). Bedaux consultants were unwelcome in the workplace and, in some instances, open hostility was expressed. It is generally agreed that the processes of study and timing should be conducted openly, a position argued by Bedaux himself. However, during the latter part of this period, at a time when unemployment levels were unacceptably high in Britain, the Bedaux company viewed it necessary to conduct some of its work in a covert manner within the workplace.[21]

Consequently, many of the assignments were conducted under a veil of secrecy, with consultants infiltrating into the factories of their clients in the guise of workers going about their normal activities. There were three primary reasons given for this (Brownlow 1972). Firstly, there was a general mistrust of efficiency measures anyway and the Bedaux system was particularly visible at that time. Secondly, there were allegations of Bedaux imitators employing techniques that were often not successful in terms of achieving improvements to efficiency; these assignments had a negative impact on the workforce. And, finally, during the latter part of this period inflammatory speeches and adverse publicity shrouded the whole Bedaux operation. For example, the *Daily Worker* was in the vanguard of the anti-Bedaux publicity campaign throughout the period, utilising headlines such as 'Fight the Yankee Speed-Up System'. To highlight this point, on those occasions when clandestine tactics had not been employed it became necessary, on occasions, for the police to escort consultants to and from their assignments (Tisdall 1982). The effects of this period on the length to which some consultants felt it necessary to go is exemplified by a quotation by Brownlow (1972); she describes a particular incident involving two Bedaux consultants:

> As an illustration of the effectiveness with which this secrecy was observed can be cited in the case of a certain consultant living in a small provincial hotel. He and his wife became on friendly terms with another resident in the same establishment, also accompanied by his wife. After several weeks of cordial friendship between the two families, the wife of one observed to the other that her husband's work 'sounded somewhat similar' to that of her own husband. Imagine her surprise when she discovered that both of their husbands were on the staff of the Bedaux company, assigned to two neighbouring clients.

Therefore, the Bedaux company viewed the situation as being so critical that not only was there a perceived need to disguise the work of consultants in the workplace but that security should be maintained even within its own organisation.

Such tactics involving the veil of secrecy are understandable when one considers the personal welfare and safety of the consultants themselves. Equally, the fear of Bedaux methods, expressed through hostility, can partly be explained by the concerns of working people in an environment where unemployment levels were high. Especially, when one considers the rarity of redundancy payments in such conditions at that time.

Industrial Strife, Break-Up and Into a New Era

The lengths to which Bedaux consultants were forced to go were the consequence of an industrial environment in which labour unrest was being openly expressed through industrial action of varying magnitude. In the early 1930s, partly because of Bedaux applications, the industrial situation worsened and open hostility became a common event.

The period of the first three or four years of the 1930s was probably the least memorable for the Bedaux company. The economy was suffering badly and this was reflected in a generally poor employment situation overall. It would be difficult, therefore, to imagine a less than ideal environment in which to conduct consultancy operations. The employment of new practices for effecting improvements to efficiency would also potentially have the effect of displacing labour. Little wonder, then, that during this period worker resistance to the introduction of Bedaux methods was at its height.

Claims by the Bedaux company of savings in unit labour costs of approximately 38 per cent did little to improve the general situation (Horn 1983). All told, 18 stoppages during the period were attributed to the introduction of the Bedaux system within firms in Britain. This was approximately one third of the total number of assignments conducted by Bedaux consultants during this period. Of these 18, five lasted in duration for periods in excess of five months, with the majority of the remainder being settled within a week (Kreis 1987). Typical of the disputes occurring at that time were those that took place at the Wolsey company plant in Leicester, Richard Johnson and Nephew in Manchester and the Rover company plant in Coventry.

Wolsey

Wolsey was a hosiery company and one of the top twelve engaged in this sector of the market. As a consequence of the work carried out by Bedaux consultants at the plant, employment practices changed dramatically; job fragmentation and de-skilling was the outcome (Littler 1982). Jobs were re-classified with some skilled functions downgraded in status to unskilled. This resulted in some craft workers being replaced by cheaper, less experienced and unqualified labour. Littler suggested that part of the problem was that a new form of process was developed, 'stretch-out', in which machine operatives that had traditionally minded six machines oversaw the operation of nine, an increase of 50 per cent to their workload. Because of this, two separate forms of resistance can be identified at the plant: supervisory and worker resistance. Supervisory resistance took the form of nonco-operation and obstruction. The attempts by Bedaux consultants to replace unco-operative foremen, either through dismissal or through moving them elsewhere within the plant, resulted in a strengthening of unity between both the supervisors and the operatives. Worker resistance was less subtle and took the form of industrial action.

The first strike at Wolsey lasted for three weeks, commencing on 10 November 1930. Even following the cessation of this particular strike, industrial action continued. This occurred in the form of short stoppages, go-slows and sit-ins following a refusal to implement the new system, together with a series of mass meetings, culminating in an all-out strike which commenced in December 1931 and continued until 12 February 1932. Management took the unprecedented action of posting a notice giving the workforce a week's notice of termination of their contracts unless industrial action was called off. Behind the scenes, however, management was critical of some of the aspects of the Bedaux application and negotiations were initiated between the two parties. Unusually, a local dignitary, the Lord Mayor of Leicester, led these. The outcome of the negotiations resulted in a compromise, reflected in an adjustment to the Bedaux application. This adjustment resulted in direct labour receiving the full bonus attributed to its efforts, with the exception of only five per cent being taken in recognition of the importance of indirect inputs. Guarantees were given to the effect that those parts of the factory that had not been subjected to the Bedaux system would remain on the old payment system for a trial period of three months following the change. The final act of compromise was the formation of a 'Works Consultative Committee' at each of the premises within the Wolsey group.

Richard Johnson and Nephew

At the wiredrawing factory of Richard Johnson and Nephew, a highly unionised workforce was engaged in capital-intensive production processes. Industrial action at this plant was a protracted affair and never reached an entirely satisfactory conclusion. This particular action is important from the perspective that the outcome at this plant was different from the majority of other industrial actions taking place during that period. Following a long period of reorganisation, a policy of job fragmentation was implemented. This included the separation of work planning from implementation, and the separation of direct and indirect labour processes.

The machine-man ratio, in similar fashion to Wolsey, had been 'stretched out' resulting in an intensification of effort and a break-up of team working. This was emphasised by the two-man operator teams being downgraded to single operator status. Here, primarily because supervisory staff was in receipt of bonus payments, supervisory resistance was less apparent than was the case at Wolsey. Worker action initially took the form of protestations, which resulted in management confining Bedaux activity to the less-unionised areas of the factory. This all occurred during the period of February 1933 to March 1934. However, at the end of this period – slightly outside the terms of reference for this chapter – Bedaux methods were applied to highly unionised departments and, inevitably, a strike ensued. This resulted in a recommendation by the Bedaux consultants to employ 'scab labour' (a non-unionised workforce brought in from outside the Company). The strike spread and eventually six hundred men were refusing to work under the Bedaux regime. The company announced its intention to employ replacement labour and the 600 strikers became effectively unemployed. The strike was over, but a penalty to Richard Johnson and Nephew followed in the form of a new labour force lacking many of the skills of the old, and it subsequently proved difficult to train the new operatives in some of the new functional tasks. Littler (1982) suggested that the cost to Richard Johnson and Nephew also included a fracturing of relations with the local community, even though ultimately output at the firm eventually increased following the changes.

Rover Car Company

The dispute at the Rover Car Company had a completely different outcome to the other two. Here, the Bedaux application had as one of its primary aims the equalisation of wage structures. These had traditionally been based on either gender (male/female) or on skill (skilled/unskilled). Equalisation, it was perceived, would remove these barriers, both in terms of pay and in terms of skill. The pilot scheme was centred in the Trim Shop where female trimmers provided the labour force for the operation. Unexpectedly, on Rover's part, the female workers resisted because of fears of speeding up.[22] Significant support was given by the remainder of the workforce at Coventry and Rover was forced to abandon its aspirations for wage equalisation (Downs 1990).

There were three main outcomes to industrial disputes relating to Bedaux applications. Either the application was continued regardless of the hostility and ultimate outcome in terms of the labour force, as emphasised through the experience at Richard Johnson and Nephew. Or, adjustments were subsequently made to the recommended outcomes of the application as a consequence of the pressures brought to bear, as was the case at Wolsey. Or finally, the application was completely abandoned, as was the experience at Rover. Each of the major disputes during this period involving Bedaux consultants fell into one or other of these three categories.

Britain was not alone, industrial disputes were also occurring in the United States for very similar reasons as those in Britain, albeit not on such a grand scale. One such example occurred at the Weyerhaeuser Timber Company Mills at Willapa Harbor. Here, a seventeen-month struggle during 1933-1935 resulted in the abandonment of the Bedaux application (Egolf 1985). Notwithstanding, not all labour saving measures during this period proved quite so contentious, nor did they necessarily result in a displacement of labour. At Mander Brothers Limited in Wolverhampton in 1932, the first forty-hour week was introduced through efficiency savings and productivity increases as a consequence of a Bedaux assignment, all without a fall in general wage levels.

There were, however, widely expressed concerns over the effects that efficiency changes had on the labour population. Consequently, two studies were carried out to determine whether the introduction of Bedaux methods had a detrimental effect on the health of those introduced to the new practices. The first of these was carried out at Imperial Chemical Industries at the behest of management following a dispute in the Metals Division. Two groups of workers were selected, one that had used Bedaux methods and the other not. Age and type of work, including general conditions were matched in both groups. The outcome of the test resulted in 'a clean bill of health' being awarded (Tisdall 1982). Similarly, the Company Medical Officer of Joseph Lucas conducted a series of tests in 1932. In this instance, groups of women workers were subjected to medical examination to establish whether Bedaux methods caused undue strain. Again, this produced similar results. Nevertheless, while some limited medical evidence failed to identify adverse effects, concern over Bedaux methods was expressed both within industry and in the Bedaux company alike, albeit for different reasons.

New Beginnings

The adverse reactions to many of the assignments conducted by the Bedaux consultants had an impact on management and personnel within the Bedaux company and morale amongst the staff suffered. Changes to policy with regards to the payment of bonuses to direct workers, an increase in emphasis on the consultation process and the implementation of new forms of service packages in less contentious areas followed as a consequence of a review carried out by the Company. In spite of this, two notable defections from the Bedaux ranks signalled a partial break-up of the team and pointed the way forward for more positive improvements to services in the wider consultancy environment.

One of the first defections was John Leslie Orr, a Scotsman of high personal integrity. Orr was one of the two earliest British recruits to the company in 1927. He considered it necessary to appraise Charles Bedaux personally of the disquiet he felt with regard to the general labour situation within those firms that had been subjected to Bedaux applications (Ferguson 1996a). In addition, he also expressed concern over his perception of the erosion of the quality of Bedaux services. This was, in his view, being the inevitable consequence of a policy of rapid expansion that necessitated a considerable input in the number of recruits to the Company without effective mechanisms for ensuring that adequate training was provided. Chance circumstances brought Orr into contact with Lyndall Fownes Urwick, via an introduction through Esmond Milward, the librarian and manager of the Management Library.[23] Milward suggested that the two men join in forming a consulting partnership, Orr to provide the expertise, and Urwick the contacts (opportunities for promoting the company) and capital.

Shortly after this, Orr was approached by the Honourable Maurice Lubbock and was invited to join him in forming another management consultancy practice. Orr, being of high principles, felt it necessary to refuse because of his on-going negotiations with Urwick. He did, however, recommend another Bedaux consultant, Robert Bryson, one of Orr's juniors in the Company whom he held in high regard. Bryson and Lubbock met and consequently in the early months of 1934 Bryson left Bedaux service and joined with Lubbock in forming Production Engineering Limited. Orr, who had agreed to join with Urwick in forming Urwick, Orr and Partners Limited, followed him in the September of that year. The winds of change had blown and this heralded wider changes, both within the Bedaux company and in the consultancy environment overall (see Chapter 3).

Notes

1. This trend continued through to the 1940s, albeit on a smaller scale, with approximately 2.5 to 3 million worker-days lost per year.
2. Flanner wrote a series of three articles for the *New Yorker* in September and October 1945, entitled 'Annals of Collaboration'.

3. Charles Eugene Bedaux was born in Charenton-le-Pont, a suburb of Paris, on 11 October 1886. As a youth, Bedaux was restless and, despite his poor educational attainments, emigrated to the United States in February 1906. His command of the English language was limited and he had very little money to spend. Consequently, his early years in America were spent in menial and labouring type employments. For example, for a time Bedaux was employed as a 'sandhog', a tunneler on the Hudson River project (Brownlow 1972). This was an extremely dangerous and physically tiring occupation that took place in confined spaces, in extreme conditions of temperature and atmospheric pressure. There was a danger that after a period of time spent underground the men involved in this form of work could suffer from a condition commonly referred to now as the 'bends'. At that time the decompression chamber had yet to be invented. Brownlow believed that it was this experience that was subsequently to provide Bedaux with the idea of including into his time-study calculations an element for the hazards of the job. However, it was associations with efficiency engineers through various later employments that wetted Bedaux's appetite sufficiently that a number of attempts were made by him to form his own management consultancy company, only the final attempt in 1918 being wholly successful. For a balanced view of the life and times of Bedaux, four accounts review his antecedents from differing perspectives. For a benevolent view of his life, see J. Christy's (1984) 'The Price of Power: A Biography of Charles Eugene Bedaux'. A review of his techniques and modus operandi can be found in C.M. Hardwick's (undated) 'Time Study in Treason: Charles E. Bedaux Patriot or Collaborator'. Finally, for a review of the work of the Bedaux company and the techniques employed by it see M. Brownlow's (1972) 'A History of Inbucon' and M. Ferguson's (1996a) 'Charles Eugene Bedaux, 1886-1944: The Man Whom "Time" Forgot'.
4. For example, Harrington Emerson had set up an office in Paris in 1914 (Kipping 1997).
5. On at least one visit Bedaux accompanied an Italian industrial engineer A.M. Morrini and three consultants from the Emerson company. Morrini had originally travelled to the United States to familiarise himself with 'modern' scientific management methods and returned to Europe in order to put in practice the skills that he had learnt (Christy 1984).
6. This was because growth in this form of consultancy paralleled similar growth patterns in the size of firms in the United States (McKenna 1995). Therefore, there was sufficient business on the home front to dampen any enthusiasm for expansion elsewhere.
7. Sir Francis Rose Price was a country gentleman, well versed in the social graces, who in addition to his business interests was a Steward at Newbury Racecourse. He had a large circle of friends who were influential in the world of business. It was through his connections that many assignments were subsequently arranged.
8. Following demobilisation from the Royal Engineers in 1919, Pleming sought further challenges abroad. He gained considerable experience re-organising and developing railway systems in the Caribbean, applying Taylor's principles during the course of much of his work.
9. A copy of the book was given to each trainee engineer of the British Bedaux company as an aid to the processes involved in industrial efficiency. This, together with a period of on-the-job training with an experienced field engineer, formed the basis of the induction training for consultant recruits. This system remained in force until a formal training manual was produced in 1930, a copy of which can be found at Appendix One to Mildred Brownlow's (1972) unpublished 'A History of Inbucon'. The 1921 version of Bedaux' the book was re-named simply 'Industrial Management'.
10. Bedaux applications were criticised on many occasions because of the over-burdening that his regime of administration and record keeping caused to the staff of client companies charged with continuing with this rigorous administrative task long after the consultants had completed their assignment.

11. The application of the techniques developed by Bedaux differed greatly from those espoused by Taylor and other American pioneers. That is because those other methods required changes to management practices; the Bedaux's system required no such prerequisite as it bolted onto the existing practices of the firm and was, therefore, cheaper and easier to apply.

12. Regardless of promises, workers were suspicious of statements that guaranteed them pay at normal rates when output failed to meet the standard. Indeed, many viewed that such a tactic of developing a base standard (norm) as a means to dispense with labour that consistently failed to achieve targets.

13. C.W. Lytle was the Director of Industrial Co-operation, New York University and Chairman of the Management Division of the American Society of Mechanical Engineers.

14. As a historical note, some of these individual(s) were the pioneers of the in-house work study departments.

15. Orr had originally moved abroad on doctor's advice because he had developed pneumonia as a consequence of being gassed during active service in the infantry during the First World War.

16. This aspect of consultancy work highlights the difference between a consultant and someone who provides advice to management. Had a management advisor conducted this assignment it would have collapsed and failed because of subsequent difficulties.

17. This information was obtained from an untitled, un-referenced INBUCON (the company name of the Bedaux company in the period after the Second World War) chart depicting the growth of the Company during the period 1923-1966.

18. This is a reference to the subsequent changes made to work-study applications and their introduction by other consultants and consultancies from the 1930s onwards in Britain (specifically see Chapter 4).

19. Northcott was an influential figure in the Institute of Labour Management.

20. The other methods reported were the Rowan System, Taylor's Differential Piece Rate System and the Emerson Efficiency System (the latter two being American in origin).

21. During the period 1930-1934, unemployment levels in Britain ranged from between 2.4 and 3.4 million workers (11.2 to 15.6 per cent of the working population); with 1932 being the worst year (Feinstein 1976).

22. Rover's view was that there was more chance of success within the Trim Shop because the female labour force would ultimately gain from the changes. However, the overriding fear was one of increased effort and, consequently, it would appear that both the consultants and the management failed to get their views across to the workers.

23. Urwick was the founder of the Management Library and had invited Milward to run it on his behalf. Orr was a regular visitor to the Library. It was Milward's suggestion that both Urwick and Orr should form a management consultancy partnership, knowing full well that Urwick was about to finish his work at the International Management Institute in Geneva due to its impending closure.

CHAPTER 4

New Directions, 1929-1939

So far, this account has reported half a century of slow evolutionary change in the history of management consulting in Britain, with change reflected in the form of services provided and in the structure of consultancy as a whole. With regard to services, consultancy concentrated initially on the financial aspects of client businesses in the broad area of cost management, but by the end of the nineteenth century production management emerged as a new form of service, largely brought about by the changing nature of management within businesses (see Chapter 2). Further developments within consultancy witnessed sales and marketing, and services in relation to management information becoming new areas of concern in the second and third decades of the twentieth century. Up to that point in time, consultants tended to concentrate on specific specialist areas, through the development of their own expertise and portfolio of services. By the mid-1920s the arrival of the Bedaux company in Britain, setting up an office in London, brought about change to the general structure of management consultancy. For the first time, consultants were organised into a company group, providing the opportunity to expand service delivery over a broader frontage. Initially, the Bedaux company concentrated on direct production efficiency and payment incentive schemes. After a few years it widened its approach to cover other areas of production management.

Because of the Bedaux company's importance in the development of techniques that became widely employed in Britain, albeit with subsequent modifications by those consultant companies that followed in its wake, the previous chapter was devoted to the work of this Company. This chapter covers the period 1929-1939 and whilst it parallels part of the time-frame associated with the previous, this is necessary in order to re-visit some of those years to view what else was going on within consultancy. The period commences in 1929 when the first wholly-owned British management consultant company was formed, Harold Whitehead and Staff, and ends at that point in time when Britain entered into a period of protracted military conflict on a global scale (1939). During the 11 years of this period

Britain's industrial environment continued to evolve and a number of significant changes occurred. Some of these changes had an effect on the shape and size of British industry; leading companies were much larger than they had been when compared to thirty years before. The Electricity Supply Act had the effect of rationalising the industry and generated the demand for electrical appliances and the subsequent growth of new industries. Other growth was reflected in increased vehicle production, specifically cars for consumers and heavier vehicles for the transport industry. House building increased through the emergence of mortgage support for private purchase and the local authority demand for social housing (Brech 2002b). This growth partly helps to explain why there appeared to be an increase in demand for consultancy services during this overall period. Within some of the other high growth businesses, for example firms producing aircraft, and those involved in electrical engineering, consumer goods and chemicals, many of them had began to employ professional managers to control both the strategic as well as the functional aspects of the businesses. The need for change came about because, whilst the merger activity of the 1930s was less vigorous than the 1920s, a significant number of mergers took place at that time. Consequently, there was an increase in the number of multi-unit enterprises generally within Britain, witnessing a greater diversification in terms of product range.

In parallel with these changes, some sectors of the economy (for example railways, electricity supply, consumer goods and aviation) were able to exploit economies of scale, occurring because trade associations had been able to exert pressure on all aspects of industrial pricing and market sharing (Wilson 1995). Consequently, overall, industrial production rose throughout the period, partly assisted by a greater demand in export markets for both goods and services. Whilst some growth could have been attributed to the rearmament programme (commencing in 1934-1935) that gained in momentum towards the end of the period, this does not explain growth more generally. One consequence of the rising output levels was a fall in the base level of unemployment, from 11.9 per cent in 1934 to 5.8 per cent of the working population in 1939. However for all that, there was still an entrenched attitude in many quarters that 'managers are born, not made', and this had an impact on the acceptance of consultancy, specifically the level to which it could be employed within firms. That entrenched attitude partly occurred because family representation was still evident in a significant number of firms, either through direct ownership or as a result of representation on company boards.

In the United States and Europe during this period management consultancy had organised itself to cope with the specific requirements of the diverse industrial and commercial environments. The situation in the United States was very similar to that reported previously with two main strands of consulting activity: efficiency engineering, and structural and organisational consulting at boardroom level (see Chapter 3). However, as this period progressed, specifically by 1930, consulting assignments at the boardroom level of the firm had become the dominant form of consultant activity in the United States. By that time, approximately 100 firms were engaged in this form of service, albeit each firm consisted of relatively few numbers of professional staff. The names of many of those firms would be recognised even today, for example Arthur Andersen and McKinsey, to name but two. As the 1930s progressed these firms grew not only in size and influence, but also in numbers, demonstrating a growth rate of, on average, 15 per cent throughout the decade (McKenna, 1995).

In Europe, specifically in France and Germany, there was less concern with the organisational aspects of businesses and more with productivity improvements and efficiency. In both those countries there were a significantly greater number of organised consultancy practices than in Britain. However, this chapter is concerned with providing an account of a period of growth in which management consulting began to expand on a limited scale in Britain through the creation of three home-grown consultancies. These consultancies, together with one other formed during the period of the Second World War (see Chapter 5), dominated British management consulting until at least the period of the late-1960s. Because of the relative importance of these companies from this point onwards it is appropriate to review the formation of each to establish the consultancy scene in the decade of the 1930s. The second part of this chapter concentrates on consultancy at a more general level in order to consider growth in the form of services provided and the size of the sector as a whole. In support of this, the chapter also examines the types of training provided to consultant recruits at that time; that was important because it was the career background of the consultants and their formalised development that had an impact on the acceptability of consultancy more generally and were factors associated with growth.

Structural Change

The eleven-year period of 1929 to 1939 was significant for management consulting because it represented a watershed in Britain. The structure of the management consultancy in the mid-1920s, such as it was, began to change irreversibly with the arrival of the Bedaux company. More significant change came about as a direct consequence of the work of this company and the negative impact that some of its work had on a number of firms in Britain; these effects were highlighted by the adverse publicity associated with industrial disputes and the lowering of morale within the British Bedaux company as a whole. Lowered morale had two main effects, the first of these was prominent defections from within the Company (discussed later in this section) and, secondly, dissatisfaction amongst senior managers to the apparent failures on the part of Charles Bedaux personally to accept necessary change. That dissatisfaction ultimately resulted in the Company being re-named British Bedaux Limited in 1936 in order to emphasise its Britishness. At the same time, the Company was floated on the Stock Exchange as a move to remove some of Bedaux's personal powers; these were seen as having a negative impact on the operations of the British firm (Brownlow 1972). Both changes were also a direct result of challenges to Bedaux's supremacy in Britain with the formation of new consulting companies in the 1930s, and this is reviewed later in this section.

Whilst Bedaux dominated the British consultancy environment in the period of the late-1920s and early 1930s, in 1929 the first wholly-owned British management consulting company was established, Harold Whitehead and Staff Limited. The Whitehead company made no attempt to compete with Bedaux because the Company had a different orientation with regard to the services it provided; these initially lay in the areas of salesmanship (especially training), sales management and marketing. At the beginning there was a reluctance on the part of the founder to operate as a consultant, even though he had established himself as a prominent figure in that field previously in the United States.[1] He was, nevertheless, persuaded to reverse his decision by the British Commercial Gas Association (BCGA) that were, at that time, looking at ways to improve the performance of its constituent members sales staff. Knowledge of Whitehead's reputation in the field of salesmanship training came from the BCGA's chairman (Francis Goodenough) through his involvement with the Management Research Groups, in particular its Boston links. Specifically, Goodenough was aware of Whitehead's successes with the Boston Consolidated Gas Corporation. Whitehead agreed to help and set about the task of recruiting a number of specialist staff members to assist him, hence the Company name. The assignment was a success and this must have whetted Whitehead's appetite because he decided to continue with his consulting work.[2] Positive publicity followed and that led to further work, with eventual diversification in the range of services provided by the Company.

In 1930 another American company established itself in Britain, partly in competition with Bedaux, although time bore witness to little threat from that direction. That company, Stevenson, Jordan and Harrison, provided services in labour and production cost planning, principally within the textile industries. The Company, however, did not include any form of work-study as the basis for conducting its analytical processes. In 1934 two further companies were formed, both wholly British and each with a founder that had previously served as a Bedaux consultant (see Chapter 3). These companies represented the first real challenges to Bedaux's dominant position and forced irreversible change to the way that consulting was conducted in Britain. The first of these, Production Engineering, was incorporated on 21 April 1934. The Chairman of the company was the Honourable Maurice Lubbock, the youngest son of the first Lord Avebury, and the Managing Director was Robert Bryson, a former Bedaux consultant.[3] Lubbock had previously had an unsatisfactory experience with the application of Bedaux methods at the firm of Dent Allcroft and Company in 1932, the glove manufacturers, where he was part owner and the Managing Director at that time. That experience was during the period when Bedaux applications were criticised and subjected to industrial action across a range of sectors (see Chapter 3). However, a more positive experience with a Canadian consultancy company, J.D. Woods and Company, when on a visit to a subsidiary company of Dent's in Canada, led Lubbock to believe that there was an opportunity to form a consultancy company in Britain, specifically a company that avoided the negatives that he endured with his experience of Bedaux.[4] Bryson was one of the two prominent defections from Bedaux, mentioned above, having personally endured the adverse reactions to Bedaux applications within a number of firms. His experiences as a Bedaux engineer had led him to believe that there was scope for improving the service, both through its application and the type of services provided.

Therefore, Production Engineering was formed to provide a wider range of services than those rendered by Bedaux at that time, including endeavouring to overcome managerial deficiencies within client firms. In addition, it positively sought the full co-operation from the personnel employed and ensured that they received the full benefits that implementation of improved methods and techniques were to attain. In effect, the Company actively sought progressive development and application of new managerial practices in the production function, including manufacturing cost control.[5]

In the same year (1934), but a few months later in the July, Urwick, Orr and Partners Limited was registered as a company. The Company opened for business in the September at offices at 23, Bloomsbury Square, in London. The founding partners, both experienced men in their own right, were Lyndall Fownes Urwick and John Leslie Orr. The Principals of the Urwick Orr Partnership were very different people in terms of both social background and experience when compared to the founders of the other companies. At the age of 43, Urwick was well off financially, and was well placed on the international management scene through his position as Honorary Secretary to the CIOS International Committee and his Directorship of the International Management Institute (IMI), 1928-1933.[6] However, his employment with the IMI came to an abrupt end in 1933 as a consequence of the withdrawal of financial sponsorship from the United States; this resulted in the closure of its office in Geneva. He was, nevertheless, less known in Britain except through his involvement with the Management Research Groups. Orr, on the other hand, was not financially independent, but had gained considerable experience within the consultancy environment through his employment with the Bedaux Company over the previous seven years and as a sole practitioner abroad prior to that within the manufacturing environment.[7] Orr was the second prominent defection from the Bedaux company.

Urwick, Orr and Partners Limited was formed to provide services in two very broad operational areas.[8] Those broad areas saw Urwick assuming responsibility for consulting in the fields of clerical management, accounting, administration and organisation; specialisms that had been reflected in his 1928 publication 'Organising a Sales Office'. Orr, on the other hand, held jurisdiction for consulting work in the areas of production management and industrial engineering, precisely those areas that were the focus of his assignments when he was employed by the Bedaux company. Based on that broad sub-division of responsibilities Urwick, Orr and Partners Limited organised itself internally with Urwick as Chairman and Orr as the Managing Director. Underpinning that structure, four main points of policy initially guided the Company (Urwick, Orr and Partners Limited 1978):

1. To develop a British approach to management consulting.
2. To exercise the highest possible professional standards of conduct.
3. To develop a service across the whole spectrum of management.
4. To obtain and maintain the goodwill of organised labour.

Those policy points highlighted the founders' belief in the deep-rooted flaws associated with Bedaux operations at that time.

To develop a British approach to management consulting A counter to the criticisms aimed at Bedaux as an American import (see Chapter 3). These criticisms were generally suggestive of the fact that the Bedaux approach was devised specifically to deal with the situation pertaining to the American industrial environment and had not been altered in any way to cope better with British industry. This was a valid criticism in the light of the autocratic stance that Bedaux adopted with regards to suggestions for change, and his personal remoteness and lack of experience of British industry at that time.

To exercise the highest professional standards of conduct A reflection of the founders' belief that the delivery of professional services would destroy the negatives associated with management consulting at that time; specifically those associated with Bedaux applications.

To develop a service across the whole spectrum of management A reference to the narrowness of the Bedaux service at that time, specifically its concentration on the operational aspects of businesses. The Urwick Orr service had two approaches. The first was to widen the breadth of the service delivery base into areas not specifically connected with direct production; this was through developing new forms of service in other areas of the firm. The second concerned the level of involvement in the firm; a move towards the strategic decision-making aspects of business, as well as other management functions.[9]

To obtain and maintain the goodwill of organised labour A statement of intention with regards to consultation at all levels with a view to reducing the risk of industrial disputes that had plagued the Bedaux consultancy in the early 1930s.

In addition to the organised consultancies mentioned above there also existed in Britain a number of sole practitioners delivering services in specific areas of consulting. Their definitive numbers at any one time are unknown but through the passage of time these individuals grew in number, collectively offering the full range of services available at that time. Therefore, the 1930s consultancy sector consisted of a small number of firms and an unknown number of specialist sole practitioners.

Consultancy Services in the 1930s

As the decade of the 1920s came to a close management consultancy in Britain was corporately concentrating most of its effort on delivering services in relation to techniques associated with production management. The majority of these services, exemplified through the Bedaux approach, were concerned with effecting improvements to the way in which manufacturing was conducted at the shop floor level; specifically in relation to improvements in operator processes. By the end of the 1920s services in production management further widened within the Bedaux organisation to encompass other areas within, the production management field. These included factory and workshop layout, and workflow management. In parallel with all this, operator training and personnel development, specifically in relation to the continuance of applications, occurred as part of the assignment process.

Harold Whitehead and Staff

In 1929, the newly formed company broadened even further the range of services provided corporately by consultants to include salesmanship training as part of consultancy's portfolio of services. This was an important addition to that portfolio because it provided a 'foot in the door' into another area of management, sales management; this was on a relatively large scale with the British Commercial Gas Association (BCGA). The importance of this development cannot be over-stressed because sales and marketing generally had received little attention in the past with regards to consultancy service (see Chapter 2) and this marked an important turning point. Another important factor of this assignment was that it was a movement away from what had become the traditional client base for the consultants, namely manufacturing and engineering companies. This was not the only occasion that Whitehead demonstrated a pioneering role in opening up new client markets.

Such was the success of the assignment with the BCGA that the Company carried out further work for trade associations, notably within retail trade associations for boots and shoes, drapers, ironmongers, and men's outfitters. However, the most notable early assignment, one that opened up another new client market, occurred in 1932. That assignment was for the Post Office, specifically its fledgling 'Telephone Service', at the request of the then Postmaster General, Mr (later Earl) Attlee (Tisdall 1982). The central feature of the work was the provision of advice and assistance in relation to sales training and business re-organisation; this led to other work in Government Departments. Another feature of this assignment, one that was to be repeated subsequently in other work, was the production of case studies and tutorial notes for wider dissemination and use. Specifically within the Post Office assignment, a handbook in six parts was published, each part 80-100 pages in length.

However, not content to stand still, the Whitehead company broadened its approach with two further diversifications in the first few years of the decade. The first of these occurred at about the same time as the Post Office assignment (1931-1932), and was concerned with what today would be called market testing or market analysis. In effect, the Whitehead company carried out a national survey of the retail selling practices of companies across 100 localities, specifically covering six retail product groups.[10] Thirty-seven in-house trained investigators were employed to sample retail outlets, and approximately 2000 customers were interviewed as representing a cross-section of the population; this was the first recorded example of the use of temporary contract staff by a management consultant company, taken on specifically to conduct a single assignment. The report published in 1932, 'The National Survey of Retail Selling Practices' (Harold Whitehead and Staff 1932a), covered 68 pages, including charts, and went on public sale as a specialist contribution to market research. At the same time it provided valuable pointers for development in retail staff training.

The second diversification occurred in 1933 when the Company was invited by Pitman's Department of Business Development to prepare a correspondence course in salesmanship. This type of work came about because of Whitehead's personal reputation within the fields of sales and marketing and because of the success of the courses in salesmanship that the Company had developed for other clients previously.[11] At the same time, the publishing side of Pitman's approached Whitehead personally and asked him to write a textbook for wider circulation. 'The Administration of Marketing and Selling' was published in 1937 and this was a major contribution to the improvement of knowledge in the management function. Therefore, by 1934 the Company had established itself as the leading provider of consultancy services in all forms of marketing and sales, including training and educational development.[12]

Production Engineering

At the outset, Production Engineering was determined to be innovative in its approach and, following the formation of the Company in early 1934, the Managing Director, Robert Bryson, went to Canada to view the work of consultants in that country, specifically J.D. Woods and Company. The purpose of the review was to gain an insight into both its management and operating practices; these included, at that time, services directed towards the use of standard costing as a tool for monitoring cost variations within production. Traditionally within consulting to that date in Britain the majority of services in cost management were specialised applications developed by sole practitioners and applied in isolation of other direct improvements in the production process. This approach was more all embracing because cost management was considered to be but one aspect of an overall process of production management; other techniques, for example production planning control, factory layout, etc., were applied in concert.[13]

The first assignment carried out by Production Engineering occurred at Watford where a small garment manufacturing business was making suede jackets, among other items of clothing. Specialist machine operators were employed to complete the process from start to finish. The client, a subsidiary of Dent's, provided Production Engineering with the opportunity to test out its new ideas. However, it did not provide it with rich rewards in terms of income; the fee charged for this assignment was 25 guineas a week, nominal only at that time. The assignment was concerned with finding more efficient ways of producing garments and cutting down on costs. While there is nothing new about this type of assignment, it does nonetheless reflect the form of services provided by consultants during that period. Following a review of the situation, the process of manufacture was changed to one of producing a more efficient and less expensive outcome. A system of part production was put in place whereby individual machine operators completed only part of the task; the work was then passed on to the next machinist in line who continued the process. This was repeated along a series of machinists until the full garment had been made (Raymond 1981). The principal consequence of such a change was the removal of the need to employ fully skilled labour, therefore there was a reduced labour bill. Such a move would have attracted an adverse reaction from the existing skilled workforce because the change would have been viewed as an attempt to de-skill the manufacturing process within the firm. Situations like this would have necessitated a careful approach on the part of the consultants in order to avoid a conflict arising; it was just such an approach that the 'Principals' of this new company had vowed to employ because of their collective experience of Bedaux methods at that time. At the heart of the approach was consultation with staff and unions where this was deemed appropriate.

The unique character of Production Engineering with regards to its methods when compared with the Bedaux company at that time was equally matched by its unique client base. From small beginnings in 1934 the Company became associated with the aircraft industry by the middle of the decade; as far as it is possible to tell this was the first recorded instance of consultant involvement in that industry. This association was heralded by an assignment conducted in 1935 for the De Havilland Aircraft Company; an important move for management consulting because, apart from its association with a relatively new and up-and-coming industry type, it preceded that time in history when aircraft production became critical for national defence (see Chapter 5).

Urwick, Orr and Partners Limited

The underlying principles associated with the formation of Urwick, Orr and Partners Limited do not need re-stating at this juncture (see the previous section), but a point worthy of note is that there was ready identification of the limitation of the skills available within the practice of consulting. For example, a stated aim of the Company was that it would only attempt to conduct assignments in areas where expertise could be found from within the organisation. Initially, the two principal areas considered were production management and industrial engineering, and clerical management, accounting, administration and organisation – fields that the founders had previous personal experience in (Urwick, Orr and Partners Limited 1978). This broad range of services marked out another turning point in consultancy on two accounts.

Production Management and Industrial Engineering   The almost slavish concentration on the visible output of consulting that was the Bedaux approach at that time, e.g. payment regimes and incentive schemes, were rightly relegated to a factor in the production process; not the visible central tenet. The principal purposes of the approach were raised productivity and improved efficiency through cost reduction and control, and these were achieved through taking a more holistic approach to consulting, embracing all areas involved in the production process.

Clerical Management, Accounting, Administration and Organisation   These represented new fields of service, bringing into play the background and support operations within an organisation where improvements to the way in which things were done could also have a direct impact on the output of the client. With regards to the organisational aspects of a business, this was a clear attempt on the part of Urwick Orr to move into uncharted waters and break the barriers associated with the more strategic aspects of a client firm. Organisation was a reflection of the distinctive approach of the Company at that time in which it was viewed that for an organisation to function at its best there should be clearly defined core areas of responsibility (Urwick 1933; Latham and Sanders 1980). Overarching this approach, was the development of written specifications to reflect the strategic roles and functions within the organisation.

In addition to the distinctive portfolio provided by the Company, there was a clear vision of future areas worthy of involvement. In parallel with this, in a similar fashion to that of Production Engineering, Urwick Orr adopted the view that involving the workforce during the consultation process would more likely produce a more positive reaction to the introduction of new methods. The Company actively sought consultation with the relevant trades unions as their central plank for this strategy, and this proved extremely successful and helped erode some of the negatives associated with the Bedaux applications of the past.

Diversification and Expansion

By 1935 the industrial engineering centred consultancies (Bedaux, Production Engineering and Urwick Orr) were beginning to expand their services and venture into new service areas where they believed that their growing expertise could add significant value to their clients. Early in that year, the Urwick Orr company was internally discussing the possibilities of forming a specialist department that would concentrate on the organisation of marketing and sales within client companies. There was a broad consensus of this approach at the first annual conference of the Company in May of that year, although no firm decisions were made at that time (Urwick, Orr and Partners Limited 1935). By 1936 a specialist marketing consultant had been employed by the Company to develop services in that field and conduct assignments. Also during that annual conference the question of conducting financial audits was also mooted. Whilst there was less enthusiasm for that suggestion, by 1936 three professional accountants had been employed by the Company to assist with the development and delivery of services in relation to management accounting and improvements to office methods, as demand for these services had far exceeded expectations. Typically, assignments were conducted in the administrative areas of manufacturing firms, within the service industries associated with insurance, advertising and trade associations, and in investment houses and social institutions. Also at that Conference, the announcement was made that a new form of service had been developed called the 'Management Audit', and that an assignment was underway in which the client was being audited following a period of rapid expansion (Urwick, Orr and Partners Limited 1936). The service was based on the principles developed by Rose (1932) in his important publication 'The Management Audit'.

The Management Audit, in succinct terms, was an overall review of a client company; in particular it was a review of its organisation, lines of delegation, managerial practices and financial control systems. The purpose of the review was to realign the company following a period of restructuring or rapid growth that may have put it out of line with its principal objective. From a financial perspective, it was a recognition of the inadequacies of formal accounting practices in circumstances that required up-to-date information in order to shape future strategy and policy decisions. From a cost value perspective, Urwick Orr expected that the Audit would cost only a fraction of the rewards gained through realignment. At the same time that Urwick Orr was developing its new services, by 1936 Production Engineering had fully established standard costing as a consultancy technique and had developed services in management accounting control (Blackstone 1980). These services would have, in all likelihood, been partly based on an approach developed by A.W. Willsmore (1932) in his book 'Business Budgets and Budgetary Control'; a publication that was known to the consulting fraternity of the day.

In addition to this general trend of expansion within management consulting, the core business of production management, in its various forms, continued to expand in Britain. Each of the companies, with the exception of Whitehead, still considered this type of service a central tenet of consultant activity. In furtherance of this efficiency objective, other developments occurred in 1937, one of which involved the creation of a service by Urwick Orr in relation to the determination of standard methods and time norms within the office environment. The utilisation of standards and time norms within production assignments had become normal practice by that time, but within clerical operations this was new. The pioneering nature of this work lay not in the principles of application, but in the development of standard methods for universal employment across the range of settings. In effect, it was a collation and analysis of categories of operations, both manual and/or mechanised, to determine: common elements based on methods improvement, standard layout and operating instructions, standard workloads with relaxation allowances, and set manpower allocations and time norms. This was achieved through shadowing clerical assignments, largely to ascertain how far common factors could be codified for future employment. Specifically, they were operations involving typing, tabulating and correspondence handing. In effect, this was an experimental approach to a technique that later became referred to as the 'predetermined-motion-time' system. The importance of this technique was that it speeded up the analytical process of determining improvements within clerical settings; the effect of this from the clients' perspective was that fees were much reduced. In reality, this was a form of early benchmarking, but as a service it was not attractive to clients and did not catch on.

Within the Bedaux company the adverse reactions to its services (reported previously) forced it to reappraise its modus operandi and the range of services that it provided. Whilst some of the negative reactions to its methods may have been of the British company's own making, the fundamental aspects of its approach were outside of its control. Changing the company name to British Bedaux Limited in 1936 had not had the desired effect and did little to endear it to the wider industrial population due to the increasingly visible personal activities of Bedaux himself at that time, even though the Company had experienced growth in demand generally for its services.[14] In 1938 the Company found it necessary to change its name again, this time to Associated Industrial Consultants, hoping to finally distance itself from its founder.

The principal effects of the change was the removal of Bedaux as company chairman and the promotion of Norman Pleming to the board, the first British employee to hold a director's appointment with the Company. These changes may have been a catalyst for the wider changes that occurred as a result of a review of the Company's scope of services and its new found freedom to modify its approach (Brownlow 1972). Two new services were developed, 'Management Accounting' and 'Temporary Services in Management'. Arguably the former of these was not new, with a similar type of service having been developed by T.G. Rose back in the 1920s (see Chapter 2) and Urwick Orr earlier in the decade, although no doubt a distinctive style would have been present in the Bedaux approach. The latter, however, was pioneering for its day as it was concerned with the deployment of consultant staff on temporary attachment in order to overcome a shortfall in management personnel. Such services are available today, but in the 1930s this was revolutionary indeed in an environment where there still remained a general reluctance to embrace outside involvement in the strategic aspects of the firm.

Before finally turning to the question of growth generally within Britain's consultancy sector, an important observation worth making is that the forgoing has described a situation in which consultant companies had generally moved towards establishing themselves as generalist providers of management consulting services; albeit within the limited range of services available at that time. The one exception so far had been that of Harold Whitehead and Staff that had tended to concentrate on services in the broad areas of sales and marketing, having become established as the foremost provider of services in salesmanship training. But even Whitehead began to diversify in the latter years of the 1930s in line with the generalist trend with four new service areas available to potential clients: 'Factory Organisation and Control', 'Warehousing and Transport', 'Office Organisation' and 'Higher Control' (Harold Whitehead and Staff undated). One noticeable absence from the descriptive content of these services was the term 'work study', or any other form of nomenclature that could be used to describe some form of 'scientific management' approach. A brief examination of each form of service will help confirm the similarities and identify the differences between the Whitehead approach and the other consulting companies operating at that time.

Factory Organisation and Control and *Warehousing and Transport* This fitted comfortably within the portfolio of services offered by the other consultancies operating in Britain at that time. The actual delivery of the services may have differed slightly, but the make-up was essentially the same. With regards to factory organisation and control, techniques associated with production planning and control, stock control, factory and warehouse layout, health and safety, security, packaging and despatch, and cost control would have been employed at the operational level. At the corporate level, each of the various strands that make up the organisation of the factory could be treated as part of a whole and brought together in an overall process in order to identify weaknesses with a view to bringing together the various elements as a co-ordinated operation. Similarly, with regards to warehousing and transport, the various strands could be treated independently where a particular problem had been identified, or they could be considered from an overall organisational perspective. In particular, these elements that made up this service concerned warehouse layout, storage methodology, stock control, receiving and despatching, security and control operations.

Office Organisation While less common at that time, this appeared to have been a similar service to that developed by Urwick Orr. The Whitehead service was particularly concerned with workflow, office layout, the deployment of equipment, and budgetary and cost control measures. In addition, it sought to mechanise clerical operations where that was possible, including the development of process improvements for routine activities. In overall terms, the service was concerned with the collection, collation and dissemination of information in support of the management decision-making process with the objective of providing executives with a greater degree of control with minimum fuss and cost.

The overarching similarity with these services and those provided by the other consultancies, possibly with the exception of the 'Management Audit' service provided by Urwick Orr, was that they were still targeted at the operational areas of a client's business. The final new service, 'Higher Control', attempted to break the mould and make inroads into the practice of management within the higher echelons of client firms. The title, however, should not be confused, nor compared with T.G. Rose's book title or consultancy service (see Chapter 2). Rose's work centred around the use of management information in the decision-making process, the Whitehead service, whilst taking into account the use of management information, was more concerned with control structures and organisational change.

Higher Control   Loosely described by the Company as a 'Business Management Service', was provided either as a 'consultative' package (e.g. the provision of advice) or as an 'operative' package (e.g. direct consultant intervention). Unusually also, the service was particularly targeted at small and medium sized enterprises, although there were suggestions that it could be applied within larger organisations where there was a perceived need for major change.

In descriptive terms, the literature suggested that:

> Harold Whitehead and Staff will undertake to reorganise the executive control of an organisation to bring it into line with the accepted principles of modern management, so that the administrative staff will secure the maximum degree of control over the various activities of the business as a whole (Harold Whitehead and Staff undated).[15]

Therefore, Higher Control was an all-encompassing package of measures to assist enterprises in the re-organisation of their businesses in line with the latest thinking in management at that time. It was a top-to-bottom approach, in contrast to the bottom-to-top functional approach of management consulting that was practised through the deployment of most other techniques at that time.

It does, however, come as no surprise that such a service should be offered by this Company because of its founder's reputation as a farsighted individual, actively engaged in improving the process of management within the management movement of the day. He was an active participant in professional circles, a prolific writer and a sought after speaker across a range of venues. The Whitehead 'Higher Control' and the Urwick Orr 'Management Audit' services were the first real attempts in Britain at raising the profile of management consulting to new higher levels within client companies. Both these packages were aimed at the strategic areas of business; this was in complete contrast to consultancy's previous concentration on the operational aspects of firms. This was a positive step forward at a time when there still remained an attitudinal stance within British firms that 'managers are born, not made' (Wilson 1995). This general widening of consultancy activity was further reflected in growth more generally and it is this aspect that the next section concentrates on before moving on to examine the professional antecedence and development of consultants within British management consulting companies.

General Growth

The principal stumbling block with regard to definitively charting the general growth in management consulting (e.g. the number of active consultants and their clients) during this period is that there is no single authority that it is possible to turn to in order to gain a corporate view. Other difficulties relate to the fact that it is not possible to identify all those engaged in a sole practitioner and small company capacity, nor have records survived in any quantities from which inferences can be made. In terms of the major consultancies featured within this chapter, the picture is somewhat different because some records that have survived assist us in this task.

Prior to the formation of the Bedaux company in 1926 it has only been possible to make a general assumption that the overall numbers of active consultants never exceeded more than about twenty at any one time. The figure of twenty was more relevant to the period of the 1920s, with the previous decades witnessing proportionately fewer numbers. This assumption has been made on the basis that very little information has been found on the activities of consultants generally prior to the formation of Bedaux. Where such information has come to light it has suggested that very few people were actively engaged as consultants as a principal form of activity.[16] There may be a number of reasons for this, and certainly the attitudinal stance of many within senior management to outside involvement in the firm would not have encouraged many to pursue consultancy as a career. Nevertheless, it may be possible to make a general assumption on the constraints to growth in the period prior to the mid-1920s.

During that period, consultant activity was generally concentrated within small and medium sized enterprises, and these were largely engineering and manufacturing firms. There is no evidence to suggest that consultants were actively working in the largest companies within Britain, specifically those companies that were identified as the 130 largest in terms of employees during the period of circa 1907 (Wardley 1999). Because of their concentration in smaller firms, consultants would have attracted much less attention than if they were involved in a successful consultancy assignment in a much larger firm. Using this knowledge, and the reluctance on the part of consultants to advertise their services publicly (see Chapters 1 and 2), then this would not have had a positive impact on growth. Conversely, because the consultant companies formed in the period after the mid-1920s tended to target much larger firms, and that significant successes led to further work (for example the Bedaux assignment at

Lyons), then this would have raised the profile of consultancy more positively and would have been a factor in growth more generally. Even, perversely, negative publicity such as that which surrounded the activities of the Bedaux company in the early 1930s may have had positive benefits in terms of raising consultancy's profile.

Regardless of whether or not the general assumptions made above will stand the test of time as a consequence of further research in this field in the future, growth in the number of consultants in the larger companies of the 1930s can be charted more accurately. The one company for which definitive records are absent, however, is Harold Whitehead and Staff. The indications are that the Whitehead company tended to rely on an element of temporary staff to cover larger assignments and in all likelihood the permanent cadre of the Company was relatively small; 'The National Survey of Retail Selling Practices' is a good example of the way in which numbers fluctuated within the Company. For the main production-centred companies more definitive records provide a relatively accurate account of growth within their organisations.

With regards to the Bedaux company (Associated Industrial Consultants), two documents help chart its growth from the mid-1920s through to the commencement of the Second World War. These documents are an un-referenced INBUCON growth chart, produced post-1966, which provides information on staff numbers, services provided and some of the major firms serviced by the Company, and Mildred Brownlow's 'A History of Inbucon'.[17] From a position of having one client and two consultants in 1926, the Company ended that decade with 40 consultants and 50 clients. Some of these clients were the leading companies in Britain at that time in terms of size, for example Imperial Chemical Industries and J. Lyons and Company. By the mid-1930s, specifically 1936, Bedaux had serviced 280 clients. Growth in terms of new clients per year steadily increased throughout the remainder of this period and by 1939 the Company consultant strength had risen to fifty.

Production Engineering experienced steady growth throughout the 1930s and from a consultant strength of one in 1934 it grew to 20 by 1939. This was brought about because of the diverse client base of the Company, for example from engineering to aircraft, and from confectionery to general manufacturing. However, this diverse range of clients brought with it problems associated with recruiting staff with the appropriate experience and background, even though a number of ex-Bedaux employees joined the Company during this period. Therefore demand exceeded supply, although this was not viewed as a problem for the Company as it highlighted for them a growing reputation and provided them with the opportunity of picking their clients (Wayne 1959). Urwick

Orr exhibited patterns of growth consistent with Production Engineering, although at a faster pace. An undated Urwick Management Centre 'Induction Notes for New Staff' document charted the pattern of growth for the period of the 1930s in terms of both consultant numbers and revenue income (see Table 4.1). The pace of growth was assisted in some large measure through Urwick's position as a leading member of the burgeoning 'management movement' at that time. In real terms, what this meant was that he gained publicity for the Company through his public appearances, journal articles and other publications.[18]

Table 4.1   Urwick, Orr and Partners Limited, Growth 1935-1938

Year	Consultant Numbers	Revenue (£)	Revenue Per Consultant (£)	% Increase in Revenue Per Consultant Based on 1935 Figures
1935	5	2,497	499	
1936	19	18,023	949	89%
1937	30	48,070	1,602	220%
1938	33	63,899	1,936	287%

Source: Urwick, Orr and Partners Limited (undated) 'Induction Notes for New Staff'

An examination of the data in Table 4.1 not only provides information on the growth of consultant numbers within the Company during this period, it also gives an indication of the revenue generation of consultants more generally. Ignoring 1934 when the Company was first set up, average growth was approximately six consultants per year. At that time, this was a significant growth rate for management consultancy when companies could only expand at the rate of demand for their services and appropriate personnel were available to recruit as consultants. Growth was also partly related to changes in attitude more generally within industry to outside involvement within the firm, the improving relations between consultants and organised labour through positive changes to the conduct of services, and the growing awareness of the availability of this form of service across the range of industries as larger firms were targeted by consulting companies in the post mid-1920s period. However, consulting was still partly constrained by its concentration in the operational areas of firms and its relatively narrow range of services in comparison with those available today.

In terms of revenue generation, Table 4.1 provides information on the overall level of revenue and the average amount per consultant on an annual basis. Whilst these figures may appear somewhat insignificant compared with today's revenue levels, in the 1930s they represented a high level of income for the Company, especially for a company that had only just commenced in business. The annual growth-rate represented by end-of-year figures based on the 1935 base level indicates steady growth. At the end of the period, the percentage increase per consultant represented a rise of 287 per cent based on per consultant revenue for 1935. Apart from the growth factors cited above and the public role of the Chairman of the Company, revenue per consultant increased as a consequence of three other factors. Firstly, there was a small increase in consultant fees during the period, although on its own this was insignificant. Secondly, the inactivity time between assignments was reduced; a factor that is just as important today as it was then. Finally, brought about by the second factor, the proportional number of assignments carried out annually by each consultant rose. It was these final two factors that had the major impact on the growth of revenue within the Company.

One positive advantage that Urwick Orr had over its rivals was the public role of its Chairman. This meant that the Company was less reliant on cold calling as a means of marketing its services than the other consulting companies at that time. Regardless of publicity or marketing approach, however, consultants increased their client base over time through the quality of the services they provided and the reputation they gained as a consequence of that. As a means of improving those services, the employment of appropriately qualified and trained personnel was a prerequisite to success. Therefore, an important aspect of the quality of service in management consulting is the training provided to consultants. The next section reviews that training in the period of the 1930s and the assumptions that underpinned its content.

Antecedence and Professional Development

Formal training for management consultants was a phenomenon of the post mid-1920s period in Britain. That was because up to that point in time consultants were largely sole practitioners who developed their own services based on previous experience and professional background. Consultants tended to be either accountants or engineers, members of a professional body with a history steeped in practical experience within their respective areas of competence. Training, when it occurred, was concerned with the background professional competence and experience of the individual. There were exceptions, of course, but these were in the minority. The arrival of the Bedaux company in Britain in 1926 brought with it a regime of training and development based on the contents of

Bedaux's 1917 publication 'Industrial Management: The Bedaux Efficiency Course for Industrial Application'. This was achieved by providing consultant recruits with a copy of the publication for their own private reading. The assumptions that underpinned this methodology were that consultants had been selected for their technical and professional competence, each were appropriately qualified and, therefore, all that was lacking was indoctrination into the ways of the Company and the techniques employed by it. As a safeguard, new consultants spent a period of time in the company of an experienced man and they only moved on to conducting assignments on their own once the Company was satisfied of their personal competence.

Arguably, this was achievable because in the early years of the Company's existence there were relatively few new consultants and the techniques employed by it were well documented and generally limited in scope. In 1930, because the number of new consultants had increased and the range of services widened, the Company formalised consultant training through issuing a training manual detailing the conditions for on-the-job training. In 1934, the manual, entitled 'Training Course for Field Engineers', was revised, probably as a consequence of the collective experiences of Bedaux engineers during the turbulent industrial environment of the early 1930s. The principal aim of the new manual was to train individuals in the range of techniques that lay at the heart of the Bedaux service through progressive instruction (British Bedaux 1934). In support of the training manual, two other documents made up the trilogy of handbooks for issue to new consultants, 'Code of Practice' and 'Outline of Terms Governing the Remuneration of Engineers of the Company'. Each had a role to play in determining the practice of management consulting within the Company and the relationship between the consultant and the client. Alarmingly, however, a glaring omission within the range of documents was any reference to consultation at all levels or any other suggested methodology to bring organised labour into the consultation process, one of the main criticisms made of the Bedaux approach in Britain at that time (see Chapter 3).

Nevertheless, the training manual provided a structured approach to training, with a course of instruction in eight parts. The first part was carried out at Head Office and was an introduction to Bedaux working practices. The remaining seven parts were carried out on assignment under the instruction of an experienced consultant. The emphasis of field training was on consulting techniques. Each part of the course was tested through a formal written examination, and the successful completion of a final examination qualified the individual as a Bedaux consultant. Production

Engineering adopted a similar approach, although less formalised than the Bedaux method.

Production Engineering's training regime consisted of on-the-job training under the supervision of a more experienced consultant in analytical techniques, work study, production control, and report writing and presentation (PE 1984).[19] The reason why training was not put on a more formal footing was because when compared with Bedaux and Urwick Orr, Production Engineering had fewer new recruits and some of these already had consultant experience. However, as the Company grew in size, consultant training became increasingly more important.

With regards to Urwick Orr, one of the stated aims of the Company was to '.... select, recruit and train suitably qualified and experienced men as consultants' (Urwick, Orr and Partners Limited 1978). To achieve that aim, and because the demand for services necessitated expansion of the Company in terms of its consultant staff, consultant training on-the-job was developed. Because some of the new consultants already had experience in consulting and because the recruitment policy of the Company meant that only men with a suitable management experience and professional background were considered, training in consultancy techniques was the main focus of consultant training. Nevertheless, because it was Company policy to make every effort to shed the negative image of management consultants at that time, then effort was expended on the softer aspects of consulting, specifically those that related to communications at all levels when at a client's premises.

In summing up, generally within management consulting in the 1930s consultants either relied on their own personal experiences and professional background in order to develop their services (in the case of sole practitioners), or they were formally trained in the techniques of consultancy (if they came from one of the main consulting companies in existence at that time). Training in management or in the peculiarities of the industries supported by consultancy was not carried out. This was because recruitment was concerned with taking into account the antecedent history of the individuals and most training, where it existed, was carried out on-the-job in the company of consultants already experienced in the management areas for which they were being employed. All of this changed during the 1940s, partly as a result of wartime conditions, when consultant training became further formalised and the importance of off-job training was recognised (see Chapter 5).

The Advent of War

The ten-year period since the late-1920s saw management consultancy enter into an era of competition between a small number of consulting companies. Positive moves were made to shed the negatives associated with the work of consultants in the early 1930s, achieved through a softening of image and a clear recognition of the human factor in the conduct of assignments. Consultancy also broadened the range of services provided and there was a general convergence of delivery among the main companies. Some companies still retained unique specialist functions, for example Whitehead's salesmanship training, but they were moving towards a generalist approach in the delivery of their services overall. Boutique, or niche consultancies, had yet to be formed, and pure specialisation, where it occurred, was largely in the hands of the sole practitioners.

During the period 1938-1939, worsening relations with Germany witnessed Britain entering into a period of build-up for war. That build-up and subsequent conflict brought with it fundamental changes to the way in which consulting was carried out in Britain. The inevitability of war and the commencement of hostilities brought fundamental changes to the client base and the type of services provided by consultants. Mildred Brownlow (1972), in her account of the history of the Bedaux company described the effects of the declaration of war:

> When war was declared we had at once terminated our consulting services in the luxury trades, and many other clients took the initiative and asked us to withdraw, because there was no purpose in continuing investigations on products or processes which would most likely be discontinued.

Consequently, the attention of consultants turned towards those firms in direct support of the war effort. New clients sought consultant services and some existing clients fell by the wayside. Another effect was simply that some firms changed their product ranges and these were in need of support at a time when re-gearing became the focus of their attention. In terms of the personnel effects, there was general confusion about what would happen in the future because this was at a time when men and women were being called up for service in the armed forces. Quite a few consultants and support staff were on the reserve list of the three services, but for those not affected in this way, that confusion still reigned. A typical reaction to this situation is exemplified through the actions of Production Engineering in its attempt at bringing order to a period of growing uncertainty: on 28th August 1939 all consultants were told '…. in the event of war you must remain on your assignment until further instructions are issued' (PE 1984).

That period of uncertainty, as the next chapter will indicate, found consultancy entering into a new era; one that raised its profile even further, break into new markets, deliver new products and irreversibly change the opinions of many in industry, commerce and government to the value of consultant services. The darkest hours of the six years of the Second World War witnessed management consultants playing their part in support of the war effort. Those who joined the armed forces faced their own challenges and those that remained faced a major task in re-skilling industry in the face of adversity.

Notes

1. Harold Whitehead was born in Birmingham in January 1881, the son of a commercial representative. Following an apprenticeship as a hardware salesman he moved to the firm of Charles Baldwin in 1901. In 1906, whilst still working for Baldwin's, he travelled to the United States in search of special window fittings for the Company. Whilst he was there he was invited by a local businessman's association to join them in discussions on American selling methods. Two further visits followed in 1908 and 1909, and on the second of those visits he was invited to design and conduct a salesman's training programme for the Young Men's Christian Union (YMCU). Because of that invitation, on his return to Britain he resigned from Baldwin's and emigrated to Boston, Massachusetts in 1910. Using the YMCU programme as a foundation for his activities, he widened his scope of training. Over a short period of time, Whitehead's reputation grew through his journal articles and other activities in the area of salesmanship. His success brought with it a daily column in a Philadelphia newspaper and he was invited to make a number of radio broadcasts. By 1912 he had established a specialist consultancy in salesmanship, retail training and sales management. Also by 1912 he was lecturing regularly at the College of Commerce and Business Administration of the University of Boston, eventually becoming a professor and head of department. During the period of the First World War, and in its aftermath, he was involved in the development of training for the United States government, initially for the Students Army Training Corps and later for war-blinded soldiers on demobilisation. Throughout the whole period he was prolific writer; notable fictional books included: 'The Business Career of Peter Flint' (1918a) and 'Dawson Black, Retail Merchant' (1918b), both concerned with fictional accounts of the principles and practices of retail merchandising and sales management. Other publications on a more practical footing included: 'How to Run a Shop' (1922) and 'The Business of Selling' (1923). Therefore, Whitehead had, unusually, for his day established himself as an academic, writer and consultant. In 1926 he carried out an assignment for the Boston Consolidated Gas Corporation in the fields of job evaluation, salary structure and salesmanship training. Whilst the form of service provided was not unusual for him at that time, the consequences of that assignment had a significant impact on his future following his return to Britain in 1929 due to personal circumstances associated with his wife's health.
2. Following the assignment, Whitehead produced a series of handbooks entitled 'Course in Domestic Gas Salesmanship' Volumes 1-6 (1932).
3. Born in 1900, Maurice Lubbock was the youngest (fifth) son of Sir John Lubbock. Lubbock was educated at Eton and Balliol and for a short time was employed in the Vickers Engineering plant at Crayford (Kent). He spent the period 1919-1921 partly at

Oxford and partly in the City with Coutts and Company. In 1919, Britain's leading glove manufacturing and trading firm, Dent Allcroft and Company, was floated on the London stock market. The Lubbock family bought a sizeable holding and Maurice Lubbock took up employment there in 1921, first as Company Secretary and then in 1922 as a member of the board of directors. The Company was going through difficult times and by 1930 Lubbock was appointed Managing Director with a mandate to secure improvements to trading, and efficiency of manufacture and performance. Lubbock's co-founder in Production Engineering, Robert Bryson, was born in 1904 and, following a mechanical sciences degree at Cambridge, worked for a period in the shipbuilding industry prior to joining the Bedaux company as a field engineer under the direction of John Leslie Orr.

4. Because Dent's had been experiencing difficulties with its Canadian operation at that time, Lubbock felt it necessary to employ consultants to review its business (Wayne 1959). As a result of the advice he received from J.D. Woods and Company, the Canadian operation was discontinued.

5. Bryson was the first Managing Director of the Company and its first operating consultant was Jack Raymond, his junior at Bedaux. Lubbock was the Chairman and two contemporaries of his, both friends from his school days at Eton, were invited to participate. These were W.L. Runciman, later to become Viscount Runciman whose family had interests in shipping, and Leo d'Erlanger, who would later become Chairman and Managing Director of the family business of Erlangers Limited, merchant bankers. In addition to these men, J.D. Woods (of J.D. Woods and Company) was also invited to join the board.

6. Lyndall Fownes Urwick was born in 1891 and was educated at Boxgrove School (Guildford), Repton School and New College Oxford. During 1913-1914 Urwick was employed in the family firm of Fownes Brothers and Company at its Worcester factory. His official job title was 'Learner', and during this period he found himself attached to one of the firm's buyers, travelling extensively throughout France, Germany, Italy and Belgium. At the outbreak of the First World War, as a reserve officer, he joined the Worcestershire Regiment. During war service, he received three Mentions in Despatches, a Military Cross and, following demobilisation with the rank of Major, an OBE. In 1919 he re-joined Fownes, this time as a partner in the firm. During the period 1919-1920, Urwick met B.S. Rowntree, the founder of the Rowntree Lecture Conferences (see Chapter 1), through sending some of the foremen at Fownes to one of the conferences. In 1922 Urwick took up an appointment in the Organisation Office at Rowntree's and in 1923 he was involved with the Office Organisation Committee at the firm charged with introducing scientific management into the work of all clerical departments; in effect Urwick performed the role of an internal consultant. In 1926, Urwick assisted Rowntree in forming the Management Research Groups and acted as its Secretary. In 1928 he accepted the Directorship at the International Management Institute in Geneva, remaining there until it closed in 1933. Throughout the whole of his life Urwick was a prominent speaker and writer on matters relating to management in its various forms, an active participant in various professional and academic bodies, and a leading member of the 'management movement'. For a detailed breakdown of Urwick's contributions to the furtherance of the management cause see Urwick, Orr and Partners Limited (1957) 'L. Urwick: A Bibliography', London, and the 'Addendum' for the period 1958-1965.

7. John Leslie Orr was born at Airdrie in Scotland on 26 May 1892. He was educated at Morrison's Academy, Crieff, and Glasgow High School. He studied mechanical engineering at Glasgow University, graduating in 1913. He was commissioned into the Highland Light Infantry at the outbreak of the First World War, and was later transferred to the Royal Artillery where he gained promotion to Major before being invalided home

after being gassed. After his recuperation, he joined a small engineering firm before being forced to seek warmer climates following the development of severe bouts of pneumonia as an after effect of the gassing. Orr worked as a freelance production engineer (consultant) in South Africa, New Zealand and Australia, returning to Britain in 1926 where he answered an advertisement to become a Bedaux engineer. When Orr left the Bedaux company he was the Sales Manager, responsible for generating new business.

8. Announcements of the Company's launch appeared in a number of journals, including *Industry Illustrated* and *Business*. However, the first client of the company came not from these announcements but from an awareness of Urwick's personal reputation and expertise in the field of management. The client was a small laundry whose owner had knowledge of Urwick through the National Federation of Launderers. The Federation journal had published in the March of that year (1934) an article entitled 'Management of Tomorrow' that was a review of Urwick's book under the same name published in the year previously, and had invited Urwick to address the annual national conference in the June; these events prompted the request for assistance.

9. Urwick had developed his visions of the future before he considered setting up in management consultancy. These visions are reflected in his 1933 book 'Management of Tomorrow'.

10. Whilst other surveys and opinion polls had been carried out prior to this date for commercial purposes, the Whitehead survey was the largest and most comprehensive that had taken place up to that point in time.

11. For example, in 1932 a series of six handbooks produced by the Company to support training in retail trades, published under the general title 'A Course of Training in Retail Salesmanship'.

12. By that time, Harold Whitehead had become one of the leading personalities in the 'management movement' in Britain, also becoming personally involved with the work of the Institute of Industrial Administration and the Incorporated Sales Managers Association. He was a regular contributor to journal articles and was often invited to speak on his specialised subjects to wide-ranging audiences.

13. In support of this approach, in 1936 Production Engineering recruited its first accountant to specialise in the development and deployment of processes in relation to manufacturing cost and expense control, and the initiation of budgetary management services.

14. The root cause of this embarrassment was Bedaux's personal contacts with leading members of fascist organisations in Germany and Italy at a time when relations between Britain and Germany were particularly strained. Bedaux's association with the Nazi regime began as early as 1935 although he had included individual Nazis in his circle of friends much earlier than that. In 1937 Bedaux became acquainted with a certain Frau Hoefken-Hempel who invited Bedaux to attend a social gathering not far from Hitler's mountain chalet in Berchtesgarten; he subsequently rented a chalet close by for the remainder of the social season. It was at this time that he became involved with a Captain Fritz Wiedemann, one of three of Hitler's liaison officers; this association lasted for a number of years. At the same time, another of the liaison officers, Captain Bruckner, also became known to Bedaux and it was Bruckner's father-in-law who later became the titular head of the German Bedaux Company (Brownlow 1972; Ferguson 1996a). Such associations, together with other events, eventually became Bedaux's downfall. Further embarrassment occurred as a result of his association with the Duke of Windsor following his abdication and marriage to Wallace Simpson, and the arrangements made by Bedaux to accompany the Duke on a fact finding visit of German industry in 1937.

15. A cautionary note: the term 'administrative' is used in this context to describe the management of the organisation and not the operations of individuals within an administrative or office setting. This was a controversial matter at the time because the term 'administration' was used by different people to mean different things. For example, it could either mean senior management within an organisation or lower level administrative functions.

16. There may have been others, for example accountants, who provided consultancy-type services on a part-time basis (see Chapter 2) or who may have dipped into consultancy at some point in their professional careers. In terms of full-time consultants very few references can be found to indicate their total numbers at any point in time and when references have been located no more than a handful occur together.

17. INBUCON was the telegraphic name of Associated Industrial Consultants and later became its trading name when a more neutral company title was sought.

18. During the second half of the 1930s alone, Urwick delivered 15 lectures at various venues (all of which led to the publication of papers), wrote 26 journal articles and produced two full-length books (Urwick, Orr and Partners Limited 1957).

19. The concept of a trainee being accompanied by a more experienced consultant was reflected in the motto of the Company at that time, 'Duo Melius Uno' (more easily understood as 'two heads are better than one'). As a reflection of that motto, the company logo was Janus, the two-faced Roman God of Gates. However, the logo was quickly abandoned when colloquial interpretations of its meaning were amusingly applied, e.g. 'two-faced'.

CHAPTER 5

Wartime Practices, 1939-1945

This final chapter in the time-phased series covering the first 75 years in the history of management consulting in Britain reviews the period 1939-1945. In but a few words, the title of Chapter Four of Mildred Brownlow's unpublished informal history of the INBUCON company, 'From Ploughshares Into Swords and Back Again', generally sums up the main thrust of management consulting activity within this period as it affected Britain's wartime industries. It is a descriptor of the major upheavals that took place prior to, during and at the conclusion of hostilities as it affected many firms within Britain and the part played by management consultants in that change process. Consulting was not, however, just to do with providing support to industry, for example this period witnessed for the first time major support to Government Departments on a scale not encountered previously.[1] Therefore, to a certain extent, Brownlow's chapter heading is misleading. That is because it may give the impression that a declaration of war on 3 September 1939, or even before that when war appeared inevitable, resulted in a major re-gearing of industry to enable industrial output to meet the needs of the crisis situation within Britain. The reality was that there was a lack of impetus to war production output, with the lessons of the First World War remaining largely unheeded.

In real terms there was very little difference during this period and a similar time frame associated with the build-up and early period of the First World War; the lessons of the past had not been heeded. Moving on from the period of build-up temporarily, the continuance of this apparent lack of impetus during the early phase of the War may be partly explained by the circumstances, both within Britain and on the front line at that time. That period attracted the label the 'Phoney War', and the seriousness of the situation was not fully recognised within Government and industry with regard to the need to improve industrial production; not only output, but also productivity. Barnett (1986) partly explains this situation through a description of Britain's dire financial straits. In early 1939 the Chiefs of Staff of the three Armed Services were warning the Government that

Britain could only win a conflict if there was a long war.[2] Conversely, the Treasury warned that it was only possible to finance a shorter campaign. Therefore, there was a conflict of interest with Britain's armed forces requiring a sustained effort over a longer period of time than was possible in terms of available cash.

Two major events brought into focus the reality of the situation and highlighted the need to take urgent action with regards to wartime production. The first of these was Dunkirk (May 1940) in which a withdrawal by the British Expeditionary Force resulted in a major loss of war equipment through abandonment and destruction on the Continent of Europe. In order to provide an effective challenge in the face of adversity, that equipment had to be replaced and a new Army needed equipping in order to make it a viable force. Dunkirk also emphasised Britain's vulnerability as an island fortress and the possibility of invasion by Germany. This highlighted the importance of an effective Airforce and Navy, and the need to increase production in aircraft and shipping.

The second event, although later in terms of time specifics, was 'The Battle of Britain' (September 1940). That event re-emphasised the need to up-gear aircraft production and the associated equipment needed to sustain an effective fighting force. British aircraft losses during the Battle exceeded one thousand and these needed replacing. Many more aircraft were damaged and there was an equally urgent need for replacement aircraft parts. Britain's management consultants, as this chapter will indicate later, played an important role in this area during the course of the War. Whilst these events increased the strain on wartime production across a range of industries, strain was further brought to bear through a disco-ordination of production across the whole range of wartime products.

A major impetus to change came about in July 1940 when the Institution of Production Engineers and the Works Management Association joined forces to lobby the Federation of British Industries (FBI).[3] This was with a view to applying pressure to the coalition Government to effect change through improvements to co-ordination of supply and demand. Because of that consequential pressure, the FBI lobbied the Government. A War Production Committee was established under the direct control of the Cabinet. The purpose of the Committee was to examine the procedures carried out by the three Services in the demand for war supply goods. However, even with such a high profile and powerful guiding force as the Cabinet there were no radical moves in the direction of co-ordination even though sub-committees were formed partly for this purpose. The FBI and the Institution of Production Engineers exerted further pressure on the Government and this resulted in the formation of the Ministry of Production in February 1942.

The Ministry of Production rationalised production and the processes associated with it and this resulted in a more co-ordinated approach for the demand of war-supply goods across the three services.[4] However, a co-ordinated approach to demand alone will not lead to co-ordinated supply, or indeed to improvements within the production process generally. These are other areas where management consultants found themselves providing services during the wartime period. In terms of overall production, regardless of difficulties with the co-ordination of demand and supply, Britain's position when compared with Germany during the first half of the War with regard to aircraft and warship production indicated that Britain out-produced Germany. It was only from 1943-1944 that Germany's production exceeded Britain's (Broadberry 1997).

This very short description of that was going on within industry and the business environment prior to and during the early years of the War is useful because it identifies some of the difficulties that management consultants had to cope with during the course of their assignments at that time. For the first time, consultants were found assisting Government across a range of functions and, therefore, this period is unique with regards to the history of management consulting in Britain. To emphasise that uniqueness this chapter has three primary aims, the combination of which tells the consultants' story for the period 1939-1945. Firstly, support to industry in various forms, the bread and butter of consultancy up to the point in time, continued throughout the wartime period. A number of new areas of involvement will be identified, as well as continuance in the traditional forms of management consulting. Secondly, part of the work conducted by management consultants within Government Departments was significant in terms of the war effort. Some of these activities will be reviewed, together with other non-war-related services. Finally, training and development for client personnel and consultants increased in importance during this period. The formation and work of Personnel Administration, initially as a training consultancy, will be examined, as well as the development of off-job training for consultants. Before moving on consultancy's support to industry, a short digression in order to review developments in the United States and Germany at that time will help bring into focus work being carried out in the British consultancy environment.

Consultancy Abroad: A Parallel Dimension

In the United States, in complete contrast to Britain, management consultancy consisted of about four hundred firms by the time of the outbreak of the Second World War. There still remained two main streams of activity within industry and commerce (see Chapter 4). By the time that the United States had entered the War in December 1941 a lot of work was being carried out within various Federal Government Departments (McKenna 1995). That work was generally directed at effecting improvements to civilian processes and production, reviewing military structures and carrying out reorganisation assignments, and overseeing and directing the expansion of the Federal Administration. Management consultants in the United States during this period clearly had a pivotal role within the heart of government, as well as in industry and commerce. There was a ready acceptance of consultancy work, both at the strategic and operational levels. This was in contrast to the British position that still reflected a situation in which consultants were largely employed within operational areas of organisations.

In Germany during this period, the ruling Nazi regime had identified the benefits of the work of consultants in a period where efficiency in armaments manufacture was of paramount importance to the war effort. An institutional framework already existed in support of the scientific management movement, typified by the National Efficiency Board, or RKW, that received most of its funding from the German Government.[5] German consultants were generally employed on the shop floor, utilising techniques that had been developed within the scientific management tradition. Consultancy was viewed as one of the primary and, therefore, important conduits in the process of effecting and maintaining change in order to improve operational performance. Consequently, their numbers increased from 320 individuals in 1942 to 700 in 1944 (Kipping 1997). The (international) Bedaux company, not to be confused with British Bedaux, which had established offices in Germany in 1927, was authorised to continue trading during the War, but under direct German control.[6] War, however, brought with it inevitable changes and it is the work of the British companies that command the attention of the remainder of this chapter.

Consultancy in Industry

Throughout the wartime period management consulting was generally classified as a 'Reserved Occupation'. This helped to resolve some of the uncertainties as to the future of consultancy, noted in the previous chapter, during the build up to war. The Ministry of Labour tightly controlled the situation and demanded regular returns from the consulting companies on the numbers employed and the disposition of all consultants. Companies were not permitted to increase the number of consultants in their employ beyond their 1940 manning levels.[7] Accepting employment restrictions, this is the first real indication from Government on the value that it attached to the work of management consultants.

Many within consultancy were on the reserve lists of the three services and a large number of these were called up for wartime service. One such individual was Robert Bryson, the then Managing Director of Production Engineering, who was mobilised into the Royal Engineers.[8] The majority of the remainder of Britain's management consultants were engaged, throughout the period, in activities either directly or indirectly in support of the war effort. Unlike 1934 when it was possible to draw a line in the sand and describe the consulting environment with a reasonable amount of accuracy (see Chapter 4), the early part of this period (1939-1940) was relatively more fluid in terms of movements in and out of established companies. The build up to war and the part played by consultant companies within it helped shape the future of consultancy, especially that part that involved consultants within industrial enterprises and in Government Departments.

Throughout the whole of this period, and for a time beyond, work-study remained the central technique for improving performance within the workplace. By the time of the commencement of the Second World War, work-study was not only being used by consultants, but a number of the larger industrial enterprises used this tool as a means of improving their internal production processes. Some firms had work-study departments and others employed management services specialists. A number of these departments were formed on the back of previous consultancy assignments and specialists had been trained in the continuance of the applications. Work-study provided an important contribution to improving operational performance and raising productivity through a structured approach to analysis and change. Brech (2002b) identifies the virtues of work-study by highlighting its value with regards to improvements to the employment of manpower and machinery, stressing the incentive benefit of payment regimes linked to targets and the development of indicators for the effective control of manufacturing costs. He also suggested that work-study provided direct indicators to effect greater mechanisation and improved layout and production flows, that included the handling of materials and components. Some of this was achieved through the development of definitive standards and the implementation of planning and progress control that helped to determine the supply of materials, components and tools into the operational programme.

Work-study, as the primary consultancy technique to improve efficiency, had been developed and improved upon from its early applications under the guise of time study (see Chapter 3). Consequently, it remained the major technique in use by management consultants throughout the whole of this period within industrial enterprises and, through modification, in some office settings. However, whilst this digression re-emphasises the importance of work-study as a technique, the work of management consultants can be explained through the work carried out by them during this period. Brownlow's (1972) general account of the period describes a situation in which firms of all types called upon the services of management consultants to help them 'changeover' from peacetime operations to the supply of war production goods. A number of these manufacturers switched their attention to other product lines, in some cases quite dramatically. For example, one manufacturer of raincoats switched over to producing barrage balloons. It was these firms that sought the assistance of management consultants. Whilst all this was true, the process was extremely complex. That complexity occurred because changing-over to other product lines (re-gearing) required input into other factors of production that were crucial to a successful transformation. One such factor, training in terms of the workforce, will be covered in more detail later in this chapter. In many instances this involved the development of a production environment from the ground floor upwards, with all the problems associated with such a task.

Barnett's (1986) description of the expansion of the aircraft industry from a relatively small affair in the mid-1930s to becoming the largest in terms of employed personnel in the engineering and allied trades by the mid point of the War is a good example of how industrial output increased to match the demand for wartime production.[9] However, an increase in size points towards the need to improve factors of production, specifically co-ordinating operations, in order to cope better with expanding demand. The use of out of date production methods and ageing equipment did little to help industry cope better with those pressures.

Specifically in terms of the aircraft industry during the early years of the War, the industry was suffering from the effects of shortages of materials for the manufacture and repair of aircraft. With regards to this historical account, there was a general shortage of light alloy extrusions. In order to produce these, a large proportion of the raw materials required had to be imported into this country. Most of these raw materials were transported by sea and a percentage of these were lost through enemy aircraft action, or surface and submarine attacks. Within the United Kingdom, the extrusions were produced on only eight presses in 1940. Brownlow's (1972) description of the situation indicated that 48 aircraft manufacturers and 5000 sub-contractors between them required the production of 500 thousand extrusions with approximately 15 specifications. Over-ordering by the manufacturers, with earlier than required delivery dates, further complicated this situation. Therefore, general confusion reigned, aircraft production was adversely affected and there was inadequate support to the war effort.

Associated Industrial Consultants (AIC) was tasked by the Ministry of Aircraft Production (MAP) to improve material control across the whole of the aircraft industry through the implementation of a priority system.[10] The first task that faced the consultants was to establish what the situation was in relation to the stocks held by individual companies. This was achieved through persuading manufacturers and sub-contractors to declare the materials that they were holding within their inventories. The next stage was to construct master parts lists of extrusions for each aircraft type within production. This was a cataloguing process without precedence up to that point in time. Both tasks were enormous, requiring all the skills at the consultants' disposal in terms of interacting with and persuading individuals of the strategic importance of the task to overall aircraft production. Once the cataloguing process was underway, and individual lists were constructed, all information then had to be collated in order to form a complete master parts list for the whole of the aircraft industry. The next stage in the process was to determine the output requirement of extrusions for industry within a given time frame (e.g. over the period of a month). This was achieved through estimating the productive output of new aircraft for each calendar month. From this estimation, the quantities of extrusions were determined through the use of the master parts list and a calculation strip. The calculation strip was specifically devised for this purpose by the AIC consultants. The calculation strip contained the quantities of each aircraft to be manufactured in a specific month. These were matched against the master parts list and the total quantities of parts were determined. Once the quantities of parts were known, orders for the manufacture of those parts could then be given to the relevant manufacturers or sub-contractors that produced them. In effect, this was a simple device for controlling supply and demand. The total quantities were then cascaded down to the manufacturers and sub-contractors that produced them. In addition to this, a supplementary allowance was added on a daily basis for repairs to aircraft damaged in action or through other circumstances. In order to achieve success, office staff worked to the pre-determined system to ensure that the cycle was accurately maintained. This overall system became known as a 'Period Batch System' and was, undoubtedly, a major success for AIC and a significant contribution to the war effort.

One consequence of AIC's involvement in the aircraft industry, primarily in terms of manufacturing potential, was that it highlighted the inadequacy of the number and deployment of presses that made the extrusions within Britain. This situation could have been exacerbated if there were any losses to those presses from, say, either normal wear and tear or through enemy action. Consequently, further presses were ordered from the United States and distributed to new sites in the United Kingdom. This was part of the Government's plan to create 'shadow factories', ongoing since before the War, as a safeguard in the event of disruption through enemy action. Other activities in the aircraft industry are exemplified by the work of consultants from Production Engineering that had previously established a strong relationship with aircraft manufacturing firms in the pre-war period (see Chapter 4). The Company's clients included: De Havilland, Armstrong-Siddeley, Fairey, Hawker, Rolls-Royce, Saunders-Roe and Short Brothers. Examples of the Company's work included helping to develop production processes for Merlin engine manufacture in the United States (these engines being ultimately for deployment within the aircraft manufacturing environment in the United Kingdom) and that of the setting up of a jet engine production line at Stoke-on-Trent for Rolls-Royce (PE 1984). Immediately prior to the War, Production Engineering had assisted Hawker and Rolls-Royce set up shadow factories for Merlin engine production for the Hurricane fighter. Consultants from Production Engineering were involved in site selection, layout, production methods, selection of plant and equipment, and the development of organisation structures. In addition, the consultants were responsible for the control and co-ordination of the work, in effect programme management (Blackstone 1980). This was the first time that the Company had been involved in a whole factory project from start to finish. A spin-off of this assignment is that it firmly established Production Engineering within Rolls-Royce and this led to numerous other assignments, including the development of a second shadow factory later.

Examples of other work in direct support to the war effort could be found within the shipbuilding industry. Specifically within Scottish shipyards, consultants from AIC developed a system of 'Forward Loading'. The purpose of the assignment was to develop a method of increasing the rate of production in order to improve overall output. This was necessary, apart from considerations relating to productivity and efficiency, because the demand for replacement and new craft was outstripping supply. Forward Loading was a method of identifying manufacturing tasks in advance, thus enabling effective scheduling and the deployment of manpower. As a consequence of this assignment, four destroyers were produced within the same time frame as the three produced previously; a 33 per cent rise in output. Similar successes occurred within factories producing motor torpedo boats in the south of England. These achievements were all the more remarkable when one considers the inefficiencies that had traditionally plagued the shipbuilding industry in

Britain. Barnett (1986) identified two primary causes of this: bottlenecks in certain areas due to poor scheduling and the inappropriate use of labour. In terms of scheduling, bottlenecks occurred within some of the production areas, for example, riveting, plating, welding and electrical work. Effective work scheduling, through advanced identification of tasks (Forward Loading), was a pre-requisite for reducing pipeline times within production. This is linked to the second cause, the inappropriate use of labour, whereby skilled artisans were employed to carry out tasks of an unskilled or semi-skilled nature, resulting in skilled workers not being directed towards those areas of greatest need. It was precisely within such conditions that consultants found themselves having to carry out much of their work.

Generally throughout the War, a large portion of the work of consultants was centred on the engineering and manufacturing sectors that had been re-geared to take account of the needs for wartime production. In overall terms, there were two aspects to this: work simplification and operator training. Whilst training is covered specifically in a later section of this chapter, a short digression at this point is necessary in order to expand upon the concepts of re-gearing and work simplification. One of the consequences of increasing production at any point in time when many of the skilled workers traditionally employed within industry had been called up in defence of their country was that there was generally a wide-ranging skill shortage. To overcome such a problem, one tactic that proved effective was to re-analyse the job and break it down into component parts. Individually these parts did not require the employment of skilled workers and, therefore, an unskilled replacement workforce could be trained to carry out the work. A good example of such a scenario was in the massive underground ordnance filling factories, employing, in some instances, more than twenty thousand people (Brownlow 1972).

For production to continue, inexperienced and unskilled operators were trained in an environment where a process of job simplification had been carried out. The first stage in the process was an educational regime to ensure that each knew their place in the overall task. The next stage was a programme of training, following the revised programme of production planning and control. Consequently, individual operators were able to perform tasks that had been in part previously the preserve of skilled and semi-skilled workers. However, none of these achievements would have been possible without the intervention of prominent individuals within Government and the support of the trade union movement.[11] Other less obvious tasks for consultants at that time included an assignment undertaken by one consultant from Production Engineering who acted as a purchasing agent abroad (United States) for those materials in short supply in this country. These included machine tools and equipment in support of a range of industries, including aircraft production. Because the United States was neutral in the early stages of the War, it was not unusual to come across German buyers carrying out similar tasks on behalf of their country (Blackstone, 1980).

It is quite easy to forget that while all this assistance was being provided during the wartime period other problems, apart from those discussed previously with regards to the workplace, hindered the consultancy process. For example, fuel was in short supply, public transport was severely disrupted and the company car had yet to be invented as a mode of transport for consultants within Britain. Consultants had a need to travel and, therefore, difficult times forced innovative solutions. Blackstone (1980) records the perils encountered by one consultant travelling between this country and the United States – not on one occasion, but twice. The outbound journey was carried out by ship in the knowledge that submarines had sunk other shipping on the same route between Liverpool and America. The return journey was even more perilous because it was not only by ship, the liner Britannic, but its upper decks were loaded with drums of high explosives. The same consultant returned to the United States in 1942 by troopship under destroyer escort. However, the return journey was the most unusual because the consultant found himself seated on a plank in the bomb bay of a Liberator aircraft travelling at 22,000 feet in arctic clothing in conditions of –50° from Montreal to Prestwick. It is difficult to imagine these conditions nowadays or the dedication required in these unusual circumstances.

Closer to home, Production Engineering purchased five motor cycles and employed an additional member of staff whose sole responsibility was making applications for petrol allocations. The motor cycles were purchased on a staff grade basis: a 500cc 'Rudge' for the use of directors, 350cc machines for supervising consultants and 250cc machines for consultants. However, amusingly, little account was taken of the riding capabilities of the senior men of the Company and the Rudge remained in a garage for the majority of the War (Wayne 1959). Whilst most of the work carried out by consultants within industry during this period was directed at the war effort, and no doubt the majority of consultants could describe similar assignments and difficulties, there still remained a semblance of normality with some assignments being conducted in areas where not all production was war related.

Urwick Orr, for example, carried out an assignment at a car production facility in Derby. The purpose of the assignment was to changeover production in sections of the plant from hand to machine fitting of parts as a result of the implementation of a partial automation process within the factory. Other assignments included the development of new forms of service. One example of this occurred during the early years of the War (January 1941). For the first time, the Urwick Orr Partnership commenced consultant services in personnel management. Previously, the only examples of assistance in this field could be found through the work of the National Institute of Industrial Psychology and the Industrial Welfare Society. Commencement of the service owed itself to an enquiry by a client, a small firm manufacturing surgical equipment mainly for War Office contracts, which had problems in relation to high labour turnover. This led to a request for assistance which in turn led to the development of services in this area.

During the period 1939-1945 the majority of work was firmly directed towards work that directly or indirectly aided the war effort. This was either achieved through direct consultant input in some form or another or, occasionally, one or two consultants provided assistance to firms through temporary attachment. The purpose of the attachment was to fill executive positions in order to bridge shortfalls caused by wartime service for senior personnel serving in the armed forces. These few examples of the work of consultants during the wartime period in industry provide a taster of what was occurring. To tell the full story a whole book would need to be devoted to that subject.

Aid to Government Departments

Times of national crisis inevitably call for measures that otherwise would not have been employed or would have evolved more gradually. One such measure was the deployment of consultants in a supporting role within Government Departments. However, a lot of the work within Government Departments during the War was of a classified nature and, therefore, very little is definitively known about the activities of consultants on many of those assignments. For example, Brownlow (1972) stated that quite a few consultants from Associated Industrial Consultants at some time or another during the War worked for various Government Departments in a wide variety of roles. Because of the classification of the work the usual practice of sending reports back to Head Office was discontinued and, in fact, little or nothing was known of the detail of the work.

The other consulting companies operating at that time provide similar stories, although one or two details have emerged through the passage of time. For example, consultants from Production Engineering were attached to Combined Operations and were involved in developing processes for the ordering and delivery of equipment to its base location (Blackstone 1980).[12]

However, the work of Urwick Orr during the period of the War within Government Departments provides a good example of the way in which consultants adapted their work in support of the war effort wherever they were needed. Lyndall Urwick realised the overall potential that Government work offered the Company and actively sought assignments with the War Office immediately following the outbreak of War. In order to raise the profile of Urwick Orr in the general area of government support, Urwick and two consultants from the Company provided voluntary assistance to the Territorial Army's Second London Division. The task involved conducting a complete review of the Division's administrative organisation and methods of working, and the initiation of a programme of improvements. Whilst these efforts were unsuccessful in terms of gaining further work, the Company's fortunes changed in the spring of 1940.

In May 1940 Urwick was invited, with three of the Partnership's clerical methods and accounting specialists, to join the Office Research Section of H.M. Treasury Investigation Division, specifically to work on an office efficiency programme. The initial purpose of the attachment was to improve methods and performance, and reduce the number of civil servants employed thus making available more personnel for the three services. This was fortuitous, as the office and general organisation consulting work, Urwick's specific area of responsibility, had fallen off, primarily because of the importance attached to direct war work in the area of production.[13]

At the time that Urwick and the consultants from the Company joined the Treasury, the Office Research Section numbered only six to eight people (Rowe 1959). The Office Research Section was the forerunner of the Treasury's Organisation and Methods (O&M) Division. During the course of the two years that Urwick remained within this Department, he and his team were responsible for a whole range of important tasks. Some of these tasks were directly related to the war effort, for example assisting with the internal organisation of the Ministry of Supply, conducting investigations for the Ministry of Shipping and working as a Treasury investigation officer in the Air Ministry. All of these areas were directly involved in the procurement, co-ordination and supply of materials and equipment in aid of the war effort. Some tasks were clearly of a more routine nature and internal to the Treasury, for example conducting a review of the volume of committee work and an analysis of messenger work within and between Departments. Other tasks involved improvements to efficiency, for example the rationalisation of the training and the supervision of typists. Some of the others had the effect of providing assistance to other Government Departments, for example carrying out clerical complaint investigations in the Home Office and participating in the Mitcheson Committee charged with the reorganisation of the Ministry of Pensions. Finally, other tasks are less easy to categorise, for example investigating the arrears of payment of balance of civil pay payments to dependants serving in the forces.

Whatever way those assignments are categorised, they were clearly wide-ranging and obviously important, even though some were not directly connected with the war effort. After two years direct involvement with the Treasury, Urwick personally no longer felt that the working relationship was satisfactory and he resigned from his post. However, he did not remain unconnected with the Government for very long because in June of 1942 he was offered, and accepted, a post in the Petroleum Warfare Department of the War Office. This was an operational appointment and Urwick reverted to using his rank of Major, being promoted to Lieutenant Colonel within a short period of time. The work of the Department was of strategic importance to the war effort and pivotal to some of the successes enjoyed by the armed forces during the period of the War. Projects involving Urwick included the development of flame weapons and the clearing of fog from airfields (known as FIDO). In the period following on from the Normandy landings, work included the direct piping of petrol by lines laid under the English Channel (known as PLUTO). This was strategically important in order to maintain the momentum generated following the breakout from the beachhead. However, by the time the Allies had advanced as far as Brussels the usefulness of the Department was at an end. Urwick applied for a discharge from his duties so that he could return to Urwick Orr.

The experiences of Urwick Orr in providing assistance to Government Departments highlighted the growing perception of the usefulness of management consultants in a range of tasks within Government circles at that time. This was probably the turning point with regard to consultant involvement within the public sector. The Second World War provided the opportunity for consultancy to prove its worth on a very broad front, emphasising the range of skills and experience held by consultants in areas that had little connection with their 'bread and butter' activities of the past. As a final thought and a reminder of the veil of secrecy that surrounded a lot of the work carried out at that time within the broad area of Government, Howell (undated) records the story of one consultant attached to the Inter Services Research Bureau, at Station 12 in Bedfordshire. The purpose of his assignment was to provide assistance in the selection of machine tools to enable special work to be carried out at the site. An amusing incident occurred when the consultant was told to report to an address in Baker Street in London. He travelled by taxi and on informing the driver of the address, he replied 'Ok Guv, Spy Headquarters'.

The period of the Second World War was important with regards to training and development. This was on two fronts in addition to the training regimes developed early in the War to cope with the re-skilling of staff. Firstly, in 1941 the first off-site training school was developed, initially, to provide training for consultants in the field of work-study. And, secondly, personnel from an emerging consulting company, which was formed in 1943 by an ex senior Bedaux consultant, developed a new and improved method of training for manual skills. These were important developments and the next section is devoted to both events.

Training and Development

In 1941 consultant training witnessed a watershed in its method of delivery. Work-study lay at the heart of methods improvement, work measurement, production planning and cost control. It was essential that all consultants engaged in that field were competent in its application. As an important component of the work-study process, consultants were required to train client personnel in the continuance of the application after the consultants had left and the assignment was complete. Other aspects of the assignment process included educating senior and operational managers on the benefits of work-study; this was achieved through appreciation courses. Kubr (1977) recognised the fundamental nature of this aspect of consultancy work and suggested that there were a number of potential types of training that could be carried out. These included on-the-job training for operatives, the training of trainers for the continuance of the application and appreciation courses for those not directly involved. He also suggested that training could be carried out either in-house, through specially devised programmes, or through the offices of external training providers.

In the period of the Second World War there were no external training providers that could support companies in the training of their staff in the field of work-study and its associated components. That was until 1941, albeit not with that intention in mind, when an ex-Bedaux consultant, at that time in the employ of Urwick Orr, William Lodge, established a work-study school in the living room of his house in Bedford. Lodge had joined Urwick Orr in 1937, he was an older man who did not wish to work as a consultant under the pressures of wartime service. The 'Bedford Work-Study School' was born and for the first time consultant training was conducted off the job. The title 'school' may seem somewhat grandiose in the light of its size and appointment; nevertheless its importance in terms of time specifics should not be underestimated.[14] The School established the principle of consultant training away from the clients' premises. The course at Bedford was of three weeks duration for up to six participants at a time. It used in-house workshop techniques for the preliminary stages, with arrangements at three local factories for the practical component of the course.

There were a number of benefits associated with utilising local factories for practical training, including: the engendering of co-operation between both the 'school' and consultants with local companies in the Bedford area, and the wider employment of consultancy techniques through a free consultancy service to participating firms, thus spreading the employment of work-study into firms which otherwise may not have used such methods.[15] In terms of content, the course consisted of a number of subject areas. Initially the course was concerned with work-study and base rate analysis, but after the War it was extended to eight weeks and included labour cost control, material cost control, planning, costing, cost control, methods improvement, time standards, factory layout, work flow and operational performance standards; all the essential tools required to provide consultants with the ability to deliver an effective work-study service.[16]

The 1940s also witnessed further advances in client training, brought about by the formation of a new management consulting company in 1943, Personnel Administration. The company was formed by a disillusioned ex-Bedaux engineer (and director), Ernest Edward Butten. Butten had a background in mechanical engineering and over ten years experience as a consultant with the Bedaux company.[17] His frustrations with the company were largely to do with his perception of its policy in terms of expansion and lack of vision in terms of resourcing. He believed that its rate of growth was unsustainable in terms of new consultants unless an effective training regime was put in place. In real terms, he probably saw an opportunity to set up on his own and follow his own ambitions in terms of his vision of management consulting. Assisting Butten in the formation of this new company were two other ex-Bedaux employees, Dr A.H. (David) Seymour and Derek McMullen. Seymour and McMullen provided the initial principal consultant force, with Butten concentrating on company philosophy and selling the consultant services. Butten had a vision and this was reflected in the Charter of the company. There were two main strands to the Charter: to create the leading organisation of its type in the world, made of authorities from the various branches of management, and to develop new procedures that would be taught to the staff of client firms, thus improving the standard of management overall (Fogg 1980).

To achieve those aims, Butten postulated two primary steps in the overall process. Firstly, to build up the consultancy side of the business in order to generate enough income to move onto the second step, that of creating a research organisation for the development of new and improved techniques. This was obviously circuitous because improved methods would lead to a greater take up in services. Therefore, Butten considered that there were two sides to the work of the Company, the delivery of consulting services and the development of research to improve service delivery overall. The aspirations of the Company detailed within the 'Charter' were limited in the first two years of the company's existence owing to the constraints placed upon the founders by their previous contracts of employment with the Bedaux company. In effect they were not permitted to practice in the same fields of management consulting as Bedaux for a period of two years. Partly because of this, at least initially, the Company developed services largely concerned with the application of new techniques in the training environment, utilising the methodology developed by one of its founders, A.H. Seymour.

This chapter has already indicated the importance of training within Britain during the wartime period and whilst the constraint placed on ex-Bedaux personnel could be viewed as negative in terms of starting a new consulting business, the service developed by the Company was opportune at a time when the training of workers was still vital to the war effort. Personnel Administration developed a new and unique method of training for operatives that was delivered away from the workplace; the majority of training up to that point in time had been carried out on-the-job. The training methodology was called 'Process Analysis Method of Training' (PAMT) or 'PA Method of Training' as a shortened title.[18] The methodology was developed by A.H. Seymour in the years prior to the formation of Personnel Administration and introduced as a commercial package in 1943. In outline, PAMT was developed through combining the principles of industrial psychology and work-study (Seymour 1968). This was achieved through a structured approach that built up the expertise of individuals through a series of phases.

Training was conducted off the job at the client's premise, possibly through a training department or school. As a preparatory step, the job was analysed to determine the elements that made it up and the various forms of dexterities involved. Specially designed training jigs and devices were constructed to test the fitness of each potential operative through a regime of aptitude testing. The type of dexterities tested included manual co-ordination, rhythmic movement, visual acuity and judgement (PA undated). Based on the initial analysis, the elements of the job were taught individually to trainees. The progress of the trainees was determined by the speed with which each element was carried out and it was only when trainees had reached 'Experienced Worker Speed' (EWS) that they progressed to the next stage. Experienced Worker Speed was the expected (normal) speed that operatives performed at within the workshop or factory and probably related to approximately 80 Bs in Bedaux methodology. Training included the use of other technologies in order to improve dexterity, for example the use of light equipment for co-ordinating hand and eye movement. The number of following stages depended upon the complexity of the job because each involved a gradual combination of elements, again progressing to EWS. It was only when all elements of the job had been combined and that EWS could be maintained throughout the working day that training was concluded. Another aspect of the PAMT approach was raising awareness of the system through introductory lectures to various grades of managers, including foremen and trades union representatives, with the view of 'winning them over' to the system and improving acceptance of it generally within the firm (Chanter 1945).

There were a number of declared advantages of PAMT when compared with training on-the-job (PA undated). For example, PAMT would lead to a reduction in scrap and waste raw materials as operators were specifically trained to avoid such costs. Other direct financial savings resulted from an overall reduction in training time when compared with on-the-job training, potentially in the region of 50 per cent (PA undated). From an acceptance perspective on the shop floor, because the trained operator was only integrated once EWS had been achieved, this reduced the likelihood that the output of the department would be brought down by the low output levels associated with on-the-job training. In addition to these benefits, PAMT could also be used to train existing workers in new skills. However, the major disadvantage of the system is that trainees added little economic value to the firm during the course of their training. Training was conducted off the job and even though it was quicker than on-the-job training, those trained on the shop floor were at least contributing towards output and whilst there was some output from training in the PAMPT method, this was less than that occurring on-the-job.

The PA Method of Training proved a success and was utilised by many firms during the wartime years and in the post-war period, although various subsequent changes in name may have hidden its true origins (the name that survived was 'Skills Analysis Training'). For example, PAMT was initially used for the training of female labour engaged in the manufacture of tail-planes for Sunderland Flying Boats. Later examples included the grinding of ball bearings for tank and aircraft engines, and for the manufacture of army uniforms (Seymour 1968). According to Tisdall (1982), PAMT was extremely successful and cut wastage by 50 per cent. At the conclusion of hostilities in 1945 the system was used to help resettle personnel from the three armed services on their discharge.[19]

The PA Method of Training provided the initial purpose for setting up Personnel Administration. It met the 'Direction of Labour' requirements and did not clash with the detailed conditions of the employment contracts of the founders with their former employer, Bedaux. At the same time it generated income and stimulated demand for services (Fogg 1980). However, the supply of training was not the only commitment that came out of the Charter. In December 1943, a Research and Development Organisation was created within Personnel Administration with the view of developing new and improved management techniques and methods for use within consultancy assignments and in the training of client personnel.[20] Therefore, Personnel Administration was a significant contributor in the field of training and development at a time when speedier and more efficient methods needed to be found to directly support the war effort. The importance of consultancy's involvement in delivering training was summed up by Kubr (1977) who stated:

> The link between consulting and training is logical and natural. Both have the same ultimate objective – to do things better – and they support each other.

The period of the Second World War was important for consultancy in terms of education and development because it highlighted the role of consultants in this field. It also set the scene for a burgeoning training environment in the post-war period when consulting company management training schools were formed by the major consultancies. These schools and the initiatives of the major consultancies led the way in the delivery of training in the broad fields of business and management (see Chapter 7). However, that was in the future, during the period of the Second World War, specifically during its closing stages, management consultants had an eye to the future and had made preparations to take their work forward at the cessation of hostilities.

Preparations for the Future

The period of the Second World War was significant for management consultancy because it demonstrated its usefulness to wider audiences in a range of settings that had previously not attracted consultant input. For example, material control within the aircraft industry demonstrated the analytical strengths of consultants, not only in areas connected with the operational environment of a firm, but at the industry level developing strategic processes that impacted upon all firms involved in the industry. There are other examples within this chapter where methodologies were developed to directly impact upon the output of firms, for example the work simplification and training programmes in those areas where re-gearing was carried out as a consequence of the direct effects of war. A parallel dimension during this period was the work of consultants in direct support of Government Departments.

As a collective, management consultants preach the virtues of effective preparation and planning as a means to improving future performance. There are two aspects to this: external preparation and planning, with regards to wider economic performance, and internally in relation to the future of consultancy. As far as the consultant companies were concerned, each of them made their plans during the latter stages of the War to set the framework for operations into a new era of peace and potential prosperity in terms of growth. This included development plans to take account of factors relating to expansion, both in terms of the size of concerns and their breadth of service delivery. In the broader context, the companies had their sights set on the wider economic environment in Britain and elsewhere in the world. A good example of this approach can be found in a survey carried out by the Whitehead company in the summer of 1944, following the successful landings in France, when there was a belief that the end of hostilities in Europe were in sight. The review was concerned with post-war planning (Harold Whitehead and Staff 1944) and had two aims. Firstly, to establish what forward planning was being carried out by commercial and industrial enterprises, and whether or not any obstacles or difficulties were being encountered. And, secondly, to seek views on Anglo-American relations after the War. The survey demonstrated the Whitehead company's professional interest in forward planning in the wider industrial and commercial environments and the likelihood of expansion into markets outside this country. Significantly, it also demonstrated that the Company was actively searching for new areas of future consultant activity.

A questionnaire was sent to the senior executives of 496 randomly selected businesses within four groups based on employee size; 169, or 34 per cent of the sampled population, responded.[21] The survey found that post-war planning was taking place within businesses, although it was largely a part-time activity. In terms of obstacles two thirds of the respondents suggested that government policy was a barrier to forward planning; this probably indicated that government attention was firmly directed towards the war effort at that time. However, there was a mixed response with regards to trade with the United States; half the respondents suggested that American companies were direct competitors within the British domestic market and three quarters felt that there was direct competition globally. Therefore, there were few indications that businesses were seeking closer co-operation with American companies. Significantly for consultancy only 40 per cent of respondents stated that they were actively seeking outside assistance with regards to their forward planning. Of those, the vast majority were in receipt of assistance from trade associations, with only one or two companies looking towards management consultants for any help.

There is little doubt that this research provided interesting information of the perceptions of the leaders of Britain's industrial and commercial businesses on the way forward at the conclusion of hostilities. The end was perceptively in sight as there appeared to be a significant amount of forward planning taking place, albeit on a part-time basis. If other consultant companies were aware of the contents of the report, and the likelihood is that they were, valuable insights would have been gained on the attitudes of businesses towards the concept of planning. The report indicated that consultant input in this process was negligible at that time. The primary reasons for this would have been that consultant companies were engaged in assignments, in the main, directed towards the war effort in some form or another. The size of the consultant force within Britain in comparison to the overall size of the task, taking into consideration the restrictions placed on consultancies in terms of growth, was small and there would have been very little flexibility in terms of directing consultants towards future planning tasks for firms. In addition, planning of this nature is a strategic task within the firm and there is very little evidence to suggest that senior managers had, in any general way, changed their perception with regards to outside involvement at the level of strategic decision-making. Nevertheless, within their own firms, each of the consulting companies had made plans in the period before the cessation of hostilities concerning their own future aspirations.

Management consulting was about to enter into a new period of growth and prosperity that would bring them up to the present day. Because of the emerging nature of consulting, specifically the complex structure that is reflected in today's spread of services and the internationalisation of the service sector as a whole, it is not possible to take forward the rest of the consultants' story as a time phased process. Therefore, the next five chapters will review management consultancy through a subject-based approach for the whole of the post-war period, with timelines indicated where that is appropriate to enhance the clarity of explanation.

Notes

1. This is not to deny the work of the Whitehead company in support of the Government within the 1930s (see Chapter 4) as that was probably the first association between consultants and Government in Britain, but the period of the Second World War

witnessed government assistance on a scale and level of strategic importance unprecedented up to that point in time. As this chapter will indicate, it marked the turning point with regards to consultancy support to government and helped to raise the profile of consultancy within government circles. Today the relationship between the management consultancy and the Government is extremely strong, with virtually all the major consultancies having specialist departments that directly service the public sector and Government Departments.

2. Whilst Barnett's exposition of the industrial situation during the Second World War is highly political and, sometimes, controversial in nature, it is a useful point of reference with regard to some of the background events on the 'home front' during the wartime period.

3. A forerunner of today's CBI.

4. Until the change, each of the three services carried out separate demand functions and individually the services used multiple channels of ordering, often with the same supplier. In terms of supply, there was little or no co-ordination with individual suppliers determining their own priorities. The initiatives of the Ministry of Production resulted in a tri-service procurement process with centralised control.

5. The RKW, or Reichskuratorium fur Wirtschaftlichkeit, was formed in 1921 and acted as the umbrella organisation for other agencies involved in the rationalisation movement (Kipping 1997).

6. Under a German Labour Front (Deutsche Arbeitsfront) initiative, the German Bedaux company had its assets seized in 1933 and was forced to cease trading (Christy 1984). The Company was re-established in 1937, but with German partners, and traded under the name Gesellschaft fur Wirtschaftsberatung (Kipping 1997).

7. The employment of consultants was controlled by statute and each of the companies maintained their manning levels in line with regulation. However, there were no restrictions on the number of individuals that were transferred to other companies, albeit for the period of war. Consequently, Associated Industrial Consultants (the old Bedaux company) saw its numbers increase from 50 in 1939 to 108 by the time of the cessation of hostilities in 1945.

8. Because Bryson was serving in Britain with the Royal Engineers he managed to maintain close links with the Company during those early years of the War. This association came to a tragic end on 16 April 1941 when he was killed in an air raid in London (Wayne 1959).

9. Barnett (1986) suggested that in 1935, 35,000 workers were involved in the aircraft industry in Britain. By 1943 the Ministry of Aircraft Production estimated that 1,750,000 people were engaged in working on Ministry contracts.

10. Technically this form of service could be covered within this publication under either the headings of assistance to Government Departments or to industry. Because the service provided was pivotal to the successful production of new aircraft it has been decided to include it within this section as an example of the work of consultants during this period within industry.

11. Prominent figures within the Government, for example Sir Stafford Cripps, convinced the unions of the importance of productivity to the war effort. Cripps was known as 'Austerity' Cripps because of his absolute commitment to the war effort and his opposition to any waste of national resources, including wasted materials and labour (Brownlow 1972).

12. Combined Operations (under the command of Lord Mountbatten), amongst other activities, was responsible for carrying out commando raids on enemy locations in the period prior to the Normandy Landings in 1944.

13. Because Urwick would not be available to fulfil his role within the Company as Chairman at an operational level this prompted some structural reorganisation internally

(he was also joint Managing Director with general management responsibilities). Orr became the sole guiding force on an operational basis, with Urwick retaining the title of Chairman even though he had withdrawn formally from active participation in the running of the Company's affairs for the duration of the War. To assist Orr with controlling the organisation, five senior members of the Company were promoted to the Board.

14. The Bedford Work-Study School did not come under the direct control of Urwick Orr because it was a private enterprise scheme operated by Lodge himself having resigned from the Company to set up the school. Nevertheless, the sole client for the School at the beginning was Urwick Orr, who contracted Lodge to conduct training for recruits of the Company or for those consultants who had not received formal training in work-study techniques.

15. A spin off of the training provided to consultants at the School was that course places were made available to personnel of co-operating firms when there were insufficient consultants available to fill all the course places.

16. By the time it closed its doors in 1961, it had trained 650 students from industry in addition to the volume of training provided to consultants.

17. Ernest Edward Butten was born on 28 July 1900 in East Molesey, Surrey, the son of a Commercial Union Insurance Company manager. Educated at St Paul's School, London, Butten enlisted in the Royal Flying Corps in 1917 where he saw war service in France (Fogg 1980). On demobilisation Butten entered Imperial College, London with a Siemens Scholarship, gaining a BSc in Mechanical Engineering. On leaving university in 1923 he became a graduate apprentice at the Metropolitan Vickers engineering firm in Birmingham. In 1925 Butten was sent to India as a member of the construction staff building a light factory. In 1926 he was promoted to General Manager, remaining in India until 1930. On his return to Britain he joined the Bedaux company as a field engineer, being promoted to the Board in 1940. Butten finally left Bedaux in December 1942 in order to form Personnel Administration.

18. It was no accident that the Process Analysis Method of Training was shortened to PA Method of Training because it firmly associated the methodology with Personnel Administration (PA).

19. In the year following the War, Butten sold the PAMT service to the TI Group of companies. The fees for the service had totalled almost £500,000, a considerable sum at that time for a consultancy service (Tisdall 1982).

20. The educational aspect was partly achieved in the post war period with the creation of Sundridge Park Management Centre (see Chapter 7).

21. Companies were grouped according to size based on the number of employed personnel: over 5000, 1001-5000, 501-1000 employees and 500 and under.

CHAPTER 6

Improving Productive Performance

Management consultancy at the end of the war consisted of five major players, the 'Big Four' and Harold Whitehead and Partners, a few smaller firms and an unknown number of sole practitioners, with consultancy consisting of approximately 250 consultants overall (Ferguson 1999).[1] Twenty years later British consultancy was still dominated by the 'Big Four', but by then there were a greater number of smaller companies and a whole host of sole practitioners of indeterminate numbers. It was estimated that management consultancy had grown to approximately 2000 consultants. By the turn of the millennium the picture had changed dramatically with an estimated corporate consultant strength of 40,000 consultants in Britain (Management Consultancies Association 2000).[2]

At the conclusion of the War there were four very broad areas of consultant activity: production engineering, including financial services and other services to industrial and commercial clients, training, support to Government Departments (largely concerned with administrative processes) and miscellaneous business services, including marketing and human relations management. Today, the Federation Europeene des Associations de Conseil en Organisation (FEACO) recognises four very broad areas: operations management, human resource management, corporate strategy and information technology.[3] As an indication of the changes that have occurred within management consultancy since the War those services provided by consultants in 1945 are now either minor categories within the various aspects of those broad service bands or they have largely disappeared, for example operator training and work-study.[4] Therefore, today's consultancy environment is far more complex than the relatively straightforward environment of 1945.

An examination of today's business environment would support the contention that business activity is generally integrated within firms and this is, therefore, a principal objective of management consulting assignments. In other words, all areas of the business attempt to work together in support of its common objectives and aims. Whilst that has really always been the case in terms of the ultimate aim of consultants at the level they were operating within firms, prior to the post-war period consulting services had tended to be task specific and bounded by a narrow range of services, so whole business integration was not possible. Therefore, in terms of this history and because of the relatively straightforward structure of the range of services provided prior to 1945 it has been possible to develop a time-phased approach within the previous four chapters. Today (2001), and indeed for the previous 30 years or so, the crossover of services has been endemic in terms of their delivery. This has come about because of evolutionary trends within consultancy over a large part of the post-war period, supported by the development and advancement of information technology. This will become more apparent as this chapter progresses. In addition, the previous chapters have indicated strongly that management consultants, up to the period of the Second World War, were generally only welcome within operational areas of businesses; wider ranging acceptance of consultancy at all levels within businesses was also part of that evolutionary process. Today, strategic change is strongly supported by improvements to sub-processes and such changes are only made possible by combining the strategic with the operational. For example, supply chain management in its complete form is concerned with the development of processes, procedures and relationships across business boundaries; it is to do with inter-linked dependencies. However, for a supply chain to be effective, and in order to raise efficiency and improve productivity overall, operational improvements within individual businesses are a prerequisite for success. Therefore, in order to best cope with those trends and provide a coherent review the next five chapters will cover the whole period from 1945 to the present day and will concentrate on specific areas of consultant activity.

The central theme, or activity, represented in each of the following five chapters is concerned with a major plank, or aspect, of the work of consultants during this overall period:

- *Chapter 6* concentrates on production services, building upon the work of consultants identified within the previous four chapters;
- *Chapter 7* concentrates on development, training and education services, an area that increased in significance through the passage of time;
- *Chapter 8* concentrates on the majority of other aspects of management consultancy, less those of information technology. It is a review of the work of consultants in the wider business field in support of

management at all levels within the firm and in all areas. A 'rags to riches' story of the evolution of management consulting; from efficiency engineering to the boardroom;

- *Chapter 9* concentrates on information technology services and the place of computers and computing within consultancy;
- *Chapter 10* concentrates on the internationalisation and globalisation of management consultancy, specifically it is an examination of how national borders have become increasing blurred over time.

Due to the complexity of management consultancy today there are limitations regarding coverage. Consultancy has expanded dramatically over the years and there are many variations with regards to the make-up of services among consulting companies; these services individually could command the attention of their own historical accounts. Therefore, it is only possible to describe the broad areas of change rather than the detail of that change. Furthermore, the sequence of the chapters is coincidental in that it does not attempt to represent an order of importance. Consulting companies do not provide services on that basis. Each type of service is provided on the basis that it meets the needs of the client at a particular point in time. There is no league table or scale to signify that any one type of service is more important than any other service within management consulting generally. However, in reality it is difficult, if not impossible in many instances, to separate one form of service from another. Today all types of services are affected in some way, either directly or indirectly, by information technology. In addition, at any given point in time or for any given client a range of services may be provided that inter-link and provide mutual support. Therefore, from this perspective, the separation of service types is largely artificial.

This chapter is about reviewing the work of management consultants in the broad area of improvements to productive performance. What that means, its definition, and how that meaning has changed over time will be developed within this introduction. The chapter is broadly constructed to take account of two time frames: 1945-1970 and 1970-2001. The reason for the split is that fundamental macroeconomic factors at the beginning of the 1970s caused a significant upheaval for management consultancy. In addition, as the period of the 1970s progressed wider changes in management thinking and practice resulted in a wave of innovation on a scale not previously witnessed in consultancy. Both these aspects will become more apparent as this chapter progresses. However, inescapably, immediately following this short introduction it is necessary to describe in broad outline the business environment and the impact of government on the work carried out in this field by management consultants in Britain over the first twenty-five years of the post-war period.

In terms of this history of management consulting, the question still remains what does improving productive performance mean? The work of management consultants to date within this account has been concerned with improving productivity, for example, output, manpower utilisation, resource usage, and production times, and raising efficiency in all areas where management consultants have been active. Those areas have included industrial enterprises, office environments and in specific Government Departments. Productivity has been to do with the balance between inputs and outputs of an organisation. Improvements are, therefore, the pro rata reductions in the quantity of inputs in comparison to the output in order to sustain current levels or increase them. However, this is a rather simplistic view and it reflects the level to which improvements have occurred previously within the operational areas of organisations. Improving productive performance can have much wider connotations and can be as much to do with the strategic aspects of businesses as it is to do with the operational. Through the process of time, as this chapter will indicate, concentration within the operational areas of enterprises lessened when compared with all other aspects of businesses. For example, improvements to efficiency and productivity through heavy reliance on functional tools, e.g. work-study, eroded over time at the expense of wider ranging processes and methods concerned with whole organisations and relationships between them, for example micro management methods eventually gave way to value chains, business process re-engineering and supply chain management. This has been a gradual change and not one marked by a particular event or definitive point in time.

With regards the breadth of service delivery, the initial concentration on the direct production environment within firms and its eventual broadening out to encompass all areas that were involved in the process was still very narrow in scope in comparison with today's consultancy activities. In other words, services tended to be specifically directed at the activities of particular departments within organisations. The Second World War witnessed some applications that were industry wide, but these related to specific processes, for example the supply of aircraft parts (see Chapter 5). Today, improvements to productive processes span the whole range of activities and are just as applicable to service sectors as they are to manufacturing enterprises. For example, supply chain management, in its very broadest sense, can mean the product process from beginning to end, e.g. from raw materials to eventual consumption, including payments and information streams. Each stage of that process being subject to consultant review overall and within and between the various stages in the process;

this is just as relevant to service industries as it is to manufacturing enterprises. This will become apparent as supply chain management is examined in more detail later in this chapter.

The fact that there has been so much change within management consulting over time owes itself to a range of drivers, both internal and external to consultancy. Three examples of drivers for change, and these were not the only ones, were: the gradual acceptance of management consultants in strategic areas of an organisation, improvements to technology generally, and the use of information technology within firms to control processes and by management consultants as a direct aid to consulting. Before turning attention to the business environment, one further change that occurred in the post-war period that requires special mention at this juncture is the bid for professional recognition.

Professional Recognition

Since the end of the Second World War, when broader changes were occurring to the corporate structure of management consultancy in Britain, there was a growing movement to raise the awareness of consultancy within business and government circles. An early attempt at forming a professional body in the period 1945-1947 through the development of an Association of Industrial Consultants was overtaken by the formation of the British Institute of Management (BIM) in 1947 and the creation of its Consultants Register in 1948. A Registration Committee controlled and administered the Consultants Register and registration was governed by a 'Code of Conduct'. The Consultants Register was primarily developed to assist prospective clients in identifying suitable consultants for conducting specific tasks. It was not developed to act as a replacement for a professional body, nor did it attempt to police professional standards, consequently there remained a general belief within the BIM that management consultants should have their own Association.

The issue of forming a corporate association was raised again during the Comite International de l'Organisation Scientifique (CIOS) conference that took place in Paris in the early 1950s (Paris Triennial Congress). The conference was attended by senior members of the leading British consultancies and during a fringe meeting of management consultants a proposition was made to create an international federation of national associations of management consultants. This presented a dilemma for the British firms because no such national association existed within Britain. On their return to England a series of meetings was held between the senior members of the 'Big Four' and as a result in 1956 the Management

Consultants Association (MCA) was formed as a form of trade association with four corporate members (now re-named Management Consultancies Association). The MCA did not, however, represent the interests of individual consultants and it was frequently mooted during meetings of the Association that that there was a requirement to form a professional body that represented the interests of all consultants.

At an Extraordinary Meeting of the Council of the MCA in November 1961 a resolution was made that an independent Institute of Management Consultants should be formed to represent the professional interests of individual management consultants. As a consequence of that resolution, on the 17th of October 1962 the Institute of Management Consultants (now re-named Institute of Management Consultancy) was granted its certification under the Companies Act. Both bodies continue to act as the corporate professional bodies representing firms and individuals in Britain. At the European level, the MCA was a founder member of the European Federation of Management Consulting Associations (Federation Europeenne des Associations de Conseils en Organisation or FEACO) in 1960 and continues to represent the interests of British management consultancy in Europe through that medium.

The Business Environment

During the period of the Second World War, industrial production was predominantly directed at the war effort. At the conclusion of hostilities this left a rather distorted industrial base that was not established in any way to support a peacetime environment (Brech 2002b). Another effect of the industrial situation of the war years in Britain, as well as elsewhere in the world that was directly affected by the vagaries of war, was that research and development had been heavily slanted towards initiatives that were influenced by the war effort. However, whilst there were spin-offs to this in terms of peacetime production, these were secondary considerations at that time. Full employment was a major cornerstone of the Labour Party's manifesto in the run up to the 1945 General Election. Once in government, the Party realised that the objective could only be attained through productivity initiatives; improvements in manufacturing, administration, and marketing and selling. This was in order to improve the competitiveness and profitability of British industry in order to create expansion, which would then create a market for new jobs and the realisation of full employment.

During the period 1946 to 1948, government working parties adopting a bipartite approach (employers and labour) were set up to examine the overall question of productivity within their sectors of the economy. As a spin-off from Marshall Aid, economic support was gained for the formation of the Anglo-American Productivity Programme to cover a four-year period (1948-1952).[5] With similar aims to the government working parties, the purpose of the Programme was to enable sector studies to take place to identify and learn from improvements that had been implemented within American companies with the objective of improving productive performance. From the perspective of productivity, and the way that businesses organised themselves and were being managed during the period of reconstruction and beyond, many of the influences in Britain inevitably came directly from the United States. This had clear implications, not only for the practical aspects of improving performance but also to management thinking within business circles. Such thinking inevitably had had long-term consequences in the way in which businesses were managed.

Government intervention through the Productivity Programme raised awareness of the need to improve productive performance generally throughout the economy and this, in turn, pointed towards the type of assistance that could be provided by management consultants.[6] The benefits of employing consultants were recognised by senior officers of the Anglo-American Productivity Programme (Sir) Norman Kipping, Director General of the Federation of British Industries, and (Sir) Vincent Tewson, Secretary to the Trades Union Congress were instructed to appoint an 'Honorary Management Consultant' to join the Council. Norman Pleming, the then Chairman and Managing Director of Associated Industrial Consultants (AIC), was invited to take up the post; this he agreed to do. Pleming was required to attend the meetings of the Council, and to review and interpret the observations of the various Anglo-American Productivity Teams.[7] Pleming's role within the Programme, together with others, was recognised as a significant contribution to the productivity movement within Britain at that time. This recognition culminated in an invitation to present the findings of the Programme and their significance to British industry to the Parliamentary and Scientific Committee at the House of Commons (Brownlow 1972).

The ending of the Anglo-American Productivity Programme in 1952 witnessed the birth of the British Productivity Council in 1953 to continue the work of the Anglo-American Programme and to provide guidance with regards to the implementation of productivity initiatives (Brech 2002b). Membership of the Council mirrored that of the membership of the British side of the Anglo-American Programme. The work of the British Productivity Council continued until the 1970s until it met its demise following the withdrawal of funding by the then Conservative Government in 1970. However, whilst there were improvements to productivity throughout the period, when compared with competitor nations Britain's performance was lacklustre. Progress for advancement was hampered internally through industrial unrest and an unstable economic situation within Britain throughout the whole period (Brech 2002b). In addition, many of the productivity improvements were achieved through attaining reductions in pro-rata manpower levels, reflected in rising unemployment, and improvements to capital equipment; during the post-war period labour productivity steadily rose throughout, although when compared with the United States improvement occurred at a slower pace until the mid-1970s when the gap began to close (Broadberry 1997). That occurred in part because British firms had failed to standardise mass production. Three explanations of that failure are: opposition by the various workforces with regards to embracing new technology, managements' failure to implement new methods and the difficulties experienced by firms in securing markets for high volume production. Nevertheless, the injection of new ideas from the United States and the work of consultants throughout this period were both factors in the rising levels of productivity generally. The effects of consultant input overall is covered in the next section of this chapter.

Productivity and Efficiency in the Post-War Period, 1945-1970

The corporate portfolio of services provided by management consultants supported the government initiatives of the post-war period. Those initiatives were developed on the premise that improving productive performance at the level of the firm through raising productivity and increasing efficiency would, it was hoped, have the effect of improving economic performance more generally within Britain as increasingly more firms optimised their performance potential. The main thrust of these improvements centred on making best use of manpower and capital equipment (Brech 2002b).

Because improving productive performance was the core service type provided by most management consultants in the period following on from the end of the Second World War, each of the major companies had a portfolio that strongly supported the objectives of raising productivity and improving efficiency within individual firms. The previous chapters have indicated how these services had matured over time and were applicable not only to industrial firms, but were also relevant in commercial operations, the administrative set-ups within businesses of all types and Government Departments. As a consequence of the experiences gained through six years of war, new services came on line and others were strengthened and improved upon. Whilst it may be labouring the point to provide endless examples of the way in which services were developed and deployed, it is appropriate to cite the work of one or two major consultancies in order to gain a general flavour of the situation.

Associated Industrial Consultants had over a period of time developed a more complex package of services in addition to work-study and payment incentive schemes. These included materials management; specifically in relation to product rationalisation and production analysis in order to improve inventory control (Associated Industrial Consultants 1963). Other services in support of the production process included: 'Production and Stock Control' (to assist in quality and stock targets), 'Distribution' as a balance between stockholding and delivery (this included plant and warehouse location, warehouse layout and design, materials handling, and vehicle fleet management), and 'Maintenance Control' with the objective of improving equipment availability. In addition to these new services, John Evans and Associates, a subsidiary company, provided services in relation to the deployment of temporary manpower, specifically specialists in work-study and industrial engineering. Harold Whitehead and Staff (now re-named Harold Whitehead and Partners), in support of the Company's objective to broaden its portfolio into the general area of production management, developed two new forms of service. The first of these, 'Factory Organisation and Production Control', was concerned with production planning and control, purchasing and materials control, time and methods study for operatives, payment incentive schemes, and site and factory layout. The other service, 'Costing and Cost Control', was to do with standard costing and budgetary control as a central feature of production planning. This brought the Whitehead company in line with the other major consultancies in terms of adopting a generalist approach to the delivery of management consultancy services. In addition to these two general areas, 'Organisation and Methods' (O&M) was offered as a technique for improving processes within the office and in administrative departments of enterprises (Harold Whitehead and Partners 1947).

Production Engineering, in a similar fashion to the other major companies, provided a range of services in support of productivity improvements within client firms. Of the nine services that were advertised by the Company at the beginning of the 1950s, four were in direct support of productivity. One other, 'Staff and Labour Administration', as far as it was concerned with operator training, partially supported this objective. The four core 'productivity' services were: 'Factory Organisation' (consisting of site selection, organisation planning and equipment layout), 'Work and Method Study' (consisting of motion study, work simplification, standards setting and payment incentive schemes),

'Production Control' (consisting of progress methods, materials control, and stores and stock control) and 'Cost Collection and Estimating' (consisting of batch and standard costing methods, and overhead allocation and recovery). One or two examples of the work of management consultants during this period, followed by a brief examination of their impact on the wider economy, will bring into focus their value to enterprises; specifically at a time when many businesses in Britain were still moving forward from the effects of the immediate post-war situation.

All of the main companies during the post-war period can provide examples of services supplied to organisations with the objective of improving productivity within engineering companies, industrial firms and commercial enterprises. In addition, the post-war period brought with it expansion in terms of the number of consulting companies operating within Britain; some consultancies were formed specifically to provide consulting services at the shop floor level. Three of the important firms formed at that time were the Anne Shaw Organisation (specialists in motion study), Industrial Administration and Harold Norcross and Partners, all three of whom concentrated on production efficiency.[8] These companies became members of the Management Consultants Association in the late 1950s, playing an important role in terms of the development and professionalisation of management consultancy at that time.

Turning initially to the successes and failures with regard to the work of consultants in the broad area of productivity in the immediate aftermath of war, there is probably no better example than the work carried out within the textile trade. For example, an early experiment conducted by Associated Industrial Consultants during this period at the firm of Joshu Hoyle and Sons, at the request of the Cotton Board, was concluded with the discontinuance of the recommended changes. Undaunted by these experiences, the Cotton Board approached Production Engineering in 1946 with a view to undertaking a further experimental application, this time at Musgrave No 7 Mill, Bolton.

The trial was carried out in the 'Cardroom' between January and July 1947. In order to gain the support of the operatives, a Steering Committee was formed that was made up of workers' representatives, a union official and members of the management (Howell undated). Assurances were given to all workers concerned that there would be no reduction in wage levels and, at the conclusion of the experiment, the then existing working methods would be re-introduced if the operatives requested it. The experiment was a success and the working week was reduced from 48 to 45 hours (Tisdall 1982). In terms of productivity: operative production increased by 39 per cent, the overall number of operatives were reduced from 39 to 31 and weekly earnings rose by 30 per cent for those remaining in employment. In

May 1948 the Cotton Board issued a full report (Cotton Board 1948); Part
II of the report contained a summary of the principal changes in the
processing and labour organisation at the Mill. The experiment attracted
considerable publicity at the time and highlighted the benefits of employing
consultants, as well as the order of savings that could be expected through
employing systematic techniques. At about the same time, 1948-1949,
Urwick Orr set up work-study training centres for the Cotton Board. At the
industry level, specifically within the spinning trades, wage structures were
developed within a range of weaving environments and this was another
area that consultants found themselves involved in during the immediate
post-war period.

Traditional payment regimes had been based on the 'Unit List Prices for
Weaving'. However, due to the apparent unfairness of the scheme a
Commission of Enquiry was set up under Lord Justice Evershed in 1945.
Evidence from members of Associated Industrial Consultants, owing to
previous involvement with firms within the trade, was submitted to the
Enquiry.[9] As a result of the Enquiry, a further Commission was set up to
investigate fully the situation. The Commission studied two proposals for
improvements, but it was the proposal that was submitted by AIC that was
adopted. The proposal had been developed through investigation and a
series of trial applications within the rayon weaving environment; the
adopted payment system was entitled the 'CMC Wage Weaving System'.
A full explanation of the methodology involved through work-study
analysis and the deployment of the new wages structure was given by R.J.
Gigli to a textile conference in Buxton in October 1947. A booklet was
produced by AIC for use by the weaving trade, containing full explanations
of the payment regime, including the allocation of bonuses and calculations
for use by the weavers (Cotton Spinners and Manufacturers Association
1949).

One further example of the way in which productivity services,
specifically work-study and production planning and control, were used by
consultants can be found within the motor vehicle manufacturing industry.
In the post-war period to the early 1960s, eight assignments had been
carried out by Urwick, Orr and Partners Limited employing efficiency
techniques. Using the example of Company A in Table 6.1, consultants
working in the 'Progress Section' of the firm made net savings for the
Company of £4,680 and £21,000 in direct labour costs. A breakdown of the
savings made overall within the industry can be found in Table 6.1 below.

These were not inconsequential sums, especially for their day, but it is
easy to lose sight of the fact that improvements are not only important
within larger companies. The work carried out within small and medium
sized enterprises can be equally dramatic when scale is taken into

consideration. For example, in 1947 an assignment was conducted at J. and S. Alexander Limited, producers of tinned foods, by consultants from Personnel Administration. Alexander's employed a staff of 58 with a weekly output of 108,000 tins prior to the assignment being carried out. The resultant outcome witnessed an increase in production to 150,000 tins (a rise of 39 per cent), a reduction in the workforce to 47 (a decrease of 19 per cent), cash savings of £6,000 per week and an increase in weekly profit of £15,000. The assignment took 29 weeks to complete and cost Alexander's £2,900 in consultancy fees (Blandford 1947).

Table 6.1   Work-Study and Production Planning and Control Assignments in the Motor Vehicle Manufacturing Industry

Client	Total Savings (£)
Company A	113,000
Company B	122,000
Company C	19,800
Company D	77,816
Company E	26,166
Company F	Turnover increased by £1m
Company G	Results not reported
Company H	38,000

Source: Urwick, Orr and Partners Limited (1962) 'Development Manual'

However, the value of consultant services overall is probably better viewed through a macroeconomic examination of their impact on improved productivity. Assistance is provided with this task through the work of Professor J. Johnston (1963) from the Department of Economics, University of Manchester in the form of a paper produced in the *Journal of the Royal Statistical Society* entitled 'The Productivity of Management Consultants'.

Economy-Wide Productivity Savings

The purpose of Johnston's paper was to develop, through statistical analysis, a model of savings (productivity) based on the work of management consultants in Britain. The study was based on a random sample of job summaries. These were produced at the end of each assignment by the consultant and agreed by the client as a fair statement of the financial benefits of the work carried out; benefits were based on a comparison between a 'reference period' (an agreed point in time prior to the commencement of the assignment) and the situation at the end of the assignment. The sampling methodology used was a sampling fraction of one in five reports or one in ten reports, with the latter fraction applying to one consulting company (not named) that did not have a complete set of job summaries. A framework for analysis was applied to each of the summaries, based on a set of pre-defined parameters: the industry or principal product, the size of the firm (number of employees), the nature of the assignment and the techniques used, the level of consultancy involvement (consultant numbers, duration and fees charged), and the results achieved. According to Johnston, there was sufficient homogeneity between the summaries of the various firms for this methodology to be partially, though not wholly, achievable. Therefore, because of that three classes of data were applied: Class A where quantitative assessment was not possible (mainly because assignments were not concerned with techniques such as work-study and were non-assessable), Class B where quantitative assessments were possible but either that section of the report was not completed or nil achievements were gained, and Class C where assessments were carried out and were quantifiable. Of the total, 37 percent were Class A, 16 per cent were Class B and 47 per cent were Class C. Therefore almost half the jobs were assessable.

This was a historical analysis, utilising the records of the four largest firms of management consultants during the post-war period. The four companies under review were Associated Industrial Consultants, Production Engineering, Urwick, Orr and Partners, and Personnel Administration. The study produced dramatic results and this prompted one commentator at the time to suggest that Johnston was '...much loved by the consulting profession' (Tatham 1964). Using measurable data, Johnston concluded that consultancy assignments resulted in average productivity improvements of over 50 per cent. In financial terms, this resulted in average net savings of approximately £14,000, with a net return on fees paid of about 200 per cent. These results were based on Class C jobs that accounted for 211 of the job summaries.

However, the real purpose of the Johnston study was to identify the impact of consultants across the whole economy. He estimated that there were approximately two thousand active consultants operating within Britain at the beginning of the 1960s. That estimation may have been overly generous in terms of the total number; nevertheless it should not detract from the importance of Johnston's conclusions (Ferguson 1999). Of those two thousand, he concluded that about three-quarters were active in the field at any one time, with 50 per cent producing measurable results in terms of productivity improvements. Using calculations based on the duration of assignments, Johnston suggested that approximately 1125 consultants were engaged in assignments at any one time that produced measurable results. His assumptions were based on an active consulting force of 1500 (three-quarters of the total), with 50 per cent engaged in Class C jobs that lasted on average 12 months. The remainder were engaged in Class A and B jobs for periods on average of four months and were, in his estimations, likely to move on to Class C jobs within the year at the average rate of 50 per cent. Therefore, it was reasonable, Johnston suggested that overall 1125 consultants within the year would be engaged in Class C jobs. He further concluded that each consultant had a direct impact on an average labour force of 110 personnel. Multiplying the consultant numbers by the involved labour force, Johnston concluded that the work of consultants directly impacted overall on an employed labour force of 125,000 workers. Working on the principle that if there were sufficient consultants in Britain (81,818 consultants) to cover the whole of manufacturing industry (9 million workers), Johnston suggested that this would produce an overall productivity increase of 0.7 per cent. Taken a stage further to include the construction industry, public utilities and distributive trades (14 million workers and 127,273 consultants), the productivity level fell to 0.5 per cent. Or, in economy-wide terms, approximately one-quarter of overall productivity achieved at that time. While Johnston does not explicitly state what period his findings were based on, the figures on employment levels within the study indicates the period of 1960-1962 (Feinstein 1976).

Notwithstanding that the figures used by Johnston to determine the size of the consultancy force in Britain at that time may be open to challenge, the point he makes is quite clear with regard to the value of consultant involvement in improving productivity. It would not have been unreasonable to expect some form of reaction to Johnston's findings at a time when productivity improvements were a central pillar of government policy. However, because his research was only published within the *Journal of the Royal Statistical Society* it did not receive any wider coverage. Some consultant firms made comment of his work (for example within the *Associated Industrial Consultants Journal*, June 1963) and non-critical reviews appeared in one or two publications (for example Tatham's 'The Efficiency Experts'), but, there was no real debate or wider publication of his findings. Looking towards the future, Johnston's concluding remarks were probably the important ones in terms of the benefits of utilising consultants:

> The real, long-term benefit of consultants, however, lies probably not so much in the measurable short-run changes in productivity and costs as in the inculcation of an enquiring habit of mind and a continuing search for even better ways of dealing with the industrial and commercial problems of tomorrow.

Johnston was suggesting that trends were indicating movements away from direct productivity work to other areas of management consulting that were less easily quantifiable in terms of measurable improvements. In other words, moving into areas where strategic decision-making was a central feature of assignments. This aspect of consultancy work is covered in more detail in the following chapters.

Changes to the direction of consultancy work, a point made by Johnston above, can be explained by examining a number of factors. Firstly, the accountant companies were beginning to emerge in the mid-1960s as serious competition for the then traditional consultancies operating in Britain. For example, in 1965 there were eleven member companies of the then Management Consultants Association (MCA) consisting of 1,636 consultants, a few months later in 1966 six accountancy companies joined the MCA raising the number of consultants to 1,930; this was a rise in the number of consultants by 18 per cent (Brownlow 1972).[10] These companies initially tended not to concentrate on productivity improvements, but in other business areas or areas where their accountancy skills could be used to good advantage. Secondly, consultancy was beginning to become internationalised with a number of leading American consulting companies gaining a foothold in Britain and these largely specialised in strategy-type assignments, for example McKinsey set up an office in London in 1959 concentrating on the organisational aspects of businesses. At the same time, British companies were exploring other markets abroad with a view to expanding their operations (this is covered in more detail in Chapter 10). Thirdly, information technology was beginning to become an important aspect of consultancy. Over time, information technology became inseparable from consultancy work (see Chapter 9). Fourthly, the use of internal specialists within larger firms (for example management services departments and internal consultancies) and the growth in the availability of training courses designed to assist firms in improving productivity at the operational level meant that proportionately there was less demand for consultant involvement at the detailed functional level (for consultancy's influence on training see Chapter 7).[11] Finally, attitudes towards consultant involvement in the strategic aspects of business were changing, with a more liberal viewpoint becoming increasingly prevalent over time. This meant that management consultants could explore and become more involved in other areas of businesses, specifically at senior management levels. Dowson (1969) highlights this point in his comparison of the revenue generated by the member companies of the Management Consultants Association for the years 1965 and 1968. Between those two years, revenue in productivity services fell by 17 per cent overall, whereas revenue in the fields of marketing rose by 8 per cent, finance by 41 per cent and human resource management by 29 per cent.

However, none of this means that services directed towards productivity disappeared. Nor that consultants en masse gave up the productivity objective. Work-study and other efficiency techniques survived into the 1980s and beyond, although their prominence waned over time with the major consultancies concentrating more on the organisational aspects of production processes. The next section takes the story forward for the next thirty years and examines some of the changes that occurred within consultancy in Britain with a view to improving productive performance.

Decline, Change and Expansion (1970-2001)

The healthy level of growth within management consultancy during the post-war period came to an abrupt end at the beginning of the 1970s. Instead of the expected increase of between 15 and 20 percent, the period of 1970-1971 witnessed a fall in demand of ten percent (Tisdall 1982). This was brought about by a world recession that impacted on Britain at a time when the economic policies of a new Conservative government resulted in a wave of industrial disputes.[12] Within Britain at that time, wage costs were rising at the same time that production output remained stagnant. This impacted on company profits, which in turn adversely affected investment. Industrial action spread, resulting in a number of national strikes.[13] In terms of investment, included within this category would be money made available to employ management consultants. This fall in demand and cancellation of management consultancy services resulted in consultant companies reviewing their activities, streamlining their operations and reducing their consultant staff. During the first two years of this period, the major consultancies shed approximately a quarter of their professional personnel; for the first time macroeconomic factors had adversely affected management consultancy in Britain.

By 1972 the decline in management consulting had been halted and the first signs of recovery were evident. However, by the end of 1973, approximately 18 months later, long before full recovery had been achieved, the war in the Middle East resulted in the price of oil quadrupling on the world market. The effects were immediately felt in Britain. A three-day working week was introduced by the Government, inflation rose to unprecedented levels and the value of shares on the stock market fell. Output dramatically fell and prices soared. The major management consulting firms directly felt all these effects; they were again forced to shed 25 per cent of their professional staff (Tisdall 1982). Within industry, companies also rationalised their operations and many managers found themselves being made redundant. Some of these managers, together with some of the redundant consultants, started up as sole practitioners. The effects of this on management consultancy were immediate and the general structure of consultancy changed to witness a growing prominence of self-employed consultants within its ranks. In effect, this was another watershed for management consultancy.

Apart from macroeconomic effects, the previous section highlighted how other factors had an impact on the way that consultancy evolved. The last thirty years of the twentieth century witnessed waves of innovation and change within management thinking and practice that had a direct impact on management consultancy in Britain, as well as elsewhere in the world.[14] Whilst these changes are too numerous to mention here in detail, and many have an impact on other areas of management consultancy covered within this history, this section will concentrate only on a number of these as they affected improving productive performance.

Following the disastrous period of the first few years of the 1970s the concentration of work in the general area of production began to fall at the expense of other services (FEACO 1984). Management consultants still provided services on the shop floor, but work in this general area eroded over time as new techniques and processes were developed to help improve the way that businesses operated strategically in an increasingly international marketplace. Work in the area of improving productive performance diversified to the extent that two streams of activities were beginning to emerge: operations and strategy consulting. This became further evident by the late 1980s and 1990s when the types of services within the broad area of production were evolving to the extent that they took account of relationships between organisations, as well as within them. This may partly explain why the slice of earnings in the general area of 'production and services' maintained consistent growth patterns throughout the 1990s, while some other areas fared less well.[15]

Innovations in management processes and practice with regards to improving productive performance became more evident during the late 1970s and beyond, and these had a major impact on the deployment of consulting services. Overarching these, and in direct support, was the prominence of increasingly more sophisticated technology, including robotic technology within manufacturing, as well as the development and deployment of computers and computing within consultancy. The end of the 1970s witnessed the appearance of Quality Circles and employee participation through opening up channels of communications between management and the workforce. Some companies saw this as a direct means of improving productivity, although there were some guarded responses to the technique suggesting that the benefits were primarily qualitative rather than quantitative (Tisdall 1982).

The period of the 1970s was one in which the breadth of service delivery widened further, especially after the disastrous few years at the beginning of the decade. As the decade progressed, seven principal fields of consultant activity emerged within the companies of the Management Consultants Association. In terms of improving productive performance, five of those areas included services, either wholly or partly, that could be deployed in support of the objective. These areas were 'Marketing, Sales and Distribution', 'Production Management', 'Finance and Administration', 'Personnel Management and Selection', and 'Management Information Systems and EDP' (Management Consultants Association 1980). In terms of Marketing, Sales and Distribution, the majority of those services would today be considered factors in the processes associated with, for example, supply chain management. Equally, this was similar for 'Finance and Administration', and 'Personnel Management and Selection'. These services, where they impacted on production, were largely concerned with improvements to operational tasks and processes, for example cost and budgetary control, inventory planning and control, and payment and personnel policies.

The only area that was wholly concerned with improving productive performance was 'Production Management'. Within this range of services, operational processes and activities within the whole range of production were covered. These services could be grouped into combinations or treated as individual packages, for example the layout of production departments and the selection of plant and equipment could be combined when consulting assignments were concerned with designing a new factory from the ground floor upwards. By and large, though, as with all other services at that time, the majority was carried out as individual services to meet specific client needs. Nevertheless, there were some indications at that time of some production-type services that could act as facilitators for bringing together a range of individual consultancy tasks into a more strategic package. Those services fell within the general area of 'Management Information Systems and EDP', and were concerned with operational research and process control systems (this is covered in greater detail within Chapter 9), albeit at that time far less advanced than similar systems today. For example, Coopers and Lybrand Associates Limited advertised services that used information technology for production and materials management planning and control systems (Management Consultants Association 1980). However, these types of services were relatively rare at that time, concentrating mainly on operational tasks within the firm because technological development had not advanced sufficiently to support complex consulting tasks across a range of environments in which the co-ordination of activities played a major role.

An examination of the range of services provided by the various companies operating in Britain at that time provide many examples of the way in which production improvement services had evolved to new levels through integrating quality processes, productivity improvements and personnel deployment. For example, Production Engineering combined organisation, control, methods and quality control as a package in support of production management within the firm, tailored to individual client needs (PE undated). The Company identified two broad groups of activity, 'management consulting' and 'consulting engineering'. Management consulting was concerned with the department and process specific aspects of production, whereas consulting engineering was more to do with the macro aspects of operational planning, factory layout and selection, and mechanisation and automation; each complimented one another. One example of the way in which combinations of services were developed to assist with specific client needs occurred on a major warehouse project at Griffin and George Limited in Manchester. Consulting engineers designed and assisted with the development of the warehouse and management consultants then used operational methods and processes to reduce the time taken for the despatch of goods by 50 per cent.

By the period of the 1980s Japanese management practices were beginning to have an impact on consultancy services worldwide. This was reflected in the use of flexible production systems that were underpinned by quality processes. Within Britain, at least for a time, total quality management, and manufacturing systems and technology were the fastest growing fields (Rassam 1998).[16] According to Tisdall (1982) all the major consultancies offered services in relation to Japanese-inspired management methods. Included within these were 'just in time' systems associated with, for example, inventory control and lean production methodologies. At first, these were not always greeted with enthusiasm because of a belief within some businesses that it was just another fad that would quickly fade away. However, trade unionists were more enthusiastic because such systems could have the benefit of opening up direct lines of communications between the employers and employees. Despite the unenthusiastic start, quality systems and processes, including TQM, have stood the test of time and have matured into an important service area for consultants today. For example in 1999, as an operational management service, Total Quality Management accounted for 1.6 per cent of the revenue gains for consultancy companies operating in the European marketplace (FEACO 1999).

Associated with TQM is 'integrated product and process development' and 'activity based costing' (ABC), with the latter acting as a reliable method for accurately reporting costs and their drivers. This was especially important in firms that produced a wide variety of products with varying specifications. Such costs, especially those relating to human effort, helped point towards areas where improvements could be made that would provide competitive advantage. The use of costing methodologies in conjunction with information technology, linking modelling processes with strategic decision-making was a growing form of service in the early 1980s. The use of these in conjunction with services directed at improving productive performance were a major cornerstone of consultancy services at that time. Advertising literature of the INBUCON company from the early-1980s, formerly Associated Industrial Consultants, emphasised the way in which automated manufacturing processes and integrated computer systems complimented grass roots production and productivity services. These in turn were supported by 'modern' cost management systems and quality management processes within the whole scope of improving productive performance.

By the mid 1980s the increasing internationalisation of businesses and the liberalisation of markets had the effect of forcing companies to review their operations within an international marketplace. In 1985 an important book by Michael Porter was published, 'Competitive Advantage: Creating and Sustaining Superior Performance'.[17] Porter suggested that companies had lost sight of the need to gain competitive advantage through their blind concentration on growth and diversification at the expense of all else. Within his book, specifically with regards to improving productive performance, he developed the concept of the 'Value Chain'. The Value Chain was, in his view, the means through which companies could examine the disparate activities of the organisation with a view to identifying those elements that could provide competitive advantage. It was a strategic tool that brought together a distinctive chain of activities within a firm that represented its key processes. These key processes were made up of 'primary activities' and 'support activities'. For example, within a manufacturing firm, Porter suggested that typical primary activities would consist of 'inbound logistics' (e.g. raw materials), 'operations' (e.g. manufacturing), 'outbound logistics' (e.g. supply), 'marketing and sales' and 'services' (e.g. after sales service). Supporting activities included 'human resource management' and 'technology development'.

From the perspective of improving productive performance, the value chain represented the first real strategic approach, albeit consisting of elements that were operationally specific. The value chain, as a consultancy tool represented the co-ordination of the primary functions associated with the output of the business within whatever market it was operating in. It was concerned with ensuring that the goals and aspirations of the business were met by its component parts through ensuring each part was integrated into the whole. Competitive advantage is gained for a company through ensuring that each element of the value chain performed better and cheaper that those carried out by its competitors. Whilst in Britain the term 'Value Chain' had not appeared within the advertising literature of British consulting companies at that time, the range of services provided by individual companies were clearly orientated towards a whole-firm approach. For example the use of modelling methodologies in distribution and other business areas suggested that a more holistic approach was adopted by consulting companies at that time. P-E INBUCON, following a merger between the two companies in the mid-1980s, advertised a whole range of services in general support of value chain strategies. In terms of primary activities, these included materials management (inbound logistics), manufacturing design and just in time production methods (operations), distribution (outbound logistics), marketing strategy and policy (marketing and sales), and quality (services). Supporting activities included the development of management information systems, human resource management, strategy development (including IT), and telecommunications and networks planning and implementation (P-E INBUCON 1988). The concept of the value chain later inspired other methodologies that integrated processes across organisations using the passage of information and monetary flows as key elements within the overall process. Such methodologies became commonly referred to as supply chain management.

During the 1990s a whole range of innovative practices and technologies were developed that either wholly or partly supported the objective of improving productive performance. These included Business Process Re-Engineering (BPR), Supply Chain Management, the Internet, electronic commerce and a wide range of e-business systems. This wave of innovations supported consultancy companies across the world in developing their own particular styles and approaches with regards to the whole process of change, as indeed did those that came before. The milestone publication by Hammer and Champy in 1993, 'Reengineering the Corporation: A Manifesto for Business Revolution', heralded the way forward for a whole range of services based on the principle of:

...fundamental rethinking and radical design of business processes to achieve dramatic improvements in critical, contemporary measures of performance, such as cost, quality, performance and speed.

In effect, this was an all or nothing approach to re-designing business processes to realign the company in order to effect wide-ranging improvements to performance. As the authors stated, this was a radical change management step on parallel unprecedented in relation to the whole organisation.

Consultants were not slow at getting into BPR, but client companies were not always willing to take such a leap of faith and consultants developed other services along similar lines whereby existing business processes were either modified (process improvement) or rationalised (process simplification). Therefore, BPR became both a service and a methodology; it ideally suited consultancy as an agency for change because of the flexible nature of the approach. Additionally, BPR as a technique was used in support of other consultancy services, linking together individual processes within companies to effect overall improvement. Some of these other processes or practices relate to the development of outsourcing regimes linked to the non-core competencies of the client firm. In the consultant context, outsourcing is a reference to the consultant acting as an agent in identifying and securing outsourcing agreements for clients where there are greater advantages and economies to be made through passing over the responsibility for specific functions and services. Some consultancies also directly provide outsourcing services themselves, largely within specialised fields related to information technology (see Chapter 9). Therefore, management consultants have played a significant role in the whole business of outsourcing, including outsourcing IT that has become a major role for many of the technology-based consultancies (see Chapter 9).

Because BPR is generally classified as a technique by many consultancies it is not publicly described as a form of service, but as a methodology employed within many of the areas associated with management consulting. A search through the literature of all the major consultancy companies worldwide would indicate case histories where BPR has been successfully applied, although equally examples could be found where assignments were less successful.[18] Business Process Reengineering, process improvement and process simplification assignments can also be found linked to supply chain management, another innovation of the 1990s. Supply chain management, in its broadest context in but a few words, is the management of the chain of processes, events and activities that, when combined, consist of a whole seamless process from start to finish. For example, the chain of events that lead to the production of a physical good could consist of a process that includes the ordering and supply of raw materials, the manufacture of component parts, the assembly of those parts into a complete product, marketing and distribution, final consumption and payments. In its broadest sense supply chain is a methodology that links organisations, companies and individuals through a network supported by multi-directional flows of information and monetary payments. Within that overall process can be found a series of sub-processes and value chains, both within organisations and between them.

Supply chains need not result in the distribution and consumption of physical products; they may result in delivery of services or the supply of information. A supply chain is to do with relationships between inter-dependent organisations and bodies that result in a sequence of integrated activities and processes that result in some form of consumption and payment of a final product or service. All the major consultancies offer supply chain management services and through the process of time the development of relationships and practices have changed through embracing new technologies and methods. For example, those relationships could be either physical or digital, or a combination of both, with the Internet and other forms of electronic information systems bridging the gap between sub-processes in the chain.[19]

There are two main strands to supply chain management, strategy and operations. The key to all aspects of the supply chain is an integrated approach, with each link in the chain working in support of the remainder. For example at the strategic level, solutions may include network design, product and customer analysis, third party logistical support and the outsourcing of elements of the chain. Operationally, supply and demand planning, manufacturing and distribution processes, warehouse design, and information technology solutions are examples of sub-activities within the chain. Today, supply chain management is inextricably linked with information technology. IT is used within all of the sub-processes as either a significant aspect of the approach or in a supporting role; simulation and modelling tools provide key information on the effects of change and there is a plethora of software tools available off-the-shelf to support supply chain processes.[20]

Supply chains can be both intranational and international at the same time; they can span national boundaries and continents. They can bring together a mix of technologies, skills and markets. They are about dependencies and relationships, as well as the multi-directional passage of information. The customer base need not be specific to any one location or industry; supply chains link the global economy through the process of supply and demand. In the final analysis, while supply chains may conjure up pictures of manufacturing industry, for example car manufacture through supplier and distribution networks and relationships globally, they can be as much to do with the provision of services, both as an aspect of the chain or as its ultimate goal. For example, supply chains can be to do with the delivery of financial, educational and informational services; they can also be to do with the activities of government and the public services. In other words, supply chains are unique; they are developed to cope with the needs of specific sets of circumstances, products and environments.

The supply chain is not just about relationships in macro environments, it is also concerned with individual aspects of the chain, bringing together two or more links in the overall process. It can now be e-enabled within a digital environment that spans industries across the world, linking customers and suppliers together in a widening range of activities. To cope with that environment, consulting companies have had to adopt a global perspective, creating their own strategic alliances and partnerships (this is covered in more detail in Chapter 10), and developing new areas of activity through the development of new skills and processes. A review of the consulting environment at the end of the millennium in Britain, as it is affected by the development and supply of supply chain services, indicates a rich mix of strategies across a range of consulting companies (Huntswood Associates 1999).

Some consultancies have consolidated their activities globally, for example Andersen Consulting (now re-named Accenture) consolidated its supply chain activities across its global community in 1998. Ernst and Young have a supply chain group based in the UK, but this is linked to its global supply chain network. The Cap Gemini Group employs a strategy of 'expert groups' across its international business, deploying services in three levels of expertise: strategic, operational and functional. Strategically value chain analysis and analytical tools to support the client's business objectives, tactically it uses modelling and mapping techniques, and operationally technology plays a major role. Other consultancies have employed strategies that group together levels or types of activities within the supply chain environment, for example PA Consulting Group offers two distinct areas of expertise; strategic development and operational improvement, as well as the design and re-design of engineering functions. Others, such as business systems developers and technology companies, provide a platform for strategic alliances, whereas some of the larger consultancy groups have these facilities internally. In terms of small and medium size consultancies, partnerships and sole practitioners, these tend to concentrate on specific aspects of the overall process, developing directed expertise in one or more areas.

Overall there is a mixed environment, but one thing stands out, management consulting is continually evolving, its knowledge base is increasing and its markets are widening. For example, e-manufacturing solutions based on software development are becoming as important with regards to supply and demand as improvements to technology. E-manufacturing in this context enables businesses to review how much demand is in the system (including the ability to follow orders through the process), where bottlenecks may have occurred and what capacity remains (Wheatley 2001). Consequently, such solutions provide definitive information on the production process that enable manufacturers to keep their customers informed on the progress of their orders. This is made possible through Internet technologies that link suppliers with customers through a digital environment; this not only improves customer relationships, but it also enables manufacturers to make best use of their facilities. Therefore, improving productive performance is as important now as it ever was, in fact it has become more so as processes span continents, industries and markets; its techniques and tools may have changed but its focus remains the same.

From a historical perspective the supply chain approach across a range of industries, suppliers, agents, technologies and customers is today's answer to consultancy's firm centred approach of the past. Interlinking networks, the passage of information and the movement of money have all replaced the productivity services that were traditionally applied in the workplace by a handful of consultants in a small number of companies. The development and deployment of management consultancy services have adopted a global perspective linking markets, suppliers and customers worldwide through an approach that has witnessed the increasing globalisation of management consulting.

Throughout the whole period, indeed ever since management consulting first appeared as a service in support of organisations, management consultants and consultancy firms have led the way in the development of management thinking and practice. The emergence of business schools, in this country and elsewhere, brought with it a new breed of individuals that have been described by some as 'gurus', many of whom have also acted as consultants combining theoretical knowledge and practical know-how (Sadler 1998). It is the combination of these influences, together with waves of innovation from business cultures across the world, for example the Japanese influences in the 1970s and 1980s, that have provided a dynamic environment for management consultants to operate in within Britain and elsewhere in the world, especially in the post-1970s era. The next chapter, 'Education and Training for Management: The Consultancy Model', develops further the post-war history of British management consulting and examines the role of management consultants in the broad fields of education and training for management. These are fields that have witnessed the involvement of consultants and consultancies throughout the whole of their history, and the British example exemplifies the pivotal role played by consultancy in this evolving environment.

Notes

1. As a reminder, the 'Big Four' consisted of Associated Industrial Consultants, Production Engineering, Personnel Administration, and Urwick, Orr and Partners. Harold Whitehead and Staff was replaced by Harold Whitehead and Partners as the Company title during the latter years of the War.
2. Of those consultants, approximately half were employed by the member firms of the Management Consultancies Association.
3. For a detailed breakdown of today's consultancy sector, see Huntswood Associates (1999), 'The Directory of Management Consultants in the UK, 1999-2000', fourteenth edition, London, Management Information Publishing Limited.
4. The Management Consultancies Association further breaks down the activities of consultancy: 'IT Consultancy', 'IT Systems Development', 'Strategy', 'Financial Systems', 'Production Management', 'Human Resources', 'Project Management', 'Marketing' and 'Economic/Environmental Consulting' (Management Consultancies Association 1999a). This is a more functional breakdown that that presented by FEACO, although there is no conflict with regard to the range of services overall.
5. The British section of the Anglo American Productivity Council was made up of members of the Trades Union Congress, the National Association of Manufacturers, the British Employers Federation and the Federation of British Industries.
6. Other government initiatives were occurring at the same time. For example, the Privy Council established a Committee on Industrial Productivity in December 1947 under the Chairmanship of Henry Tizard to advise government on any research being carried out in the natural and social sciences; the results of which could assist with the objective of improving productivity within the economy. The first report of the Committee (Committee on Industrial Productivity 1949) pointed towards the services of management consultants as an appropriate medium through which to improve levels of productivity. However, it also noted that at that time there were relatively few management consultants operating within Britain and that the benefits of the services would only be felt by their clients, and not the wider economy.
7. In conjunction with his opposite number from the United States, he produced a report on the whole of the Productivity Programme. The basis of this report was used to develop the book by Graham Hutton (1953), 'We Too Can Prosper'.
8. Anne Shaw was born (1904) and educated in Scotland. Her father was killed on active service in 1914 and her mother was a Member of Parliament. She studied for a University of Edinburgh Diploma in Psychology and Social Science, and her achievements witnessed her being awarded a scholarship to the Bryn Mawr College for European Women in Philadelphia (1927-1928). One of the visiting lecturers at the college was Lillian Gilbreth who invited Anne Shaw to join her consultancy practice for the purpose of study and gaining experience in method and motion study. This she did, but on returning to Scotland in 1929 to spend Christmas and New Year at her family home a subsequent request for a working visa to return to the United States was met with difficulties because of the economic situation within America at that time. However, following an introduction to the Works Director at Metropolitan-Vickers Electrical Company in Trafford Park (Manchester) she was offered and accepted the opportunity to initiate 'method and motion study' applications in the Company's 'Meter Department', staffed mainly by women and girls. From the outset, her work involved consultation with the operatives and their supervisors, and as progress was achieved the outcomes were fed into the joint consultation process (this included consultation with the unions). In the light of the scheme's success, the project was extended and in 1933

Anne Shaw was promoted to Chief Supervisor of Women, with a special mandate for the application of methods and motion study on a programmed basis throughout the production and assembly departments of the firm. Her involvement with the unions bred a co-operative relationship that was to endure through the rest of her professional career. By 1937 Metro-Vick had become increasingly involved in supplying defence equipment and this necessitated expanding its production facilities and workforce. This led to the development of systematic operator training in order to supply personnel for the Company's factory at Trafford Park and the 'shadow' factories that came into being from 1940 onwards. In 1942 an official request was made by the Minister of Aircraft Production (Sir Stafford Cripps) for the training facilities to be made available to personnel from other companies, and in particular for Anne Shaw's services to be available for training other personnel in methods and motion study techniques. The Company agreed and Anne Shaw became a member of the MAP Production Efficiency Board. This proved a very successful and highly valuable contribution to the national war production effort as well as providing her with an extensive range of contacts within manufacturing companies. During 1944 Anne Shaw wrote for publication by the Production Efficiency Board 'An Introduction to the Theory and Application of Motion Study'. In 1952 it was expanded into a full-length textbook published commercially as 'The Purpose and Practice of Motion Study'. Her last involvement with the Productivity Efficiency Board was at the Efficiency Exhibition staged by the Ministry in London in October 1945, having already ceased employment with Metro-Vick pending the birth of her third child in the summer of that year. She formed the Anne Shaw Organisation in November 1945, providing efficiency services with specific emphasis on training. She was awarded the CBE for her contributions towards efficiency in the war-time setting, but probably for her the greatest recognition came with development of facilities for the exchange of experiences and problems in the method and motion study context with those practitioners engaged in that field. Initially, this was called the Anne Shaw Society, but rapidly progressing to become formalised into 'The Motion Study Society' (March 1944), with Anne Shaw as its chairman.

9. Since 1937 wages for weaving were determined by a 'Unit List of Prices for Weaving'. Certain sections of the weaving trades (for example coarse weavers) were viewed as being particularly ill rewarded under this system (Brownlow 1972). This was largely because the 'List' took no account of the skill of individual weavers or of any modernisations carried out by the individual firms. In effect, this meant that the List was inflexible and failed to meet the needs of a changing industry.

10. For a survey of accountant involvement in various areas of business, including their historical involvement in consultancy, see W. Habgood's (1994) 'Chartered Accountants in England and Wales: A Guide to Historical Records'. For a general historical review of accountants within management consultancy see D. Mathews' (1998) 'The Business Doctors: Accountants in British Management from the Nineteenth Century to the Present Day', *Business History*, Vol 40, No 3, July, and T.A. Wise's (1960) 'The Auditors Have Arrived', *Fortune*, November. Or for an example of some company histories see E. Jones' (1995) 'True and Fair: A History of Price Waterhouse', R. Kettle's (1957), 'Deloitte & Co. 1845-1956', and T.A. Wise's (1982) 'Peat, Marwick, Mitchell & Co.: 85 Years'.

11. For a historical view on the growth of management services see E.F.L. Brech's (2002b) 'Productivity in Perspective, 1914-1974' and T.J. Bentley's (1984) 'The Management Services Handbook'.

12. Industrial action occurred partly because of the Government's policy to remove wage controls through industrial relations legislation (Tisdall 1982). The first serious industrial action was the national dock strike that resulted in the declaration of a national emergency by the Government at that time.

13. These included an unofficial miners' strike, resulting in the loss of more than a million working days, a strike by local authority workers, the national postal workers strike in 1971 and a strike by the National Union of Mineworkers at the beginning of 1972 (Tisdall 1982).
14. For a detailed graphical summary of the broad changes within business and management during the twentieth century see '75 Years of Management Ideas and Practice', *Harvard Business Review*, September-October 1997.
15. According to miscellaneous sources of data held at the Management Consultancies Association, the main growth areas during the 1990s were IT Consulting, IT Systems Development, Corporate Strategy, Finance and Administrative Systems, Production and Services, and Project Management. Human Resources, Marketing, and Economic and Environmental Studies services either grew more slowly or fell proportionately as a percentage of the total.
16. Its predecessor, Total Quality Control, inspired Kaizen, a system of continuous improvement through co-operation between managers and workers (Imai 1986).
17. Porter was himself a consultant and an academic at Harvard Business School.
18. Many of these case histories can be found in the publicity documentation of the consulting companies or on the Internet within the web sites of consultancies that use this medium to advertise their services. A search through those companies associated with the Management Consultancies Association reveal a rich tapestry of cases associated with improving productive performance.
19. Relationships such as B2B (business to business) and B2C (business to customer) are typical of those that consultants develop today for their clients using e-business systems within the digital economy.
20. Many of the major consultancies have strategic alliances with business systems companies and software houses, others have their own information technology divisions and bespoke solutions can be and are developed to meet specific customer needs.

CHAPTER 7

Management Education and Training: The Consultancy Approach

In 1961(a) Urwick suggested that the delivery of training and the transference of knowledge was an almost 'natural' consequence of consulting work and, therefore, an inevitable by-product of management consultancy. He stated:

> The long term objective of all management consultancy is education.

He qualified that statement by stating that:

> The only complete management consulting job is the management consulting job that leaves the client's managerial staff re-educated, alive, educating themselves.

This may have been a somewhat personal view of the work of consultants but the transference of skills and knowledge remains today, as it has always been, a central tenet of consultancy work (Obolensky 1998a).

This second in the series of five subject-based chapters reviews the work of management consultants in the broad fields of education, training and development for the period 1945 to the present day.[1] The consultants' contributions in those very broad fields are embedded in the whole ethos of consultancy as well as the historical situation. In line with the structure of all the other chapters in this publication, the first objective is review the historical situation, specifically what was going on in these fields more broadly within Britain. Having established the general situation, the contribution made by management consultants will be identified through two distinct time phases (1945-1975 and 1975-2001). The purpose of reviewing these two time phases is to develop the notion that management consultants have always played an important role in the delivery of education and training for management; that that role is unique and it represents a particular model of training and development, one that is described in this account as the 'Consultancy Approach'.

Historically the long-held belief that 'managers are born, not made', cited often within this account, meant that in-bred qualities lay at the heart of good management and that what was required was some form of coaching in the job. That dominant ethos in Britain, until at least the 1930s, did little to help identify the need for management and business education and training at a formal level. There were some departures from this popular belief, for example in 1924-1925 the Institution of Mechanical Engineers introduced a compulsory section (Section C) in its membership qualification syllabus entitled 'The Economics of Engineering, including Workshop Organisation and Management', but generally the ethos held. It was not until the late 1920s and the 1930s that there was a wider movement in education and training in Britain, but then still at the professional level. These wider movements were found within the engineering institutions and the management associations of the day.[2]

The Institute of Industrial Administration (IIA) launched its professional studies and examination programme in 1928, with tutorial arrangements at four technical colleges. The take up was poor, probably because of the demanding nature of the syllabus. In the 1930s the Councils of the three Management Associations formed in that decade (Office, Purchasing, Works) and the longer established Labour Management Association collaborated on a syllabus with common and specific elements. The four section syllabus was only agreed in 1939 and was then postponed by the outbreak of the War. Tutorial sessions for the IIA syllabus continued throughout the War when circumstances permitted. Later commentators suggested that overall situation with regard to management education and training at the national level was unco-ordinated. There was little on offer other than the qualifications of some professional institutes (cited above), and the pre-degree and degree courses taught at some universities; these were only weakly linked to business and management (Keeble 1992).[3] This is a description of a situation in which there was a common element, 'management', but the qualifications could only be obtained generally outside of working hours at the expense of the leisure time of the individual (Keeble 1992; Millerson 1964).

During the wartime years some initiatives by the Ministry of Labour and National Service witnessed some tutorial programmes at technical colleges in personnel management and industrial relations, as well as in foremanship. Significantly, during the War there was a weakening of the general ethos that management was an in-bred quality, brought about by the pressures of the manufacturing supply situation and this prompted interest in serious study for management. Some members of the Council of the IIA were strong advocates in obtaining support for a national qualification from the Further Education Division of the Board of Education (re-named the Ministry in 1945). This manifested itself in September 1945 when a meeting was convened by the Minister that included representatives of the management institutes and associations. He agreed to their request for a national review through a committee chaired by Lyndall Urwick. A consultative document was produced by August 1946 and the formal report was published in Spring 1947.

The implementation of the national syllabuses (Certificate and Diploma in Management Studies), mostly taken at evening classes, implied the death-knell of the prevailing ethos. Until 1966 the newly formed British Institute of Management (1947) held administrative responsibility on behalf of the Ministry, but because of emerging complexities in the programme fundamental changes took place in 1961.[4] At about the same time as the Urwick Report was published, private industrial and commercial initiatives and sponsorship lay behind the foundation of the Administrative Staff College at Henley-on-Thames and the launch of a course in general management for senior personnel.[5]

In 1951 a specialist team of the Anglo-American Productivity Council visited the United States to study the provision of management education. They found that in stark contrast to the provision in British universities, many American universities had departments named 'Business Schools'.[6] Also at the beginning of the decade, the Privy Council's Committee on Industrial Productivity identified that the industrial and social relations aspects of management as appropriate subjects for review. A panel was formed under the chairmanship of George Schuster (Schuster Panel) who concluded that current knowledge was inadequate and accordingly commissioned a series of research studies at selected universities. The outcome of the research was published later in the decade in a series of booklets by the Department for Scientific and Industrial Research entitled 'Progress in Industry'. Those findings and the burgeoning spread of interest in management as a subject led a few universities to inaugurate short informal courses for managers, directors and others. The limited extent of the university involvement overall was demonstrated in 1961 by a paper delivered by Professor R.C. Tress at the Federation of British Industries' conference on 'Stocktaking in Management Education'. Advances in management education and training had been hampered by attitudes in academia and business that reflected the opinion that management was not a subject suited to an academic approach. For example, this was stated in 1957 by the University Grants Committee in their quinquennium report

1952-1957, but was variously discussed with mixed outcomes on numerous occasions elsewhere.[7]

Fortuitously, just a couple of years later, a meeting between Keith Joseph MP and John Bolton led to the formation of 'The Foundation for Management Education' (FME) and a radical change in the general situation of management education in Britain.[8] The objective of the Foundation was to foster, promote, fund and provide support for the introduction of management studies in British universities. At about the same time as the formation of the Foundation, a group of businessmen in the Midlands were discussing the possibility of developing a business school within a local university and had developed preliminary plans for its formation. That initiative was known to John Marsh the newly appointed Director of the British Institute of Management, as well as the aspirations of the FME. Securing the goodwill of both parties to have their intentions independently reviewed so as not to dissipate energies or engender confusion, Oliver Franks undertook a review of their efforts and recommended the formation of two business schools at London and Manchester. A joint effort by the FME and the Federation of British Industries resulted in a wide-ranging appeal to companies for funds in the setting up of the schools. The appeal produced more funds than expected and was matched pound for pound by the Ministry of Education; the two schools were founded and inaugurated, as recommended, in 1965.

Under the stimulus and support of the FME, the inauguration of management studies courses at an appreciable number of universities occurred during the decade, including the provision of Bachelor degrees, and later the initiation of Master degrees in various configurations. That expansion can be viewed in the reports of the FME, the BIM 'Conspectus of Management Courses' (principally the 1968 edition) and in the BIM/Gower 'Yearbook of Management Education 1975-76'.[9] By the 1968 edition of the 'Conspectus of Management Courses' it was becoming commonplace to see the titles such as 'School of Management', 'Centre for Management Studies', 'Department of Industrial Administration' or 'Department of Business Studies' within some university organisations; this reflected a more serious approach to the delivery of educational courses in the fields of business and management.

Alongside the expansion of management education in the universities a similar expansion was occurring among the further education colleges, with the 'National Diploma in Management Studies' as the key course. The Ministry's formation of 'The Council for National Academic Awards' in 1964-1965 oversaw a new policy permitting approved further education colleges to provide courses in Bachelor degrees in management ranking equally in status to university colleges. By the end of the 1960s and into the

1970s courses in management had become overall the fastest growing subject, with a considerable proportion being conducted during daytime academic hours, either full or part-time.

In the latter years of the 1960s there was increasing interest and involvement of the industrial and commercial sectors, reflected in the work of the Confederation of British Industry, the British Institute of Management and the National Economic Development Organisation. The first two organisations demonstrated that involvement in 1967-1968 by the formation of a 'Council of Industry for Management Education' into which the FME was invited. Therefore, by the end of the 1970s, management education and training had taken off as a serious subject for study.[10]

The Historical Situation of the 1980s and Beyond

In 1986 the National Economic Development Council, the Manpower Commission and the British Institute of Management together sponsored research into management education and training. The purpose of the research was to examine what was going on within competitor countries as a comparator with the provision of management education and training in Britain at that time. The competitor countries reviewed were the United States, Japan, France and West Germany, with the output of the research being an official publication entitled 'The Making of Managers'. The information obtained through the research was subsequently published in a book in 1988 under the title 'Making Managers' (Handy et al). This was important research because it established the position in Britain at that time.

As far as the British experience was concerned, the author of the chapter, Charles Handy, developed the notion that there were three models of management education and training: the 'Corporate Approach', the 'Academic Approach' and the 'Professional Approach'.

The Corporate Approach A method of staff training to meet the business needs of the organisation. Within this general model, individuals were trained to meet the immediate functional requirements of their roles. However, this form of training delivery was, primarily, only usual within larger organisations that had their own training departments – more recently (for example, in the 1980s) management consultant companies supplemented in-house training programmes.[11]

The Academic Approach A replication of the American form of business education, with a jungle of courses in a range of qualifications taught at different levels across the whole academic community. In the mid-1980s, the situation was confusing because of the individual's inability to chart a clearly defined path through the range of qualifications and courses.

The Professional Approach A description of a methodology that enabled individuals to 'earn while they learned'. In general terms, it was a mixture of training and education leading to a graded series of qualifications with the objective of gaining membership of an institution. For those with occupations outside of the general management field, such education and training consisted of modules or aspects of management and business within the general framework of the occupational qualification.

Handy suggested that the whole spectrum of management education and training within Britain was unco-ordinated and difficult to subsume into a general model. Whilst the situation has changed since Handy's study, for example the Internet has widened the availability of education and training across a whole range of subjects, and business and management courses are more readily available, arguably there is still a plethora of courses and qualifications without a defined progressive path. Therefore, Handy's three models are still largely true today, but the dividing line between each has tended to blur.

Today, education and training is provided in a number of ways: full-time, part-time and at a distance (for example correspondence courses, through the Internet, etc). Using Handy's models, academic institutions provide a range of courses at pre-degree, graduate, postgraduate and doctoral levels in various subjects linked to business and management; these can be both taught or research based. Within colleges of further education, certificates and diplomas in business and management, specialised subject-based courses and a range of seminars and workshops are also available. Some of these colleges act as an annex to a particular university, with higher education courses mirroring some of those provided by the host. Private training institutions tend to cover the whole range of courses; including some having links into the universities and further education colleges. National vocational qualifications and other nationally recognised qualifications, at varying levels, are also on offer in business and management, and many of these are connected with the professional qualifications of various institutes. Many courses are provided that have no such national recognition, even though they may result in the awarding of a certificate of some form or another. Within commerce, industry and government, training is available internally at a school or by some other arrangement, or through some form of external provider; these courses are either specifically designed for the organisation (bespoke) or are provided for wider audiences. Whilst this is only a snapshot of what is on offer, the whole spectrum of education and training associated with Handy's three models is just as applicable today as it was in the mid-1980s. What has changed is the volume of courses on offer, the medium through which those courses are taught and the overall blurring of the three approaches. Within this environment, individual management consultants and consultant companies can be found providing direct and indirect management education and training.

What has not changed is the lack of recognition of the work of management consultants in the whole process of education and training for business and management. This chapter attempts to reverse this situation, putting forward the case that management consultants throughout their history have played a unique role in the delivery of education and training, and that role should be considered an additional approach to Handy's three models, the 'Consultancy Approach'.

Education and Training during the Post-War Period (1945-1975)

Each of the preceding chapters has described examples of the involvement of management consultants in the areas of management education, training and development, either directly or indirectly. Consultants have always been involved in both the development of theory and the application of management practice. In very broad-brush terms, two forms of delivery mechanisms have been used by consultants in the dissemination of knowledge towards the objective of providing services in education and training for managers. These mechanisms are best understood from the perspective of two distinct roles.

Direct Role Training delivered as part of an assignment or through formal training courses (either at the client's premise or at a training school), the provision of tuition through correspondence courses and assistance provided to companies in setting up their own training operations. Importantly, coaching by consultants during the course of an assignment was the dominant feature of on-site direct training support during the whole period. Included within this general role is the work carried out by consultants within the professionalisation process of various occupations and assistance to educational institutions in the furtherance of their programmes.

Indirect Role Knowledge provided through the delivery of lectures to professional and other forms of groups, and through publications of various types. In addition, it will be shown that the work of consultants was continued either deliberately or through imitation at the conclusion of assignments, and this represents another form of indirect input.

In order to develop an understanding of the roles, and the way in which they fitted in with the general working practices of the consultancy companies, a short historical digression will help paint the scene for the period prior to the post-war period.

Using the concept of roles, the preceding chapters have identified the work of consultants generally within their indirect role in terms of their contributions to the furtherance of the management cause through their articles in journals, books and public speaking. All of these aspects are exemplified through the work of Urwick and other consultants as part of the management movement, although consultants have generally been prolific contributors through this medium.[12] The other aspect of the indirect role, imitation by practitioners, is an almost natural consequence of a consulting assignment and this will always be the outcome of the work of management consultants; especially when assignments have been successfully carried out or a positive relationship has been established between the consultant and the client's staff.

The story of the direct involvement of management consultants in management education and training commences, in some small way, with the first known recorded incidence of a management consulting assignment in the late-1860s; this continued to be the case with regard to the work of sole practitioners and consultancies thereafter (see Chapter 2). One of those sole practitioners, Edward Tregaskis Elbourne, was active in the professionalisation process for management as well as being a direct contributor to the academic process at that time. The formation of the Bedaux company in Britain in 1926 raised the level of training to a more formal level as an important element in the delivery of consultancy services. Specifically with regard to operator training, the training of supervisors, appreciation courses for senior management and the selection of appropriately trained personnel to continue the application at the conclusion of the assignment. These individuals became the forerunners of the management services and training departments of some of Britain's major companies. A good example of this was the work carried out by Bedaux consultants at Imperial Chemical Industries from 1929 in the area of work-study and the creation of training departments in its aftermath (Faraday 1961; Ferguson 1996a). Consultancy companies formed in the period after Bedaux followed similar examples, although through the process of time the range of services widened and so did the scope of training during assignments. The one exception to this general rule was Harold Whitehead and Staff which, in 1933, was invited by Pitman's

Department of Business Development to prepare a correspondence course on salesmanship (see Chapter 4). During the build-up and the period of the Second World War, consultants played a significant role in training and re-training personnel in the operator skills required for producing war-supply goods. Whilst each of the consultant companies during that period directed effort towards the training of operatives and their supervisors in this changing environment, that effort is exemplified by the work of consultants from Personnel Administration and the development of Process Analysis Method of Training (see Chapter 5).

In terms of management education and training, as previously mentioned, probably the most important innovation during the wartime period was the opening of the Bedford Work Study School for consultant staff and client personnel. The real importance of the school was that it partly provided the inspiration for the introduction of management training schools run by the consultant companies in the period after the War. From small beginnings the consultant companies launched their management training schools in the years following on from the Second World War.

The management consultant companies had long harboured ideas for the creation of training centres to provide a supporting platform to their work in the operational fields. This was in a similar vein to that of improvements to management practice being also a motivating force in the development of some of the consultant services (Ferguson 1999). Mosson (1965) provided a description of the form of training carried out within these schools:

> What many of these institutes have in common is the country house atmosphere, the idea of a withdrawal from active participation in the affairs of industry and commerce to discuss management matters with other managers, to exchange experience and compare notes.

The emergence of these schools occurred at a time when the consultant companies themselves had identified the importance of training away from the workplace. Urwick, Orr and Partners Limited, utilising their experiences at the Bedford Work-Study School and the personal ambitions of its founder, formed a management training centre at Slough in 1947. This was initially for the provision of training for consultant recruits and client staff in work-study and related subjects (Sanders 1994). The Slough Training Centre was the first external management training school set up by a consultant company in this country and both centres (Slough and Bedford) operated in parallel in the ensuing years. Initially, at Slough there was just one course of eight weeks, within a short time a number of specialist options were included that broadened the scope of the training.

These options were production, marketing (known at that time as distribution) and finance (known at that time as control); a general management course was added to the curriculum in the mid-1950s.

The major contribution to management training, however, came through the setting up of the Urwick Management Centre that was established at Baylis House following a conversion programme in 1957-1958. The Urwick Management Centre was formed because the Slough Training Centre became too small to support the demand for providing training services. Its inadequacy eventually stemmed from the fact that it was a listed building and, consequently, the Company was unable to expand the premises. Associated Industrial Consultants (AIC), the old Bedaux company, formed a 'College of Management' in 1953 at Dunford College in Sussex. Later, in 1957, AIC provided training services at Bush House, moving subsequently to larger premises at Bilton House in Ealing. This became known as the AIC Staff College. Bilton House was a non-residential centre and, partly as a consequence, training was also conducted on a dispersed basis at other venues. These included, for example, Manchester, Glasgow, Portsmouth and Midhurst. The staff of the 'College' was made up of experienced consultants of the company who, according to Brownlow (1972), had received special training and had an aptitude for teaching. Supplementing the permanent staff, lectures were provided by practising consultants, operational managers and trade union representatives. In addition, some clients of the company provided historical sketches of the work carried out by AIC. To assist with the delivery of lectures, various teaching aids were applied: the use of films, models, case histories of actual assignments, management games, seminars and syndicate work. Training was thus provided in the following forms (Brownlow 1972).

Site Training Bespoke training conducted on the client's premises by AIC staff for specially selected personnel (for example foremen and/or charge hands). Training would normally include course work, seminars and/or lectures.

General Training Usually non-residential modular training for one or more client staff on an existing AIC staff training course or postgraduate course. Or a bespoke client training package delivered non-residentially at the AIC Staff College.

Central Training Residential courses provided by AIC at either the Staff College or other suitable venues. Courses were usually of two or three weeks in length and included guest speakers and evening discussion sessions.[13]

Production Engineering, the next consulting company in terms of longevity, during the war years conducted off-job training for two or three major industrial clients. Consequently, as a logical extension of this experience, in 1953 facilities were developed at Park House at Egham in Surrey for both P-E consultants and client personnel. In parallel to this training was also delivered at the London Headquarters of the company at Grosvenor Place; formal training courses were established making use of the previous experience of consultants in the field. Such training was developed, utilising what was considered by the Company to be up-to-date thinking in both functional and management subjects (PE 1984). Similarly in 1953 Personnel Administration obtained a building suitable for the establishment of a management training centre. Sundridge Park, at Bromley in Kent, opened its doors in 1953 for the purpose of training managers in short courses appropriate to their roles. As a testimonial to the demand for the delivery of training at Sundridge Park, this survived as a management training centre until relatively recently.

The final company whose work featured strongly within the first few chapters of this publication, Harold Whitehead and Partners to use its post war title, unlike the other consultancies did not create a management training centre. Nevertheless, it did consider training to be a central facet of the service it provided. The Company had been actively engaged in the delivery of training through correspondence courses in salesmanship and this was an important aspect of its work. The Company also provided sales training in the more conventional way at a wide range of venues throughout the country.

In general terms with regard to the work of management consultants, it is possible to argue that what was on offer was not an education but a regime in which the exchange of information was facilitated to provide advancement in management knowledge. In other words, the consultants had facilitated the process of management development at a more formal level. However, the creation of management training centres was a major step forward at time when little else was occurring in the furtherance of management education and training within Britain. The effort of consultant companies in the field of management training was confirmed during a conference arranged by the Federation of British Industries (1961) on 27 April 1961, cited earlier.

At this conference, representatives of British universities, colleges of further education, the Henley Management Centre, Government Departments, interested parties from business and the consultant community reviewed and debated the situation with a view to taking forward the issue of management education and training. Certainly the evidence provided by the universities and further education colleges confirmed the situation described by the commentators referenced in this history in that an ad hoc array of courses with no defined progressive path was the general situation that still existed at the beginning of the 1960s. The conference, aptly named 'Stocktaking on Management Education', did enable precisely that to occur. Lyndall Fownes Urwick (1961) represented the management consultants and provided a background paper detailing the services provided in this field by the then members of the Management Consultancies Association (MCA).[14] As a consequence of this paper, it is possible to identify the services provided by consultants, within six principal areas which are summarised in Table 7.1 for the period between 1940 and 1960.

Table 7.1   Direct and Indirect Educational Inputs

Educational Input	Prior to 1956	1956	1957	1958	1959	1960	Total
Direct Inputs:							
Student Weeks of Management Training	11858	6725	8220	8672	9217	10360	55052
Student Throughput	2276	942	1401	1603	1549	1547	9318
Firms Assisted in Starting Their Own Management Training Regimes	99	33	34	44	50	50	310
Indirect Inputs:							
Summary of Lectures Delivered	1815	470	367	359	332	443	3786
Summary of Books and Booklets Produced	64	15	17	17	15	17	145
Summary of Articles Published	257	63	81	83	70	81	635

*   Data on student weeks and student throughput prior to 1956 was not available for Associated Industrial Consultants and Personnel Administration.

Source: L. Urwick (1961a), 'The Part Played By the Management Consultant'

In terms of the direct role of consultants, 'Student Weeks of Management Training', 'Student Throughput' and 'Firms Assisted in Starting Their Own Management Training Regimes' are the categories associated with this field. With the exception of assistance provided to firms, most of the direct inputs were made possible through the formation of the consultant company training schools by the member companies of the Management Consultancies Association (MCA) in the post-war period. These inputs could be categorised as falling within two broad headings:

Functional Methods and Techniques   For example work-study, organisation and methods (O&M), production control and method-study.

Specialist Subjects For example general management, finance, marketing and operational research.

With regards to duration, these courses lasted from a matter of days through to a number of months, with the orientation towards specialist subjects becoming more prevalent through the passage of time. It is through an analysis of this data that it is possible to develop the concept of trends.

An important factor to emerge from Table 7.1 is the take-up rate for training courses ('Student Throughput'). This initially increased for the first few years (1956-1958) and then levelled off for the remainder of the decade. The principal reason for this was as some courses were changed, or were replaced by others in some of the centres, their durations tended to lengthen as either more detail was added or additional modules were included. In addition, there was a growing emphasis on specialist management subjects that tended to be of longer duration than the functional method and technique orientated courses. There was an overall growth of 54 per cent in the number of 'Student Weeks of Management Training' for the period between 1956 and 1960. Whilst the average indicated an annual growth rate of approximately 11 per cent per year, this may be somewhat misleading as trends within individual companies fluctuated on a yearly basis, even though generally growth was the dominant feature. In terms of the other form of direct inputs, 'Firms Assisted in Starting Their Own Management Training Regimes', there was a growing trend in the period 1956 to 1960. In percentage terms, there was a rise in demand of 51 per cent over the five years, or in real terms a 10 per cent rise on a yearly basis, although there were similar fluctuations between companies to that of 'Student Throughput'. When compared with all else that was going on in the wider world of education and training for management within Britain the consultants' contribution was clearly important, at least during the period of the 1950s, and previously. Turning to the indirect inputs, these appeared less progressive. In fact, in some large measure the data indicates a trend in which at the mid-point within Table 7.1 there was a fall in the level of output. There is no real reason why this should have occurred, other than possibly the increased demand for consultant services generally during this period would have prevented time being spent on these indirect outputs.[15]

A review of the situation in the 1960s and 1970s with regard to the member companies of the MCA indicates that the importance of direct training inputs in terms of courses provided to client staff and other customers was a significant feature of consultant practice. For example in 1963 there were 265 training courses run by the member companies of the Association.[16] By 1972, 10 years later, this figure had increased to 882, a growth rate of over 300 per cent. This mirrored the growth rate in consultancy generally, with the types and range of courses provided paralleling the development of consultancy. From the mid-1970s, even though the number of member firms of the MCA increased, the overall total number of courses began to fall. This may be partly explained by the increase in training providers generally within Britain and also partly because the restructuring within consultancy that occurred as a consequence of the macroeconomic shocks during the early years of the 1970s (see Chapter 6). The consultants had played a significant role, but attitudes were changing. This is reflected in the range of educational and training providers, not the least of which were the universities, which were becoming increasingly important as management education providers. Therefore, whilst the heyday of the consultants was over in terms of their pivotal role, they had provided in some large measure the impetus for change and remained an important contributor generally. Their growing numbers, the types of services provided and their training inputs were all-important features. This peculiar combination of training methods was reflected in their model of training delivery, the 'Consultancy Approach'.

Another feature of the first 30 years of the post-war period, and one that continues to the present day, is the prominence of education and training providers that also offer consultancy services. The 1972 edition of 'The Register of Management Consultants and Advisory Services to Industry' recorded 34 educational and training institutes providing such services (Smith 1972). These included university business schools, technical colleges and private management schools. Arguably, the majority of these only provided advisory-type services and many use business titles unconnected with the originating institute; quite often only one or two personalities within the organisations provided the lead for these activities (Rassam 1998). Nevertheless, the activities of the business schools, and the research conducted by them and on their behalf, was an important feature of consultancy's contribution to management education, training and development.

Education and Training from 1975 to the Present

By 1975 British consultancy was beginning to recover from the two waves of disruption that witnessed consulting numbers dramatically fall and the structure of consultancy changed to reflect a greater prominence of sole practitioners (see Chapter 6). In terms of the model of education and training developed within the previous section, the 'Consultancy Approach', the 26 years of this period to the present day has not witnessed a change to the basic model. If anything, the activities of consultants during this period had the effect of strengthening the validity of the whole Approach. That is because as consultancy began to rapidly expand the incidence of involvement in education and training also expanded as a parallel effect. Probably the best way to understand this is to return to the consultancy model of education and training and review what was going on within this 26-year period.

Unlike the 1950s when there was relatively little going on generally in education and training for business and management, with the consultant companies providing a significant input into the process, today the situation has changed; there is now a plethora of providers, using a whole range of methods, at various levels with greater access to a wider population. Within that whole environment, management consultants still provide education and training services within the two broad roles identified previously: 'indirect' and 'direct' roles.

In terms of the makeup of the 'indirect role', three important features were previously identified as representing the consultants' input: imitation or copying, public speaking, and the creation of publications of various types. Firstly, dealing with the question of imitation, or the copying of the consultants' methods, this will continue as long as consultancy itself continues. This is an inevitable, almost natural, consequence of the delivery of a service, especially when that service involves the use of a technique and the application of it was wholly successful; although the same can be said for many other services, not just consultancy. At the same time, imitation need not just be the result of the delivery of a service directly, it can occur through knowledge of a particular approach or technique being implied or described through some other medium. This natural consequence of consultancy work links into the second feature of the indirect role, the delivery of lectures or some other form of public speaking and representation.

This aspect of consultancy work is just as prevalent today as it ever was; the difference today is that there are many more consultants and consultancies prepared to provide this indirect form of service. For example it has become increasingly common for the major consultancies to develop the use of seminars, workshops and other forms of personal interaction to bring together groups of individuals and companies in order to air a particular subject or theme. One visible aspect of this type of work can be found in trade fairs or exhibitions where the use of seminars and other variously described events are a popular method of creating an open forum to describe and discuss a specific subject or form of service. Many of these have an educational or developmental theme, and professional bodies and associations may sponsor some of these. Arguably, such events could be considered as a form of public service, although knowledge of such activities and wide attendance at the venue would do little harm to the marketing efforts of the consultant companies concerned.

The final aspect of the indirect role relates to the publication of various materials that are available to wide ranging audiences. Generally, these have been in the form of articles, papers and books. The pioneering consultants used this form of public medium as a method of getting their message across to both professional and non-professional groups. Today the conventional methods described above have become increasingly more important as a medium to demonstrate new and existing ideas, methods and approaches. A search through journals, magazines and publication lists will reveal a dearth of materials on a broad frontage. For example, there are a number of journals in existence in Britain that specifically deal with the issues surrounding management consulting, including identifying new techniques and services that are being developed. These include *Professional Consultancy* (the journal of the Institute of Management Consultancy), *Management Consultancy* and *IT Consultant*. Journal articles in trade, business and management publications are a common aspect of this type of approach, and these are supported by an increasing list of books provided by management consultants and their companies on a whole range of business and management topics. Many of these have become important contributions to management thinking and practice, and in the world of business some of these represent 'best sellers'. Some can also be attributed to fads, but many others have stood the test of time (some of these are referenced within this publication). These more conventional methods have been supplemented by the Internet that provides a greater access to materials, quite often free, to anyone who can communicate through that medium. As a test of this, a search through the Internet sites of consultancies will reveal the availability of papers, case studies and service details that provide ranging information on the whole range of topics that are of interest to the consulting community and the businesses they support. Many of these items have become periodical publications developed by the consultant companies or they are produced as a result of a specific event, topic or activity.[17] Therefore, in general terms, the indirect role of consultants has become more important over time, today representing an approach to knowledge dissemination that is now unrivalled when compared with any other point in time in the history of management consulting in Britain. Nevertheless, whilst the indirect input into management education and training has become increasingly important, it is the direct role of consultants that provides the most visible and obvious contribution to management education, training and development.

There were seven aspects of the direct role identified earlier in this chapter:

1. Training provided during assignments.
2. Coaching of client personnel.
3. The delivery of training through formal courses.
4. The development and application of correspondence courses.
5. Assistance provided to companies in setting up their own training facilities.
6. Direct assistance provided to educational institutions.
7. Involvement in the professionalisation process.

Each aspect of that role still applies today, but as is the case with the indirect aspects of the Consultancy Approach these have become increasingly important features of management consulting services. This can be emphasised through examining each in turn and describing the consultants' contribution.

'The Official Yearbook of the Institute of Management Consultants' (1996), before the demise of the publication more recently, described each of the nine specialised areas of management consulting according to the Institute's own categorisation and identified the contribution of its Registered Practices with regard to the provision of training services.[18] Within those nine areas each of the Practices were marked according to their contributions; Table 7.2 below summarises those contributions.

Table 7.2 indicates that on a functional specialism basis an average of 76 per cent of Registered Practices provided training services as part of their portfolios; that scale ranged from 68 per cent for Information Technology to 83 per cent for Human Resources. Whilst this is not representative of the whole of management consultancy, it does nonetheless provide an indication of the importance of training as a key aspect of management consulting. However, it is not possible to judge from this data how that training was delivered or what it consisted of, only the significance of it overall. To do that, each of the aspects of the direct role will have to be examined in turn.

Table 7.2   Institute of Management Consultancy Registered Practice Training Consultancies, 1996/97

Functional Specialism	Total IMC Registered Practices by Specialism	Training Consultancy	Percentage (%) of Training Consultancies by Registered Practices by Specialism
Business Strategy	228	167	73
Human Resources	185	154	83
Finance and Management Controls	116	87	75
Information Technology	129	88	68
Marketing	134	101	75
Manufacturing and Business Services	129	95	74
Environmental Management	28	21	75
Quality Management	143	114	80
Design	19	15	79

*   Very few Registered Practices were associated with only one Functional Specialism; the majority provided services in at least two or more specialist areas.

Source: Institute of Management Consultancy, 'Consulting 1996/7: The Official Yearbook of the Institute of Management Consultants'

Training Provided During Assignments

Management consultants often provide training as part of their assignments, especially when specific techniques are employed, as there is a need to transfer skill or knowledge. Consequently many consultancies are dual functional in the sense that they not only provide consulting services, they also deliver training directly in the techniques associated with the assignment. That can either occur during the assignment or as a separate function away from the client's premises. In terms of training provided during assignments, according to Obolensky (1998a) linking implementation with learning improves the likelihood of long-term success. For example, training in project management skills for implementation personnel within a client firm may be more effective if training is carried out within the project environment rather than sending individuals on courses separately. Many consultancies will provide training as part of the change process thus providing additional benefits to those harvested from the change. Such benefits are linked to the quality of implementation and the quality of learning (Obolensky 1998a). However, this dual functional approach not only applies to project management, many consultancies will provide on-site training during assignments as a part of the overall process with key members of the clients' staff. In addition, in order to spread the message more widely, group seminars and workshops are also tools that can be and are employed by consultants to ensure overall acceptance of the change.

Coaching of Client Personnel during Assignments

One important aspect of consultancy assignments from the very beginning has been the role of consultants in coaching of client personnel during assignments. This can be easily confused with the delivery of training, but there is a clear distinction between the two approaches. Coaching is to do with the direct transfer of knowledge from the consultant to personnel within the clients' firm through the personal experiences of the consultant during the course of an assignment, whereas training is more to do with teaching and is, therefore, a formalised event. Coaching is less formal and ad hoc, but is nonetheless important with regards to the success of the application in hand and the continuance of it into the future (Mulligan and Barber 1998). The importance of the consultants' role as a coach should not be understated, it is both supportive and based on experience, and a vital ingredient in the overall success of a project. However, coaching is a personal trait, each consultant will apply their own style to the process. Consulting companies may offer guidance or set guidelines, but ultimately the breadth, depth and quality of coaching is dependent upon the experience and qualities of the individual consultant.

The Delivery of Training through Formal Courses of Instruction

Training and coaching carried out during assignments is strongly linked with the third aspect of the direct role, the delivery of training through formal courses of instruction. There are primarily two types of training courses, bespoke training (those courses developed with the particular needs of a client in mind) and programmed training (those that form part of a catalogue provided by consultancies). Most consultancies in Britain will provide or recommend training of some kind or another, and some consultancies specialise in the delivery of it. This latter group of consultancies is generally classified under the human resources function within catalogues or in agencies that supply information on management consultants. In the 1999-2000 edition of 'The Directory of Management Consultants in the UK', over 1,250 firms provided training in some form or another (Huntswood Associates 1999).[19] These ranged from the major consultancies to the small and medium sized firms, as well as sole practitioners, smaller partnerships and those on the fringes of consultancy. Training is offered by these firms in specialised subjects where the firm is a niche player, or in a range of subjects from the specialised to the more general. Some of these firms have their own training establishments, or they use temporary venues on either a regular basis or more casually (temporary venues also include client premises). Many offer both facilities, especially where it is more appropriate to provide regional training away from the consultancy's main centre of learning. The schools of management developed by the leading consultancies featured in the previous section of this chapter have now all closed, but other centres have replaced these as the training function has expanded. One or two of the major consultancies, those that generally describe themselves as 'global', have developed their own business schools and a number of business schools have developed their own consultancies.

The Development and Application of Correspondence Courses

One aspect of the provision of training services not specifically covered within the delivery of training through formal courses of instruction is the development and application of correspondence courses. The previous section highlighted the unique role of Harold Whitehead and Partners in this particular approach in the first half of this period and prior to that in the 1930s (see Chapter 4). However, on-line learning through Internet and Intranet technologies are the more modern equivalents within today's digital environment, making extensive use of network systems for a global approach to this form of training. This type of approach can involve the use of on-line study materials in various forms, but can also include other facilities such as e-libraries for materials that have traditionally been supplied in hard format. Many companies have, with the help of management consultants, set up their own e-universities where a whole catalogue of courses is on offer to their employees. Equally, universities and other learning institutions have made use of this form of technology to support their distance learning programmes. A number of consultancies have specialised in this form of service, for example A.T. Kearney and its parent EDS, in partnership with other service providers have delivered a number of e-learning solutions for their clients. The development of the e-learning environment has been recognised by a number of global companies as a positive supplement to the training and development strategies for their own staff development programmes.

Assistance Provided to Companies in Setting Up their own Training Facilities

The development of an e-learning environment is one aspect of the consultants' involvement of assistance provided to companies in setting up their own training facilities and operations. A number of consultancies specialise in this form of consultancy work, providing a whole range of services from identifying the training needs to designing the training environment. Major companies and smaller firms alike offer services that include training needs analysis using a variety of methods that may involve surveying, interviewing and workshops. Other forms of services that are provided by these consultancies and others in Britain include course design, curriculum planning, strategic delivery planning, and course evaluation and validation. More specialised services may include 'train the trainer', vocational guidance and readiness programmes for 'Investers in People' accreditation. In addition to those services that directly relate to the delivery of training, some specialised consultancies, for example W.S. Atkins, provide services in the design, construction and alteration of training facilities. Therefore, management consultants are involved in all aspects of the training environment in addition to directly providing services in relation to the delivery of training identified above.

Assistance Provided to Educational Institutions

In addition to consultants providing training to industrial, commercial and governmental organisations they have always maintained strong links with educational institutions; indeed many academics are consultants and many consultants are also academics. In the post-war period, management consulting has witnessed the emergence of business school consultancies in which education and consulting share a common platform. Therefore, it would seem almost natural for management consultants to provide direct assistance to educational institutions. That assistance can come in many forms, in fact most aspects of both the direct and indirect roles of consultants are connected with this relationship in one form or another. The most obvious form of connection concerns the relationships between consultancies and education providers in terms of partnership arrangements. Another form of relationship concerns educational institutions providing courses in management consulting. Whilst the range of courses may not represent the core functions of the institutions they are, nevertheless, important to the development needs of management consultants.[20] Therefore, there is, and always has been, a strong link between management consultants and education and training providers within Britain.

Involvement in the Professionalisation Process

The final aspect of the direct role of consultants in the education, training and development of managers concerns the consultants' involvement in the professionalisation process of various institutions. There have been changes to this aspect of education and training since the earlier periods in the history of management consulting. That is because consultants now have their own professional institute for individual consultants and full-time management consultants are less likely to consider other institutions as their primary professional bodies. What that means in general terms is that consultants have been less active in terms of the professionalisation process within other institutes corporately, which was one of their main avenues of involvement in the past. Having said this, consultants do provide services to professional bodies as fee-paying clients, especially in the development and application of training services and strategies. Other areas of involvement include the delivery of accredited training towards professional qualifications, with individual consultancies specialising in specific subject areas. Therefore, this aspect of the Consultancy Approach still applies, albeit the type of support provided may have changed.

This examination of the Consultancy Approach for the second half of the post-war period has confirmed the contention that the consultancy model still applies. A comparison of the situation now with the first thirty years of the post-war period further indicates that, whilst the input of consultants into the processes of education and training is less significant than it was then on a more general level consultants remain important contributors to the education and training of managers in Britain.

Notes

1. This chapter is largely based on Chapter Six of M. Ferguson's (1999) 'The Origin, Gestation and Evolution of Management Consultancy within Britain', and (2001) 'Models of Management Education and Training: The Consultancy Approach', *The Journal of Industrial History*, 2001, Vol 4, No 1.
2. In consultation with members of the Institute of Industrial Administration, the engineering institutions in 1934-1935 inaugurated an optional subject for study and examination entitled 'Fundamentals of Industrial Administration', with Section C remaining compulsory. It was a broad-based approach to industrial, commercial and

financial practices, together with an introduction to the basic aspects of manufacturing management. Candidates who gained a Higher National Certificate were entitled to sit the 'Fundamentals' examination which was endorsed upon their qualification. This proved to be a popular avenue for career advancement.

3. This situation is confirmed by Charles Handy (1988) in the mid-1980s in which his models of management education and training pointed towards three different 'Approaches' (Corporate, Academic and Professional), each of which contain choices that do not appear to support a progressive career path for the individual.

4. Whilst the Certificate and Diploma in Management Studies was viewed as a positive step forward, only 810 Certificates and 640 Diplomas had been awarded by the beginning of the 1960s (Keeble 1992). In 1961 a revised Diploma in Management Studies, with the Certificate no longer offered as a formal qualification or course, witnessed a greater take up than its predecessor.

5. Attendance at the College, now known as the Henley Management Centre, was particularly strong amongst senior personnel from the nationalised industries and some government departments, as well as from large industrial and commercial enterprises.

6. British universities generally had no involvement other than tutorial provision in Bachelor degrees in Administration, Commerce or Economics.

7. This was also a topic of discussion at the Federation of British Industries' 1961 conference and this attitudinal stance was well highlighted in J.F. Wilson's (1992) 'The Manchester Experiment: A History of Manchester Business School 1965-1990'.

8. John Bolton was the owner and operating head of a progressive electronic engineering design and manufacturing company. Unusually for a Briton at that time he had gained an MBA degree from Harvard University Business School. He continued to serve the School in a part-time tutorial capacity and was keen to see a similar top-level educational system in British universities. Keith Joseph had become aware of Bolton during the course of a visit to the United States that included Harvard, and on his return got in touch with him with regards to that objective. Having gained the support from a group of large-scale British industrial and commercial companies, both men designed and established the Foundation for Management Education that was inaugurated in 1961.

9. The 'Conspectus' series of booklets covered seven editions from 1953 through to 1968. The first three editions were titled 'Education and Training in the Field of Management' (1953; 1954/1955; 1956), with the final four editions titled 'A Conspectus of Management Courses' (1960; 1963; 1965; 1968). The booklets contained information supplied to the British Institute of Management by the training providers themselves and there was no attempt by the Institute to provide a judgement on the quality of education and training delivery. However, whilst the content and format of each edition varied, education and training providers fell within three broad groups: universities, colleges and independent centres. These covered between them courses within the areas of general management, functional management, management techniques, management skills, background subjects and the qualifications of the professional institutes.

10. For a full and detailed account of management education and training in Britain for the period 1852-1979 see E.F.L. Brech's (2002e) 'Education, Training and Development for and in Management in Britain'.

11. This is the only indication provided in Handy's three Approaches of the work of management consultants and, then, only within the context of a supporting agent within the Corporate model.

12. For example, see the input of Lyndall Fownes Urwick in this indirect approach to management education and training in Urwick, Orr and Partners Limited (1957) 'L. Urwick: A Bibliography'.

13. The training school survived until the demise of the Company in the 1980s when it was subsumed into P-E.
14. The member companies of the MCA at that time were Associated Industrial Consultants, Production Engineering, Urwick, Orr and Partners Limited, Personnel Administration, Harold Whitehead and Partners, Harold Norcross and Partners, the Anne Shaw Organisation, and Industrial Administration Limited.
15. With regard to the situation in the United States at that time, Urwick (1961b) suggested that American management consultant companies were less active than their British counterparts in terms of delivering services in relation to management education and training. The reason why this may have been the case was that both consulting environments were markedly different. In Britain at the beginning of the 1960s the dominant form of consultancy work was operational consulting and training featured prominently in that type of service. In the United States, on the other hand, strategic level consulting assignments were more common and these did not tend to attract a direct training element.
16. Data based on information obtained from the annual reports of the Management Consultancies Association for the period 1960s through to the 1980s.
17. For example A.T. Kearney's *Executive Agenda* periodical is available on-line at http://www.atkearney.com or in hard copy on request. Other examples include the *McKinsey Quarterly* that provides subject-based articles and can be found on http://www.mckinseyquarterly.com.
18. The Institute no longer produces the Yearbook, but information can be obtained either directly from its London offices or through its web site at http://www.imc.co.uk.
19. In addition to the consultancies within the human resources function, over 400 firms also provided services in sales training. As a comparator to indicate growth, two definitive references provide an indication of the importance of training today as central element within management consulting. The Management Consultants Association (1978) 'Statistical Information for 1978' indicated that the then member companies provided 605 training courses amounting to 37,364 training days in 1977. Whilst the member companies represented only part of the overall total of operational consultancies, they were important players in the UK at that time. However, more generally the 1983-1984 edition of the 'Directory of Management Consultants in the UK' identified over 200 firms offering management training and development services and over 50 firms provided sales training as part of their portfolios (Management Consultancy Information Service 1983).
20. The Institute of Management Consultancy has a list of 'approved course providers' that include Ashridge Management Centre (MSc in Organisational Consultancy), University of Salford (MSc in Management Consultancy), Sheffield Business School (MSc in Organisational Development and Consultancy) and the Management Consultancy Business School (MSc in Management Consultancy). Other institutions include the University of Strathclyde (Certificate in Professional Development in Management Consultancy) and the Civil Service College (Diploma in Consultancy Practice). Some of these courses are full-time, while others are part-time or through distance learning.

CHAPTER 8

From Efficiency Engineering to Strategy

An examination of management consultancy today reveals that there is no consensus corporately on what each aspect of consultancy is made up of with regard to the breakdown of services. This is further complicated because each consulting company describes its range of services in a manner peculiar to its own organisation. For the purpose of this history, and to maintain links with previous chapters, it will be more appropriate to continue to describe two main streams of consultant activity: operations and strategy. As a cautionary note, often there is little distinction between the two streams within the range of services provided by individual consultancies and they can only generally be separated by the level within the client organisation that the services are applied. Further complications arise because within those two main streams every aspect of consultancy is resident in some form or another and both streams may be represented in concert within individual consultancy tasks; these complications will become more apparent as this account progresses. The title of this chapter, 'From Efficiency Engineering to Strategy', is an attempt at describing, in but a few words, an evolutionary process within consultancy that witnessed a growing acceptance of the role of consultants at all levels within client organisations. Chapters 2 to 5 described consultancy in its infancy, identifying very much the operational nature of much of the work that was being carried out. Unlike the United States with its parallel development process (see Chapter 2), consultancy in Britain travelled a single road, evolving over time to gradually subsume all aspects of client businesses into its corporate portfolio.

The first two chapters of the post-war period (Chapters 6 and 7) concentrated on specific areas of activity (production and education), because those activities represented the main thrusts of consultancy work to the end of the Second World War. This chapter has a more general theme and attempts to review the growth of management consulting by examining the evolution of service delivery in the post-war period to the present day. This will be achieved through an examination of two specific time frames (1945-1980 and 1980-2001), representing appropriate periods of time for descriptive purposes. In a similar fashion to the preceding chapters, a short historical digression of the situation within business during the post-war period will provide the necessary background information to put into perspective the work of consultants.

The conclusion of the Second World War did not bring with it any dramatic changes to the way in which management practice was conducted within businesses. In fact, according to Wilson (1995), continuity was as much a feature of that period as change. Nevertheless, the period as a whole did witness evolutionary change and some of that change was reflected in the increasing prominence of concentration within businesses, supported in some large measure by merger activities throughout the economy (Channon 1973). In parallel with this, especially within those businesses whose origins could be traced back to the United States, there were changes to the way that businesses were organised to reflect a multi-divisional structure; but according to Bostock and Jones (1994), the pace of change in British companies was much slower than in their American counterparts.

The fields of business strategy and management are extremely broad, and a period of five and a half decades of change is a significant task in its own right in terms of providing an explanation of what was going on. However, there are a number of indicators that can be used to provide examples of some of the wider changes that occurred within businesses throughout the whole of this period; these indicators include concentration, merger activities and the changing nature in the way in which businesses organised themselves. Dealing with each in turn, concentration remained a prominent feature of the post-war period and Wilson's (1995) analysis of this phenomenon confirms the rising trend towards greater concentration throughout the whole period. From a macroeconomic perspective, this had the effect of creating an environment in which a smaller number of firms had a significant foothold within product areas, thus eroding wider competition through the creation of ologopolistic trading structures throughout the economy. In some large measure, concentration was assisted through merger activity that, as Wilson points out, would not have reached such proportions without it. Mergers occurred to satisfy both the aggressive and defensive strategies of businesses, enabling firms to enjoy greater economies of scale. In part, this was supported by government initiatives where such mergers were seen to strengthen the British economy. In parallel with this, greater internationalisation of production witnessed a large number of foreign subsidiaries establishing themselves in

Britain during the whole period, occurring at the same time as British firms were internationalising their own operations.

There are some links between these changes and those occurring with regard to the way in which companies organised themselves. The multidivisional form of organisation, pioneered in the United States, became a growing feature of large-scale businesses. An examination of the situation in Britain of the top 100 companies by Channon (1973) indicated a rising trend towards multidivisional structures throughout the 1950s and 1960s, in fact for a time these changes were the 'stock-in-trade' of a number of consultancies operating in this country. Whilst initially these companies tended to have American roots, a growing number of British businesses emulated this organisational practice. This afforded greater control opportunities in an environment where increases in scale, product range and geographical dispersion required firms to adopt a more sophisticated form of organisation (Wilson 1995).

All of these factors are important to understanding the way in which businesses were evolving throughout the period and the changes taking place to management practice within them. Apart from these broader changes, there were criticisms relating to continuity being as much a theme of this period as change. For example, within some companies, merger activity was seen to be to do with protecting the firm rather than facilitating dynamic growth (Wilson 1995); this meant that some mergers were not pursued with the vigour that the opportunities provided. This occurred even in those companies where the multi-divisional form had been adopted, forcing Channon (1973) to conclude that there was a resistance in some quarters with the result that some of the negative features of the holding company situation had remained.[1] Furthermore, Wilson (1995) suggested that companies were more concerned with short-term gains than with long-term growth, at least until the 1970s, a situation encouraged by attunement to the short-term market price of shares rather than the dynamics of the business environment. Arguably this situation is extant within many companies today, valuing shareholder support in the short-term rather than long-term growth. Assuming that this is correct, in those firms where short-term gains were considered important the level of involvement by outside sources (management consultants) would have been limited to achieving only that objective.

This very broad-brush account of the dynamics of business and management, in but a few words, belies its underlying complexities. Much has been written on the subject in the more recent past, and no doubt will continue to be written into the future. It is within this spider's web of complexity that the role of the consultant for the overall improvement of management performance can be found. This chapter is, therefore, about the integrated nature of management within the whole organisation and the role of the consultant in the overall process. Before examining what was going on within the two time frames described within this introduction, it would be useful to recap the position of consultancy at the end of the wartime period. That is with the exception of services directly related to productivity (including training services in a range of subjects), a subject covered in detail within Chapter 6.

A Stock Take of British Consultancy

Three-quarters of a century of management consulting in Britain to 1945 brought with it an evolutionary process that was tied in with the concept of non-acceptance of outside involvement in the firm. In some large measure, the dominant theme was that 'managers are born, not made', and this led to consultants only concerning themselves with the operational aspects of the firm. This attitudinal stance only slowly changed over time and it was through that change process that consultants were able to 'spread their wings' and involve themselves in areas outside of direct production.

The first indications of the broadening of consultancy services occurred in the 1920s with the work of Wallace Attwood in the areas of salesmanship, sales promotion and publicity, and sales management. Another consultant at that time (specialising in medium-sized manufacturing enterprises) was T.G. Rose who developed a service that was concerned with the consolidation of financial and operational information of the firm with the view to enhancing overall management control (see Chapter 2). These examples are the first indications of real diversification in areas outside of direct production management and whilst they were breaking new ground their overall impact was limited because of the small-scale nature of consultancy within Britain at the time.

By the end of the 1920s, with the formation of Harold Whitehead and Staff, salesmanship, sales training and sales management became an important feature of consultancy work in Britain. This aspect of consultancy was broadened even further by the mid-1930s with Urwick Orr's venture into marketing and sales, and eventual formation of a marketing department to specialise in those areas. In parallel with these developments Harold Whitehead and Staff ventured into market research, and market testing and analysis in the 1930s. The Whitehead survey on retail selling practices typifies the pioneering spirit of the Company (Harold Whitehead and Staff 1932a). The mid-1930s also witnessed further changes to the corporate portfolio of services provided by management consultants with the development of the 'Management Audit' by Urwick Orr. The

Management Audit was pioneered a few years earlier by the consultant T.G. Rose who authored a book in the same name in 1932. The Audit was an overall review of a client company; in particular it was a review of its organisation, lines of delegation, managerial practices and financial control systems. This was a deliberate attempt by Urwick Orr to make inroads into areas that had been previously considered taboo because of the negative attitudinal stance within businesses to the work of consultants in the higher management fields. In a similar vein, although with even broader intentions by the late 1930s, Harold Whitehead and Staff had developed a new form of service called 'Higher Control'. Once again the work of T.G. Rose and the publication by him in the same name in 1934 pioneered the development of strategy-type services in management consulting. The Whitehead service was primarily, although not exclusively, directed at small and medium sized enterprises. It was concerned with re-aligning businesses following some form of significant change or growth within markets to re-optimise performance through a top to bottom approach, linking objectives and aims with operational performance. Finally, the late-1930s also witnessed the development of temporary manpower services by Associated Industrial Consultants to help client firms overcome a temporary shortfall within their management ranks. These services are readily available today, but in the 1930s this was pioneering work (see Chapter 4).

The period of the Second World War, like all national emergencies, brought out the pioneering spirit of management consultants at a time when 'needs must'. This was reflected in some of the major project management-type tasks conducted during the period of the War that included the re-gearing of industrial establishments for new products (see Chapter 5). Even though consultancy by-and-large concentrated on direct war production activities, the period also witnessed assistance provided to Government Departments on a significant scale that marked a turning point in terms of opening up a new industry group for consultancy. Another first occurred in the second year of the war with the development of services in personnel management, as opposed to personnel as a resource that was the subject of techniques such as work-study. Urwick Orr started this service in response to a request from a firm that was suffering from high labour turnover (see Chapter 5). Today, human resource management is a central feature of the work of most of the major consultancies, with some consultancies specialising in this aspect as their principal form of service. Finally, the wartime period was significant in terms of the development of management training services. Whilst this has always been a major feature of consultancy work, off-site training really only came into existence during this period through the work carried out at Bedford (see Chapters 5 and 7).

This short stock-take of the situation within management consultancy for the first 75 years or so of its existence has highlighted how management consulting evolved slowly over that period of time. The specialised services of consultancy outside of the production function were developed by individual firms to exploit liberalising attitudes within businesses. The notion of defined areas of consultancy expertise, for which each company developed its response in terms of specialised services, had yet to be born in 1945 because at the heart of the majority of assignments was techniques associated with efficiency. Exploitation in wider markets occurred through opportunity and pioneering spirit.

Evolutionary Change, 1945-1980

The situation in the aftermath of war was one of growth as the major consultancies, the 'Big Four' together with Harold Whitehead and Partners, the other major consultancy at the time, were joined by a number of smaller firms, partnerships and sole practitioners. One or two of Britain's leading accountancy companies began to develop consultancy services in the first few years of the post-war period; 20 years later these challenged the 'Big Four's' dominance of the British consultancy market. By the early 1950s there were a number of definitive service areas within management consulting in Britain: production, training, marketing and sales, human resource management, financial services and strategy. Leaving aside production and training, these are covered in Chapters 6 and 7, the remaining consulting services were grouped within the latter four service areas (Harold Whitehead and Partners 1947; Urwick, Orr and Partners Limited 1951; PE 1953; Brownlow 1972; Ferguson 1999).

Marketing and Sales Each of the major companies had established either specialist departments or employed specialist consultants to cover a range of services within these two related areas of consultancy. However, within those areas each of the companies offered a different range of services, largely determined by the longevity of the departments and the experience of individual consultants within them. In terms of strategy, services included the determination of sales and marketing policy, sales and market forecasting (both nationally and internationally), and sales organisation. Operational services included pricing policies, sales promotion, sales techniques and review, and specialised training services.

Human Resource Management All of the established consultancies had a similar range of services on offer; this is unsurprising as each of the major companies matured with similar experiences of the British industrial environment. Strategic services included recruitment and selection (specifically executive selection), and HR strategy. Operational services included policy development, job evaluation, welfare policy development, HR administration and the provision of training services for all grades of personnel.

Financial Services   These were largely concerned with budgeting, estimating and cost control, although services in management accounting and financial administrative systems were becoming increasingly important. In support of these services, and in parallel to them, was the development of methodologies in relation to management information. These included data collection and analysis linked to objectives and target setting, and the routinisation of reporting processes and functions.

Strategy   There were two main forms of strategy services, the Management Audit and support to client firms involved in merger activities. The Management Audit has already been discussed within the introduction to this chapter, but services to companies pre- and post-merger was beginning to become an important strategic area for management consultants. Pre-merger services included investigations and planning, whereas post-merger was largely to do with recovery when the expected benefits had not been realised.

Most of the other types of services provided at the beginning of the 1950s can easily be grouped under production and its related areas. At the beginning of the 1950s there were five broad fields within management consulting in Britain, with training fitting in each of those areas on a subject-by-subject basis. The 1950s were a period of expansion, both in the number of consultants and in the range of services provided, with strategy becoming a definitive field in its own right. The 1950s was also a period when one of the first major American consultancies set up an office in Britain, McKinsey and Company in 1959, being quickly followed by others as part of their own internationalisation strategies. Using the four broad areas highlighted above, a review of the period 1950-1980 will indicate that the management consultancy was becoming increasingly important to organisations as an independent and objective force in improving business performance.

Marketing and Sales

The demand for consultant services in Marketing and Sales from the 1950s onwards was an important contribution to the growth of management consultancy. According to Tatham (1964), whilst British consultancies may have been slow at taking up opportunities within the marketing and sales fields earlier in their history, the demand for specialist consultants in the 1950s and early 1960s emphasised the importance of this form of service to consultancy. Examples of growth within these fields are emphasised by the number of consultancies that developed either their own subsidiaries or specialised divisions. For example, P-E set up a marketing development subsidiary in 1952, followed a year later by Personnel Administration (PA Consulting Group) who developed a sales and marketing division (Tisdall 1982).[2] The importance of marketing and sales increased through the passage of time as an export product for British consultancies. This occurred because of the immature nature of marketing in some of the exporter countries for which they were providing services (the internationalisation and globalisation of consultancy is covered within Chapter 10), specifically in Britain's overseas territories (Tisdall 1982).

Throughout the whole of this first half of the period, indeed throughout the remainder of the history of management consulting, each company developed its own particular style and expertise within Marketing and Sales. As the period progressed other aspects of the business process became extricably linked with marketing and sales, for example distribution within some companies was viewed as an essential element (P-E undated), and this in turn fed into the production process. For some companies marketing and sales were central aspects of their portfolios and for others it represented a growing proportion of their revenue. Throughout the period, innovations within individual companies led to a broadening of the whole approach. For example, Urwick Orr discussed the possibilities of developing a 'Marketing Research Unit' in the late 1950s and early 1960s, later initiated with a view to develop intelligence on consumer and industrial markets (Thompson 1961). The Company's vision in relation to the Unit extended into three distinct areas of activity: 'Market Studies', 'Product Studies', and 'Marketing and Selling Effectiveness Studies'. 'Market Studies' was concerned with investigating markets to determine their size, and the current and potential future trends. Specifically for individual clients, it was also to do with market penetration and market coverage. 'Product Studies' was concerned with investigations to establish for clients their current competitiveness, and the need for expansion and diversification or the rationalisation of their product ranges. 'Marketing and

Selling Effectiveness Studies' was more to do with strategy, specifically sales policy, planning and organisation.

By the beginning of the 1970s there were over 330 management consultancy and advisory firms, of all sizes, offering marketing and sales as portfolio items (Smith 1972). This represented a significant growth in this type of service since the end of the Second World War when marketing and sales was emerging as a specialist field within management consulting. By 1980 60 per cent of the member companies of the Management Consultants Association, representing the major management consulting firms in the United Kingdom at that time, offered marketing and sales as definitive aspects of their service portfolios (Management Consultants Association 1980).[3] Therefore, throughout the first half of this whole period, Marketing and Sales represented a growing and important management consulting service area, as indeed it continues today.

Human Resource Management (HR)

Generally referred to as personnel management at the time, Human Resource Management as a corporately recognised aspect of consultancy work really only came into being in the post-war period in Britain as an emerging area of consultancy. There were examples from previous periods, but these services tended to be ad hoc. By the end of the 1970s Human Resource Management (personnel management and selection services) represented 20 per cent of consultant income, becoming particularly important at times of scarcity in terms of the availability of personnel with the right qualifications and experience (Tisdall 1982).

Throughout the period Human Resource Management services matured into three very broad areas: Personnel Management (including industrial relations), Personnel Selection, and Development and Training Services, the latter being covered within Chapter 7. Taking the first two broad areas in turn, Personnel Management was largely to do with employment policy, organisation, personnel planning, job evaluation, and industrial and human relations. Because of the very nature of management consulting work, there were different approaches among consultancies, with some specialising entirely in Human Resource Management or in Personnel Selection Services (recruitment and headhunting). Using the example of Associated Industrial Consultants (INBUCON), with a long history of HR, in May 1961 an Industrial and Human Relations Division was formed by the Company (Bocock 1968; Brownlow 1972). Work fell into two main fields: Industrial Relations and Personnel Services, with a particular style emerging that became the Company approach.[4] For example, not only were the services provided for industrial and commercial clients, by 1965 nine trade unions had also become clients of the Division, with advice provided on their administrative structures and internal procedures. A particular approach adopted by the Company was the development of the 'Human Relations Seminar'. The Seminar brought together individuals from the trade unions, business, politics and academia to engage in debate and to share knowledge in the field of human relations; according to Brownlow (1972) the event was always over-subscribed. The more usual work of the Division centred on the identification, description and understanding of all things that make up human behaviour within a firm; they were concerned with attitudes, communications, motivation, financial and other reward systems, training and all other problems that relate to human behaviour within the workplace. Therefore, assignments usually commenced with a comprehensive review of the conditions pertaining to the individual firm.

From a more strategic perspective consultants from the Division provided services that reviewed the organisation structure of a firm with particular emphasis on personnel manning. 'Manpower Planning Assignments', as they became known, were carried out in businesses of all sizes to provide for both continuity and succession. The other aspect of the HR function, 'Executive (Personnel) Selection', was also the product of earlier periods, but only on an ad hoc basis. In recognition of the demand for this form of service the Executive Selection Division was formed within Associated Industrial Consultants in 1958. There were three main strands to the work of the Division:

- Executive search and selection;
- The maintenance of a punch card co-ordinating index of senior and specialist personnel;
- International Salary Survey.

The core business of the Division was to search for and select appropriate personnel for a client to fill some senior vacancy within a firm. In support of this function the punch card co-ordinating index was developed and maintained as an intelligence system, being gradually built up through the process of time, containing information on suitable personnel for future approach and possible re-deployment. From a job description the index was searched and if suitable applicant(s) could not be found, the post was advertised. Once located, applicants were tested and a report was submitted to the client for its consideration.

In parallel to the executive search service, and partly in support of it, the 'International Salary Survey' provided clients with information on the current scale of financial rewards. This survey was compiled through partnership arrangements with a number of agencies abroad and provided salary information on a range of countries in Europe (including the United Kingdom) and elsewhere in the world. In addition to providing salary information, it also produced data on taxation and the cost of living in the range of countries covered. The work of INBUCON exemplified the range of services provided by the major management consultancies engaged in the full aspects of HR management during the period.

Corporately, there were approximately 330 management consultancy and advisory firms offering services in Human Resource Management by the beginning of the 1970s. The majority of these provided Personnel Selection Services, but there was a growing number of specialist service providers that solely concentrated on this form of activity; overall approximately 350 firms provided selection services (Smith 1972). By 1980, 80 per cent of the member companies of the Management Consultants Association were involved in Human Resource Management, all of whom provided personnel selection as part of that service (Management Consultants Association 1980).[5]

Financial Services

The penultimate form of service provided during the period to 1980, Financial Services, sometimes referred to as Finance and Administration, is an area that grew into a specialism over a period of time. According to Tisdall (1982), the demand for financial services increased throughout this period from 20 per cent of income in the 1960s to 30 per cent by 1980. Growth occurred in parallel with the fall in demand for production efficiency services utilising techniques such as work-study. In the first half of this period to about 1960, services in finance and administration were concerned with functions such as:

Administration   Office mechanisation, clerical methods, operational research and, increasingly, the use of computers.

Finance   Policy and planning, budgeting, costing and management accounting.

By the beginning of the 1980s, the Management Consultants Association (1980) identified the scope of services in this area as:

Administration Organisation and methods, including procedures and office mechanisation.

Finance Financial control (including management accounting, budgeting and profit planning), financial modelling, investment evaluation, and costing and estimating.

Management information systems and information technology services were grouped within their own specialism entitled 'Management Information Systems and Electronic Data Processing'; this was clearly in support of greater specialisation and growth overall within consultancy more generally.

Because of the potentially wide-ranging nature of financial and administrative services, and their separation within most consultancies, no two portfolios were the same. Some consultancies provided services in what they described as management accounting and office administration, although the substance of the service was that of finance and administration. Each consultancy developed its own particular style and range of services, although within the major firms most of the areas identified above were covered. Typical of the services provided by management consultants during this period were those of P-E. The Company separated finance and administration as portfolio items, with the range of services provided represented as 'Management Accounting' and 'Office Administration', reflecting both the strategic and operational aspects of financial and administrative management (PE undated). Throughout the period there remained a strong link between financial services and production management, and it was only as the period progressed that the strategic aspects of financial management began to take a more central role within the range of services provided by the Company.

Reviewing initially the first half of this period, the work of the PA Consulting Group in industrial firms typifies much of what was going on within consultancy. One aspect of the work of the Company in this field was its 'Standard Costing' service; this was a method of obtaining financial information based on developed standards within the client firm. These standards were either determined by PA as part of a wider service or supplied by the client in a directed assignment. Standards were 'Attainable Standards', based on realistic expectations, or 'Ideal Standards', a developed model for which expectations were less certain. From the standard it was possible to monitor performance on a specified time-span basis, providing early warning of any deviations from expected outcomes. Therefore, key financial information was routinely available to effect the management decision-making process; such information included (Lamond, 1948):

- Costs relating to products and total output to determine sales policies;

- Actual expenditure to determine excess costs and where they occurred;
- Profit levels and margins.

As the period progressed, services became more sophisticated, specialised and wider ranging. Typical of the services provided at the end of the 1970s and beginning of the 1980s were those of INBUCON that strongly linked financial systems with business continuity and planning (INBUCON undated). Administratively, INBUCON's services ranged from effectiveness programmes through to reviewing staffing levels in all administrative areas. Effectiveness programmes included Organisation and Methods, organisation review, communications processes, office layout, and training for all staff grades. From a financial perspective, services included cost reduction programmes, specialist financial services and economic feasibility studies. Specialist financial services included advising the client on various aspects of the business relating to taxation, acquisitions and mergers, and insolvency. As a parallel activity, economic feasibility studies included evaluation of regional development plans and comparative economics. In support of these services, the development of client-specific management information systems provided the necessary data to support the business processes of the organisation. INBUCON employed specialist staff, including economists, and had a strategic partnership with the accountancy firm of Edward Moore to support its worldwide operations. The work of the PA Consulting Group and INBUCON throughout this period typified what was going on within the major consultancies in Britain.

Corporately within Britain, there were approximately 300 management consultancy and advisory firms offering financial services by the beginning of the 1970s; many of these firms had firm foundations within accountancy (Smith 1972). By 1980 16 out of the 25 member companies of the Management Consultants Association provided financial services of some form or another (Management Consultants Association 1980). Without exception, each of those member companies that had been formed by accountancy firms provided comprehensive financial management services.

Strategy

This is the final area of consultant involvement identified as a cornerstone of consultant activity for the period prior to 1980. Strategy services were less readily identifiable as a stand-alone service prior to the 1980s because no such categorisation had been corporately made. Strategy services could be found represented within each of the main areas of consultant activity and were recognisable through the level to which they were applied within the client firm, as well as their impact globally within the organisation. Strategy consulting was not a product solely of the post-war period, Chapters 4 and 5 point towards earlier examples of their application. In terms of their frequency and their breadth they only became a significant aspect of consultancy during the post-war years, and then only gradually becoming a main aspect of consultant activity in Britain.

One of the major difficulties with describing strategy consulting is the potential range of services that could be selected as being representative of that objective. Each area of consultancy could be represented and it is really only in the last twenty years or so that consultancies have advertised strategy services as a distinctive element within their portfolios. Because of this complexity and in order to gain a flavour of what was going on at the time, a number of service forms act as exemplars of the type of services provided. Taking the 1950s and 1960s as the starting point, P-E provided services in business organisation and planning. During the 1950s, assignments relating to organisation review and planning were generally ad hoc in nature and in support of other aspects of consultancy work. A number of prestigious clients sought the services of the Company at that time; these included Rolls-Royce Limited, British European Airways Corporation, Vickers Armstrong Limited, and many other major aircraft manufacturers. However, a 'Business Planning and Organisation' service formally commenced in the early 1960s, partly as a consequence of the greater internationalisation of businesses within Britain (PE 1984). One or more of the following business effects were typical outcomes of the consultancy assignments:

• Organisational decentralisation, either to create regional or divisional hierarchies;
• Internationalisation of operations;
• New financial control processes;
• Diversification of product range.

Production Engineering believed that many of the problems associated with businesses partly occurred through an inappropriate organisation structure and, therefore, it was towards this aspect of the business that the service was primarily developed to deal with. In support of this objective, another form of service, the 'Management Audit', was utilised as a technique to provide some of the necessary information on which to make judgements in terms of appropriate structures. The Management Audit, as far as P-E was concerned, was a method of reviewing the objectives of the firm in combination with its structure and financial policies.

At the same time that P-E was developing its business organisation and planning service, James O. McKinsey and Company set up an office in London in 1959 to deliver services in organisation and boardroom management (Tisdall 1982). The Company had previously carried out an assignment in Venezuela for the Royal Dutch Shell Group and its first work in Britain was a continuation of that, with the office opening at its conclusion. However, there are a number of misconceptions about the extent to which McKinsey challenged the established British consultancies within Britain at that time. This was emphasised by the fact that McKinsey provided services in a specialised area of consulting that had not fully taken off by that time and the Company had relatively few operational consultants when compared with British firms; only 15 by 1962 (Kipping 1996). Where McKinsey stood out was the publicity that the Company attracted as a consequence of its high profile clients and the effects it had on businesses through their visible reorganisation. Its clients included the major tobacco companies, Shell, ICI, Dunlop, the Post Office, the BBC, and British Rail (Channon 1973). In addition to McKinsey, other American consultant firms, for example Booz-Allen and Hamilton, and Arthur D. Little, also mounted a European challenge during this period.

The McKinsey 'flagship' service at the time was the reorganisation of client firms into a multi-divisional structure (M-Form); the services were fully underway from the mid-1960s onwards. A survey carried out by Channon (1973) of a hundred large firms in Britain indicated that multi-divisional structures had been adopted by 13 per cent of the firms by 1950, these numbers rose to 30 per cent and 72 per cent in 1960 and 1970 respectively. He found that McKinsey had been the major driving force behind these changes, with British subsidiaries of American firms being the first to adopt the change. A significant impact of the change process was that it helped firms grow within their own product areas and also to diversify into others. Channon calculated the level of diversification within the same group of companies: 25 per cent by 1950, rising to 45 per cent and 60 per cent in 1960 and 1970 respectively. What McKinsey achieved for British consultancy was raising its profile and identifying the benefits of using consultants to effect changes to the strategic aspects of a clients' business. However, the situation became critical for British consultant companies in terms of the McKinsey challenge when public institutions, for example the Bank of England, looked towards American consultancies for help rather than the established British firms. In 1968 questions were asked at Prime Minister's Question Time, and a full-blown debate followed in the same year with regard to the apparent unfair treatment and disregard of British consultant firms.

Less visible than the work carried out by consultants in effecting major organisational changes of the type mentioned above, but no less important, were the services developed by consultancies in support of strategies in relation to the high-level objectives of companies. Typical of these services were the Management by Objectives (MbO) service developed by Urwick Orr that had a span of implementation that stretched for over 20 years between 1963 and 1984.[6] MbO is exemplified by the work of Peter Drucker (1989) who stated:

> What the business needs is a principle of management that will give full scope to the individual strength and responsibility and at the same time give common direction of vision and effort, establish teamwork and harmonise the goals of the individual with the common weal. The only principle that can do this is management by objectives and self control.

The service commenced operationally in 1963, although it had been in development for some years before. The principle of MbO was that the strategic aims of the client were cascaded downwards through the organisation. In concept MbO was a strategic service, in practice it became largely operational with strategic level services following on in later years. The concept was a flexible approach based on tailored solutions that met the specific needs of each individual client (Cullen and Buttery undated). There were five basic service packages dependent upon on client needs (Ferguson 1996b):

1. *First Major Installation of MbO*   The complete MbO package, including training, seminars and pilot installations.
2. *Training and Counselling Approach*   A part-time consultancy package that included the training and counselling of senior managers.
3. *Second Generation MbO*   A recovery package initiated when the initial installation had failed through the identification of problem areas and the application of remedial action.
4. *MbO Audit*   A review of organisations that had adopted MbO and directed re-vitalisation where required.
5. *MbO in Non-Profit Making Organisations*   A tailored package in those organisations where profit was not the primary motive.

Two general principles of application were observed: client personnel were trained to participate as fully as possible in the installation process and the whole process was conducted in a way that there was an observable change in the behaviour of the management of the organisation. However, not all applications of MbO were conducted organisation wide, some were only applied to specific departments, or within specific locations or in specific groups of the organisation.

Throughout the 22 year life span of the MbO service at Urwick Orr, consultants of the Company carried out 408 assignments; for a breakdown by years see Table 8.1.

Table 8.1   Number of Assignments involving MbO

Year	Total Assignments
1963	5
1964	8
1965	8
1966	13
1967	28
1968	34
1969	50
1970	62
1971	60
1972	37
1973	26
1974	33
1975	16
1976	15
1977	6
1978	2
1979	0
1980	2
1981	2
1982	0
1983	0
1984	1
Total	408

Sources: Ferguson 1996a; Urwick, Orr and Partners Limited 1984a

Individual assignments varied in duration on a scale between half a week to 182 weeks and the number of consultants employed on each assignment also varied between one and eleven (Ferguson 1996b; Urwick, Orr and Partners Limited 1984a). The demise of the service occurred for a number of reasons, but at the heart of these there existed a general lack of understanding of MbO within management circles generally in Britain, some firms still did not accept consultant involvement in the strategic aspects of business and the introduction of computer-based information systems that replaced many aspects of the MbO service. The heyday of MbO occurred in the late 1960s through to the beginning of the 1970s and represented a significant contribution by Urwick Orr to the strategic direction of the client companies involved.

This first period has drawn attention to the evolution of 'strategy' consulting within Britain, and the growing acceptance of consultant involvement in the higher management functions of businesses and other organisations. This trend continued past the 1980s with strategy eventually becoming a distinctive field of management consulting in its own right.

Evolution, 1980 to the Present

The beginning of the 1980s did not immediately bring with it any dramatic changes to the way in which management consulting activities were categorised corporately within consultancy. Once again it was evolutionary forces that brought about change. The Management Consultants Association's (1980) 'Scope of Services' identified seven fields of management consulting activity:

1. Organisation Development and Policy Formulation.
2. Marketing, Sales and Distribution.
3. Production Management.
4. Finance and Administration.
5. Personnel Management and Selection.
6. Economic and Environmental Studies.
7. Management Information Systems and Electronic Data Processing (EDP).

Twenty years later, consulting services in the new millennium draws attention to the way in which services have evolved in Britain. Whilst the basic structure remains largely unaltered, 'IT Consultancy' and 'IT Systems Development' replaced Management Information Systems and EDP, and two new areas, 'Project Management' and 'Economic/Environmental' services, have appeared. Other fields have had some cosmetic name changing and the range of services within each have broadened. From a revenue perspective, the main difference is the changing nature of the pro rata share of each field of activity over time. Each of the categories has been a major winner over time, but recently project management has suffered from a fall in revenue (Management Consultancies Association 2000). However, overall consultancy has demonstrated consistent growth, typically revenue returns increased by 19 per cent in Britain in 1999 (FEACO 1999).

The pattern that emerged for the final 20 years of the twentieth century confirms the contention made within the introduction to this chapter that there are two main streams of consulting activity; Business Strategy and Operations (referred to by some companies as performance improvement). The term 'business' is used in this sense to generically describe all organisations regardless of whether they are conventional business organisations, not-for-profit organisations or government bodies. Overarching these two main streams of activity, and bridging them, are consulting services in relation to information technology (see Chapter 9). In parallel with this evolutionary process, and inextricably linked to it, are the evolution of markets and the overall structure of management consultancy. Historically, management consulting within Britain was concerned with domestic markets, but through the process of time consulting operations expanded into markets outside of the United Kingdom through the establishment of local offices and operations. More recently many of the major consulting companies have re-organised themselves on a global basis linked to fields (aspects) of consulting activities (this is covered in greater detail in Chapter 10). In terms of the remainder of this chapter those aspects of consulting related to productive performance (covered within Chapter 6), personnel training (Chapter 7) and information technology (Chapter 9) have been largely disregarded in this section because they are covered elsewhere within this history. To continue the theme developed within the chapter, strategy and operations will each be examined as the two broad streams of consulting activity.

Strategy

One of the principal problems with Strategy as an aspect within consulting is that it can be resident within each of the fields of consulting in the portfolio of services provided by individual companies. In addition, there is no consensus with regard to the range of services identified by the professional institutions related to consultancy and in the various catalogues of consultancy services that are published in this country. Even when strategy as an activity is separated from the remaining fields, strategic-type services can still be identified within those fields. Strategy is both a field in its own right and an aspect of each of the other fields of activity. Based on that premise, strategy can mean one of two things. It can relate to the high level strategic decisions taken by an organisation in terms of developing plans and processes to position itself within a market with a view to keeping ahead of the competition, sometimes referred to as the grand strategy. But, it may also relate to an aspect or part of a business and re-tuning it in line with the business-level strategic decisions; Obolensky

(1998b) suggests that this may consist of one or more moves within a specific area of the business, referring to the concept as pure strategy. Therefore, each grand strategy may be supported by a series of strategic moves and it is this differentiation that partly explains why strategy as a consultancy service both stands alone and is resident in each of the other consultancy fields.

Business strategy is one of those fields of consultancy that has witnessed steady growth within Britain in terms of revenue. From an income stream of £98m in 1994 revenue rose to £490m in 2000, representing an overall growth rate of 500 per cent in the seven years (Management Consultancies Association 1996, 1998 and 2000). The term 'strategy' was probably a product of the mid to late 1980s and even then it appeared to have been used guardedly within individual British consulting company portfolios. Typically, at the beginning of the 1980s, strategic services tended to be labelled 'General Management', 'Business Appraisal', 'Corporate Planning', 'Organisation', 'Diversifications', 'Corporate Services' and 'Mergers and Acquisitions'. According to the 'Directory of Management Consultants in the UK 1983-84' (Management Consultancy Information Service 1983) the position in the first few years of the decade witnessed the major consultancies of both British (including the larger British accountancy firms consulting businesses) and American in origin specialising in these fields. In addition to those companies, a host of small and medium sized firms also provided strategy services. Using the Directory's classification, services in 'General Management' were provided by over 120 firms, with in excess of 150 firms providing services in 'Business Appraisal', 130 firms in 'Corporate Planning', 90 firms in 'Acquisitions and Mergers', and 80 firms in 'Diversification'. The major consultancies were largely involved in the majority of service areas, whereas the smaller and medium sized firms tended to be more specialised. By the mid to late 1980s strategy services were openly provided using that nomenclature and typical of the services provided at that time were those offered by INBUCON.

INBUCON had a five-stage approach to the delivery of its strategy service involving key areas and aspects of the business process: defining the objectives, developing the strategy (grand plan), determining internal strategic changes, the operational review of key areas and the development of the business plan (INBUCON c1986). Underpinning the INBUCON approach was the use of analytical tools and techniques, dependent on client needs, that may have included: 'competitor analysis', 'portfolio analysis', 'environmental analysis', 'market research', 'strengths/weakness analysis', 'financial modelling' and 'post improvement potential'.[7] Typical strategic outcomes would have included acquisition, diversification, rationalisation or specialisation. The client list of the Company boasted some of the major organisations within Britain at that time, including oil companies, government organisations, media companies, financial institutions (including the major banks), and a whole range of manufacturing and service companies.

By the end of the millennium, at the corporate level of management consultancy, strategy incorporated services within the areas of business transformation, merger and acquisition, e-commerce, knowledge management, and a range of strategy services relating to business development and modelling (Huntswood Associates 1999).[8] At the heart of service delivery were the major global consultancies, international firms and larger domestic companies. Within the other fields of activity, services such as risk management, corporate recovery, IT/IS strategy, outsourcing, branding and supply chain strategy were all typical of strategic-level services provided by the whole range of consultancies operating in Britain. However, strategy services are but one aspect of the diverse portfolio currently provided by British management consultancy companies and other consultant firms operating in Britain and elsewhere in the world.

Operations

The second stream of consultancy, 'Operations', includes the remaining aspects of the corporate portfolio; these, like strategy, evolved over time. Generally they were concerned with business improvement and exploitation in the range of areas that make up the business processes of an organisation. Typically the first half of the 1980s bore witness to an eroding production engineering market based on the functional techniques that had traditionally been associated with the operational aspects of businesses (see Chapter 6). Emerging out of this changing environment were the broad fields of financial management and administration, human resource management and marketing, together with production services un-reliant on traditional techniques (Management Consultancy Information Service 1983). For the generalist consultancies, these represented the main fields of activity throughout the 1980s, but each field was extremely broad and only the major consultancies provided services that encompassed the majority of these. Using the Management Consultancies Association classification of services that fit within the scope of 'Operations', namely 'Financial Systems', 'Human Resources', 'Project Management', 'Marketing' and 'Economic/Environmental', it is possible to describe in broad outline the evolution of these services through to the present day.[9]

Financial Systems More commonly referred to as financial management and administration at the beginning of the 1980s, financial systems was concerned with various aspects of financial management, including management accountancy, and cost and budgetary control. The administrative element of the service was wide-ranging encompassing individual services such as organisation and methods, office management and planning, information and library retrieval systems and word processing. Also within that range of services could be found a growing element concerning the use of information technology, specifically feasibility studies, computer audits, operations research and management information systems. Other aspects of the service within some companies may have included telecommunications as well as other forms of communications. Well represented with regard to the financial elements of the service were the management consulting arms of the major accountancy companies and some small and medium sized specialist financial consultancies. The administrative element was covered by a broad range of consultancies, some specialised, others generalist; also within this group were the major generalist consultancies and the financial specialists. The remaining services, those relating to information technology, communications and management information systems, tended to be provided by specialist consultancies, together with a number of the others that had developed their own specialised departments to cope with this growing field. The one exception to this rule was management information systems because of its link with strategy formulation and review. Here, a number of the international consultancies, primarily of American origin, were strongly represented together with the major British companies and a range of specialist consultancies with strong links with information technology (Management Consultancy Information Service 1983).

The distinctive nature of the financial and administrative range of services meant that information technology was playing a growing role, not only with regard to solutions, but also in terms of tools and techniques; especially with regard to the development and use of computer modelling methodologies. Therefore, there was a mixture of the old and new, with traditional services such as organisation and methods interacting with the burgeoning business information technology market. By the mid to late 1980s, there was a distinctive separation within most company portfolios between administrative and financial systems and information technology. At the turn of the millennium, within the financial function, a number of the aspects of the service are shared between strategy and operations depending upon the level to which they are applied within individual organisations and the nature of the service within individual consultancies. Certainly, some aspects of finance can be employed at both levels, for example risk management, outsourcing, business process re-engineering and corporate recovery provide examples of these. Other service areas may include corporate restructuring, performance measurement and a host of financial services. Each of the major consultancies is strongly represented within the financial service area, many of which originated from an accountancy background. Inextricably linked with financial services today is e-commerce, as well as all other aspects of consultancy.

Typically the major consultancies offer a range of services that include business finance and recovery (including enterprise resource systems), project finance, real estate valuation, corporate value consulting and advice on mergers and acquisitions. A number of consultancies organise their businesses along global lines, sharing experience across industries and international markets; typical of these is PricewaterhouseCoopers that has a global financial team. Services related to 'Administration', whilst unavoidably linked to finance and information technology, are treated as separate offerings by many consultancies of all types and sizes. They can encompass a whole range of areas from back-office applications to complete re-engineering of enterprises, to realignment in changing market conditions. Included within this group of services are those related to the employment of technology and the mechanisation of manual processes. From the perspective of value to consultancy, the Management Consultancies Association (2000) records a doubling in income over the three years from 1998 to 2000, although a large portion of this is undoubtedly related to the application of e-commerce systems and other e-business processes.[10] Financial systems logically also have a relationship with Human Resource Management in many respects, with a history of combination stretching back as far as the birth of consultancy itself.

Human Resource Management   Largely referred to as personnel management until the 1980s, Human Resource Management had a number of clearly defined strands during the early 1980s. The two main strands, personnel management and personnel selection, distinctive fields in their own right, were often combined in company portfolios to represent the personnel function. Personnel management incorporated a number of distinctive fields that could be classified as personnel services (typically, planning, evaluation, industrial relations, communications and, organisation structure and development), psychological services (attitude surveys, psychological assessments, counselling and performance appraisal), financial services (incentive schemes, remuneration strategies and pensions), training services and other services (for example, health and safety policy development and implementation). Personnel selection, on the other hand, was concerned with executive search, personnel recruitment and advertising. These two main strands of activity progressed through the 1980s, both as parallel activities and as combinations dependent upon the approach adopted by individual consultancies. For example, some consultancies developed single departments or divisions to cope with the human resource aspect as a single entity, while others separated the functions.

INBUCON, for example, had a separate 'Personnel Services and Selection Division' for executive recruitment and personnel search, while human resources in general was the concern of 'INBUCON Human Resources'. Many smaller consultancies and niche players specialised entirely in aspects of the HR function; a search through the inventory of niche consultancies within the 'Directory of Management Consultants in the UK 1983-84' reveals the number of small and medium sized firms specialising in the various aspects of the range of services within the personnel function at that time. For example, over 90 firms supplied services in 'performance appraisal' and 100 firms in 'counselling', but only about 14 firms provided services in 'graphology'. Of those firms, less than half a dozen feature today as medium sized consultancies and very few of the very small firms specialised in more than one area. However, of the mainstream services at that time such as 'general personnel management', 'industrial relations', 'management development and training', and the 'recruitment services', a number of today's larger consultancies are represented within the 'Directory'. Strategic services, such as 'manpower planning', and 'organisation structure and development', witnessed many of today's global and international consultancies, for example McKinsey, being involved in providing services of that nature. Therefore, Human Resource Management attracted a wide range of consultancies of all types and sizes, some very specialist and others providing general services across the whole range.

The noticeable aspect of Human Resource Management at the turn of the century is the virtual disappearance of payment incentive schemes based on traditional methods of detailed job analysis and methods improvement; these were still evident during the 1980s as an important part of the personnel function. Moving on to the 1990s and into the new millennium there are still two main streams of activity (HR and Recruitment), the principal differences relate to the spread of services, the differentiation between operations and strategy, and the dominant involvement of information technology across the whole range. All of the larger firms operating in the United Kingdom provide HR services, and the overwhelming majority of these are involved in both operations and strategy. Typical of the services provided by consultancies are those delivered by the PA Consulting Group whose portfolio is strongly aligned to supporting strategic change through gaining best value from personnel resources. One aspect of the service unique to the Company is its proprietary Personality and Preference Inventory (PAPI) to assist with the recruitment, selection and development of staff. PAPI is an assessment process based on questionnaires, analysis and review. PA Consulting Group provides a service that permits the licensed use of PAPI that includes software, assessment materials and consultancy support.

Human Resource Management, including personnel selection services, is one aspect of consultancy work that is provided, in some form or another, by most consultancies of all sizes. Consequently, the Management Consultancies Association (1996, 1998 and 2000) has recorded a dramatic increase in revenue for its member companies from 1994 to 2000 (from £40m to £151m). But, surprisingly, Human Resource Management has witnessed an eroding share of European revenues from 6.2 per cent of the share of consultancy in 1999 to 3.9 per cent in 2000, even though recruitment and selection increased as a proportion of European income (FEACO 1999). This erosion of share may have been due to a re-classification of some services within FEACO towards a bias in Information Technology where it is difficult to separate out the field of consulting from the technological aspects for statistical purposes.

Project Management The third aspect of consultancy work within the Management Consultancies Association classification of 'Operations' services featured in this section is an area of consultancy work that has largely been the product of the post-1970s as a formal service offering.[11] Project management is concerned with the management of all aspects of a project, including its planning, organisation, implementation and control. Project management can also mean programme management, which involves the co-ordination and control of multiple projects or events within a process of change. At the beginning of the 1980s, the 'Directory of Management Consultants in the UK 1983-84' (Management Consultancy Information Service 1983) recorded about 170 consultancies offering services in this aspect of consultancy work. The great majority of these firms were small and medium sized enterprises, with the larger consultancies not specifically offering project management as an aspect of their portfolios at that time. Many of those consultancies were providing services either in an advisory role, acting as an independent agent for the client, or in a consultancy role with the consultant actively involved in the management of the project. Also at that time, assignments were largely concerned with physical events, such as the construction of a physical project, or a project that required change in management control. However, project management as a category of consultant service did not differentiate between programme and project management in terms of form of service, although at a practical level such differentiation would have been difficult to avoid. Therefore, many of the assignments conducted in the name of project management were in fact programme tasks.

Through the process of time, the orientation of projects changed to reflect the growing prominence of information technology within enterprises, therefore increasingly project and programme assignments were concerned with the implementation and application of technology, either directly or indirectly. Equally, project management as a form of service grew in parallel with this change in orientation. For example, between the years 1994 and 2000 the revenue from project management assignments of the member companies of the Management Consultancies Association rose from £44m in 1994 to £119m in 2000, although a comparison between 1999 and 2000 indicates a fall in revenue generally by 31 per cent from £172m in 1999 (Management Consultancies Association 1996, 1998 and 2000). This may represent a re-categorisation of services from Project Management to Information Technology where a large proportion of project management services may now be recorded statistically within individual firms. Growth is also generally reflected within the 'Registered Practices' of the Institute of Management Consultancy during the latter period of the twentieth century. Approximately 50 per cent of all firms provided project management services within each of the nine specialisms identified by the Institute (Institute of Management Consultancy 1996).

Just as consulting has two main streams of activities, strategy and operations, so this structure is reflected within the area of project management. As a generalism, strategy is aligned to programme management, whereas operations are concerned with project management. Those consulting companies that offer both programme and project management services tend to reflect that separation, with multiple projects residing within programming tasks. Whilst no two companies provide support to clients in exactly the same way, there are a range of individual services that can be found among them. Within project and programme management these can include the provision of professional advice, direct project support (including management), the deployment of temporary project management staff, the use of project management tools and, in the majority of instances, project management training. Other services may include configuration control, risk assessment and management, financial control, third-party management, and contingency planning. In effect, management consultants provided services in all areas that encompass project and programme management; some consultancies specialise within specific sectors and some others specialise within a defined range of consulting activities. Overall, though, programme and project management is one of the major growth areas of management consulting in Britain.

Marketing The penultimate aspect of consultancy work covered in this section, Marketing has a relatively long association with management consulting in Britain (since the mid-1920s, see Chapter 2). At the beginning of the 1980s, marketing, sales and distribution tended to be linked as a group of activities (Management Consultants Association 1980). Ignoring the distribution aspects of the service, marketing and sales were concerned with business forecasting, economic and market research, product planning and development, pricing, sales organisation and control, sales promotion, and training. Within the broad field of marketing itself, there tended to be three main strands, consumer, industrial and export marketing, with each strand related to the two broad streams of consulting, strategy and operations (Management Consultancy Information Service 1983). At the level of operations, services such as market research, social and economic research, pricing, sales promotion, and sales training were typical fields of activity. At the strategic level, services included economic forecasting, diversification strategy and new product development. As was the case with other fields of activity within consulting at that time, it is difficult to definitively establish the dividing line between strategy and operations, largely because the makeup of services within individual portfolios, regardless of title, were and are specific to organisations.

By the mid to late 1980s, the division between the two principal streams of consulting activity were beginning to become clearly defined within the portfolios of the major companies. For example, P-E INBUCON (1988) 'Market and Business Development Service' consisted of market strategy and policy, acquisitions and diversifications, and corporate image services as strategic offerings. By the 1990s, customer relationship management, market positioning and brand management featured strongly as services within the marketing field. Within the major consultancies, services tended to be offered either in marketing generally or in customer relationship management specifically, with individual firms organising their operations accordingly. Customer Relationship Management (CRM), sometimes referred to as customer management or relationship marketing, is concerned with the development and maintenance of relationships between the supplier and the customer, although there is probably no common definition of CRM. Traditional views of marketing were largely concerned with the development, enhancement and management of aspects of marketing such as pricing, promotions and products. CRM, on the other hand, tends to be a holistic approach combining strategy with operations with the view of retaining as well as developing a customer base. Today, the overwhelming majority of CRM services are inextricably linked with technology through e-business solutions and it is the role of the consultant to not only develop the culture but also provide and implement the solution. Small and medium sized firms, including niche consultancies, tended to follow similar patterns of operating, other specialist firms generally concentrated on specific aspects of the marketing service. In terms of revenue, the marketing field has been subject to growth throughout the whole of the latter half of the 1990s.

In the period 1998-2000, revenue among the member companies of the Management Consultancies Association increased from £37m in 1998 to £61m in 2000. A similar growth pattern was witnessed in the period overall from 1994-2000 when revenue rose from £14m in 1994 to £61m in 2000 (Management Consultancies Association 1996, 1998 and 2000). From a European perspective, the share of consultancy revenue generated through marketing fell by 0.3 per cent of the total in 1999 when compared with the previous year, although it still represents four per cent of total income overall in European consultancy (FEACO 1999).

Economic/Environmental Services The final category within this section, these services are probably the most difficult to definitively categorise. In the 1980s, there was clearly no direct link between the two forms of service and neither tended to be specifically definitive in their own right, largely being aspects (or fringe services) of other fields of consultancy. For example, economic feasibility studies, consisting of economic feasibility planning and regional development planning advice and consultancy, economic forecasting and economic research, were generally encompassed within the field of finance and administration or marketing. Environmental services, largely unrecognised as such when compared with those provided today, were concerned with areas such as energy management that was subsumed within the tradition of productivity services or financial management (INBUCON undated). Energy management tended to be concerned with savings to the underlying costs of running businesses; the motive being cost reduction rather than energy conservation. Both forms of services were linked through information technology and the ability to model change scenarios before selection of final solutions. Other links included financial management and marketing, where the profit motive often became the driving force for the selection of appropriate solutions, and through localised environmental issues related to health and safety in the workplace.

At the beginning of the 1980s, taking each aspect in turn, economic services were generally the preserve of specialised consultancies, largely small-scale, although one or two of the emerging medium sized consultancies, for example Touche Ross, provided some services as specialised functions. Environmental services were similarly serviced, although there was less involvement in this field generally amongst consultancies at that time (Management Consultancy Information Service 1983). Even services in Health and Safety were only provided by 30 small and medium sized consultancies. As the 1980s merged into the 1990s, both aspects began to take on greater importance as specialisms within consultancy generally. In terms of revenue growth, the Management Consultancies Association (1996, 1998 and 2000) recorded a span of income from £20m in 1994 to £48m in 2000, an overall growth rate of 240 per cent in seven years, or an average of 26 per cent per annum. The one year in which revenue dropped was 1996 when there was a down turn from £23m in 1995 to £18m in 1996; at that time this represented 1.6 per cent of overall revenue for the MCA. Part of this growth may have been due to the major consultancies themselves developing specialised sectors and adopting a more global approach to the delivery of their services. The majority of the global and international firms provide a range of services in both aspects of this field, however as with all other fields of management consultancy there is very little commonality in terms of both their description and range.

The PA Consulting Group provides what it describes as 'Environmental Services' in a combined range of financial and environmental subject areas. These include the development and implementation of environmental strategies, and the economic analyses of environmental issues.[12] Lorien Consulting's 'Environmental Engineering' services include noise assessment and energy utilisation within its portfolio. Other consultancies, for example Pagoda, specialise in specific areas associated with environmental issues. In Pagoda's case, its Energy, Natural Resources and Development team provide services in those areas around the world. These include various forms of analyses in the areas of finance, risk, environmental impact and energy efficiency. Other services include planning, support and strategy, organisation change and training. Finally, other consultancies that predominantly organise themselves on a global basis, for example PricewaterhouseCoopers, have a network of specialists across the world. PricewaterhouseCoopers 'Environmental Services' covers three main aspects of environmental risk: compliance and prevention (assessment, verification and post-operational support), environmental performance (design and implementation of solutions, financial performance improvement, and environmental issues relating to product lifecycles), and policy and strategic support (strategy development, public policy support and support to eco-industries). The Economic/Environmental services field is clearly an up-and-coming aspect of consultancy work and one for which there are good indicators of future growth, especially if current trends are continued.

On a national scale, management consultancy has demonstrated patterns of growth in most fields of consultancy work. Using the member companies of the Management Consultancies Association as an indicator of growth, definitive data exists to support this contention, see Table 8.2.

Table 8.2   UK Consultant Revenue, 1994-2000

Year	Revenue (£m)	% Improvement on Previous Year
1994	931	
1995	1084	16%
1996	1460	35%
1997	1814	24%
1998	2243	24%
1999	2498	11%
2000	3207	28%

*   Revenue includes income for outsourcing/facilities management.

Sources: Management Consultancies Association (1996, 1998 and 2000)

From an overall examination of the period 1994-2000, United Kingdom revenue grew substantially in each of the years even though growth fluctuated yearly. A more detailed tabular view, described partly within this chapter under the fields of consultancy covered, provides for a review of consultancy on an activity-by-activity basis, see Table 8.3.

Each field associated with management consultants in the period 1994 to 2000 has demonstrated growth over the whole time frame, but for one or two activities growth was not entirely consistent for the whole period. What this chapter has demonstrated is that it has proved difficult to clearly separate strategy from operations; both have grown together over the post-war period, with strategic services present within each field. At the same time, at the heart of each field today lies information technology, either directly or indirectly. The evolution of the utilisation of information technology and its place in consultancy is the subject of the next chapter. There it will be demonstrated that computers and computing have been associated with management consultants for almost all of the post-war period, with their position within consultancy growing in importance with each passing year.

Table 8.3   UK Consultant Revenue (£m) by Activity, 1994-2000

Field/Year	1994	1995	1996	1997	1998	1999	2000
IT Consultancy	258	263	280	254	341	285	465
IT Systems Development	213	208	186	247	407	316	469
Strategy	98	138	229	238	284	325	490
Financial Systems	81	115	128	160	188	210	389
Production Management	84	82	107	163	152	151	218
Human Resources	40	61	65	78	60	72	151
Project Management	44	50	49	97 ·	119	172	119
Marketing	14	26	39	42	37	56	61
Economic/ Environmental	20	23	18	40	31	40	48
Outsourcing	79	118	359	495	624	871	797
Total	931	1084	1460	1814	2243	2498	3207

Sources: Management Consultancies Association (1996, 1998 and 2000)

Notes

1. A 'holding company' was a means of retaining control of an organisation following change (merger) in order to continue the approach adopted in the past. For example, in terms of a family-owned firm, members of the family would retain prominent positions on the board, thus ensuring the maintenance of continuity and control. Channon argued that features of the holding company manifested themselves in lack of co-ordination, poor planning, ineffective control and out-of-date reward systems.
2. According to Tisdall (1982), the interest in marketing and sales partly came about because of the lifting of restrictions on newsprint in the post-war period, innovations in colour printing and, from 1955 onwards, the use of television as an advertising medium.
3. Of the 25 firms of the Association, 15 offered services in marketing and sales. The remaining firms were, by-and-large, either specialised consultancies or accountancy company firms that tended to concentrate more on financial and information services at that time, rather than the broad spectrum of generalised consultancy.
4. According to Brownlow (1972) the Company got off to a slow start with developing an Industrial and Human Relations Division because it had always viewed activities in the personnel field as a normal aspect of consultancy work requiring no special treatment.
5. By 1980 the Management Consultants Association categorised Human Resource Management (including selection services) within a number of sub-categories. These included: personnel policy formulation, personnel planning, industrial and human relations, executive and staff selection, personnel advertising, salary formulation, job evaluation, and personnel training and development.
6. The background and history of the MbO service within Urwick Orr had its roots in the mid-1950s with the development of a service called 'Improving Managerial Performance' (known within the Company as i.m.p.). The service was based on a

framework of financial and profitability reviews via a mechanism of budgetary control; the service involved an element of coaching for senior management personnel on the dynamic aspects of their responsibilities. The programme was launched in Leeds through a series of seminars. Ultimately, this was a two-pronged strategy, a consultant service and an educational programme. In-built into the overall strategy was the emphasis on responsibilities in relation to marketing and management accounting. The seminars proved popular, however, the parallel consultant service was less so (Ferguson, 1996b).

7. These analytical methodologies were developed specifically to review different aspects of the business process as it affected each individual client: *competitor analysis*, a review of market share, product range, strengths and weaknesses, pricing policies, etc.; *portfolio analysis*, a review of present and future profitability potential; *environmental analysis*, industry trends, technology, sociological changes, economic forecasts, etc.; *market research*, customer profiling, customer needs, price sensitivity, etc.; *strength/weakness analysis*, typically a review of the capabilities of strategic areas of the business; *financial modelling*, 'what-if' analyses using computer technology; *profit improvement potential*, operational review potentially resulting in productivity improvements, cost reduction, etc.

8. Business development and modelling is a reference to a series of services that included competitor and market analyses, scenario and business modelling, strategy development, portfolio analysis and a range of top level strategic techniques and performance methodologies.

9. The scope of services is described within the Management Consultancies Association (2000) 'President's Statement and Annual Report'. The remaining services (IT Consultancy, IT Systems Development, Strategy and Production Management), as previously stated are dealt with elsewhere within this history.

10. The revenue for the member companies of the Management Consultancies Association for the period 1998-2000 within 'Financial Systems' is recorded as £188m (1998), £210m (1999) and £389 (2000). From a European perspective, where financial advisory services are separated from e-commerce solutions for statistical reporting purposes, financial advisory services were subject to a fall in the share of consultancy revenue overall from 3.6 per cent in 1999 to a projected share of 1.4 per cent for the year 2000. Services in information technology, however, were projected to rise by over 10 per cent in 2000 (FEACO 1999).

11. In real terms, most consultancy assignments could themselves be considered projects in their own right, with the consultant acting as the project manager for the process.

12. PA uses decision analysis tools to determine the costs involved in compliance with environmental regulations.

CHAPTER 9

Information Technology and Management Consulting

Today the term information technology (IT) is synonymous with the use and deployment of computer technology, and the physical use of information technologies has become commonplace within the overwhelming majority of environments within business and in other organisations. In management consultancy, IT is inextricably linked to all the fields of activity for which consultants are associated, having also become the principal definitive field in its own right.[1] Therefore, it has become difficult to separate out the work of consultants from IT or IT from their work; IT companies have consulting arms, consultancies have IT divisions. Chapter 8, specifically Table 8.3, identified the importance of IT in terms of revenue, and each field of activity directly and indirectly is subject to the application of information technology.

Information technology, in the broadest use of the term, pre-dates the computer and has been linked with management consulting for a large part of the twentieth century in some form or another. Using the example of the office, technology has been employed in office environments for the routine processing of information since at least the nineteenth century. In terms of the time frame associated with this history, there were probably three main strands to the early information technologies concerned with the mechanised office and, unsurprisingly, these represent the three main uses of today's office computer for routine applications (Campbell-Kelly and Aspray 1996):

- *Word Processing* Previously carried out on typewriters is today the mainstay of office automation packages;
- *Information Storage* Previously handled by manual recording and filing systems is today collated by, for example, database programmes;

- *Financial Accounting and Analysis*   Previously carried out by mechanical adding and punch card accounting machines is today assisted by the use of spreadsheets or enterprise management systems.[2]

The office environment represents one of the main avenues for the employment of information technology today. The office environment and the administration of businesses were areas that witnessed the involvement of consultants from the early days of their history. Services in accounting, office mechanisation, and the handling and manipulation of information were important functions of many of the early consultants and consultancies. During the 1950s consultant involvement in office automation, indeed office automation in general, consisted of mechanising routine functions, thereby merely adding speed and some scope to those routines. However, in the post-Second World War period the link between consultants and information technology had tended to be strongest through its association with computer technology. Today IT is generally used as either a driving force for change or in support of the change process itself. In order to understand the position of IT in consultancy a selected knowledge of the history of computing is a necessary pre-requisite to understanding its evolutionary role within consulting.

Taking the computer as a device rather than as a function, in the period prior to the appearance of the first electronic computer, analogue machines were designed and used to model scientific and engineering problems where mathematical calculations were either difficult to carry out or were time-consuming in the extreme.[3] The majority of analogue machines had but one purpose, although through the passage of time some machines were developed that were multi-functional. The electronic computer can be said to have owed its origins to the scientific-military situation of the Second World War (Campbell-Kelly and Aspray 1996). The first electronic computer built in Britain using digital processing was developed in 1943 at Bletchley Park for the purpose of code breaking; the machine was called Colossus.[4] Programmable computers were developed towards the end of the War, still with a military purpose. These early machines were extremely large and were driven by valves and it was a number of years before transistors replaced valves thus reducing the overall size of the machines. The first computer built with a business purpose in Britain was the LEO (Lyons Electric Office) in the early 1950s at the behest of J. Lyons and Company. This came about because the Company had a strong interest in new technology, coupled with a desire to improve its office management techniques (Simmons 1962).[5] A review of available technologies in the United States by a team from the Lyons company led them back to Britain and Cambridge University's Mathematical Laboratory and an experiment on a new machine known as EDSAC (Electronic Delay Storage Automatic Calculator). The First LEO computer, LEO 1, was built from an adapted EDSAC machine. Lyons used LEO 1 for payroll compilation and wage payments, coming into service in 1953. It was also being looked at from the very early days to provide integrated management information, including its use for production planning, progress control and distribution within the Bakeries Division. By August 1954 LEO had undertaken a payroll compilation for another major manufacturing company and this was the first instance of a service bureau application (time-share) in Britain (Brech 2002c).

Early computer programmes were a product of the 1950s and a number of computer languages were developed during the decade. Also during the 1950s British companies began manufacturing computers, including Ferranti, Marconi and English Electric, but these were overshadowed by larger American firms that included IBM within their ranks (Coopey 1999).[6] The 1950s and 1960s was the era of the second generation of computers and the application of stored programmes provided some flexibility on their use within businesses.[7] Second generation computers used transistors in place of the vacuum tubes. The period also witnessed the concept of time-sharing coming into wider effect; this provided a number of agencies or users with the ability to simultaneously take advantage of computer technology without the vast expense of investment, giving the illusion that each user was the sole operator at that time. This was the same period that the leading management consulting companies in Britain began to develop an interest in computing and, it will be seen, heralded the commencement of IT as an important aspect of consultancy work; although it was mainly from the 1960s onwards that the serious application of IT consulting got underway.

The 1960s witnessed the arrival of the minicomputer at a fraction of the cost of mainframe units, thus removing some of the financial arguments sustaining the justification of time-sharing. However, time-sharing continued and expanded, especially within small and medium-sized businesses through to the 1970s and 1980s. The main financial advantage for these businesses was that the cost of a time-share was much less than the cost of purchasing and maintaining its own computer system. The period of third generation computers was marked by the creation of the semiconductor, electronic components mounted on a silicon chip, and the development of a central operating system that allowed computers to run a number of programmes at the same time. Computer Aided Design (CAD) was also a significant development in the 1960s, although initially operated through mainframe technologies until the 1980s, and this became an important area of involvement for management consulting companies.[8]

The 1960s also witnessed the introduction of industrial robotic machines in factory environments with the employment of the first of these by General Motors. Robots controlled by computer programmes offered the benefits of cost reduction through replacing manual labour in tedious and often uncomfortable environments. The employment of robots offered other benefits through spawning a whole new industry, creating specialist employment, improvements to management control over the production process and the raising of productivity levels. Today robots can be found in factory environments throughout the world, most visibly in car production plants, and the automation of production processes is an important aspect of consultancy work within modern-day production management.

The development of the silicon chip revolutionised computer design as it became possible to place an increasing number of components onto just one chip. This meant that computers could be manufactured smaller, the larger the number of components on one chip the smaller the machine and this had a positive impact on reducing cost. In 1971 Intel developed the 4004 that mounted the major functions of the computer on one small chip that was capable of being programmed to meet customer needs. This had the effect of revolutionising the application of computer technology to the extent that smaller units could be manufactured for personal use, expanding the usage of computers into consumer and business desktop markets. The advent of the first personal computer, Altair, occurred in the mid-1970s with the development of kits for self-assembly. This innovation was shortly followed by the launch of the Apple 1 personal computer.

The formation of the Microsoft company in the 1970s, initially to develop machine codes, was a seminal event in terms of software development. At the beginning of the 1980s IBM introduced what was considered by many as the first functional personal computer for home and business use, being pre-built and requiring no self-assembly. The Microsoft company developed the operating system MS-DOS (Disk Operating System) for residence on the IBM machines; MS-DOS provided the bridge between hardware and software. The introduction of the Macintosh in 1984 was a huge step forward in modernising the personal and business computer fields and this heralded the way forward for the development of the graphical interface for the personal computer.

By the mid 1980s MS-DOS was firmly established as the principal operating system for the personal and business computer markets, any graphical interface would either have to replace it or work in concert with it. Given the spread of MS-DOS and the volume of programmes written with MS-DOS as the operating system, it was little wonder that it remains one of the principal desktop operating systems extant today. A whole range of graphical interfaces appeared on the market and in 1985 the first version of Microsoft Windows was released for IBM compatible computers. Other versions of Windows followed and operating systems were also developed by other companies, including a proprietary system by IBM itself. The information technology environment of the 1980s was extremely competitive with a whole range of technologies developed and released to satisfy the home and business communities.

The 1980s and 1990s witnessed rapid developments in Local Area and Wide Area Networks (LANs and WANs), acting as a stimulus for moving away from main frame computer technology towards distributed localised computing systems capable of sharing information across a community. The 1980s also witnessed the advent of a global communication system that revolutionised the business and information environments; the World Wide Web or Internet as it became commonly known. Whilst not a product of the 1990s, it was a technological development that impacted upon the decade and continues with a vengeance to affect many aspects of personal and business life throughout the world. Such technology supports a global networking community, capable of communication through e-mail systems. The Internet brought with it a whole range of supporting technologies that included web browsers to act as search engines, encryption to provide security for users and firewalls to offer protection. The Internet, and the technologies associated with it, has directly benefited the wider business community through the introduction of systems that support electronic business processes. Previous chapters have identified areas of consultancy that are directly supported through the gains made by exploiting the Internet and other networking systems. These include, for example, Chapter 6 and supply chain management, Chapter 7 and e-Universities, and Chapter 8 identifying each of the other areas of consultancy and their association with information technology.

This very quick gallop through the history of information technology in the post-war period, covering computer systems, software, networking, robotics and the Internet, amongst other areas, provide some indication of the dynamic environment that consultants have operated in throughout this whole period. This outline review provides only a series of snapshots, it cannot provide the whole picture. Nevertheless, it does give an indication of how emerging technologies were and are used in direct support of consultancy operations, and indeed in many instances acted as their focal point.

This chapter is about the involvement of consultants with information technology, encompassing all aspects of their work in the post-war period. Taking into consideration the nature of the evolution of computing and the waves of innovation associated with it, there appear to be three main phases concerned with the work of consultants through to the present day. The next section, 'The Application of Early Computer Technology, 1945-1970', marks the first phase and describes the early involvement of consultants in information technology, and the first stage of development in terms of the establishment of a definitive aspect of consultancy work. The second section, marking the second phase, is concerned with the work of consultants during the period 1970 to 1990, prior to the wider development of the Internet and the arrival of e-business solutions; it was that period in time when IT services were expanding into all aspects of consultancy work.[9] The third and final phase of consultant involvement is the subject of the last section, 1990 to the present day, and is concerned with the Internet and the advent of e-business in all its guises. It is also a statement of the present day, providing a description of consultancy services into the new millennium. Each of these three phases represents evolutionary trends, not only in technology but also in its wider usage by the management consulting community.

The Application of Early Computer Technology, 1945-1970

The historical situation with regard to information technology to 1970 was marked by developments in main frame computer units. These early machines were large, although getting smaller through the passage of time, expensive to purchase and their scope was limited. The first business computer, the LEO, appeared in the 1950s and this signalled a turning point in terms of a direction away from developments for scientific and military use. The broadening of development in information technology during this first period included time-sharing, early computer programmes, the opportunity for integrated management information systems, early robotic machines and the creation of programmes in support of computer-aided engineering (CAD/CAM). No wonder, therefore, that in the mid-1980s Halton suggested that the world was experiencing a new form of Industrial Revolution, brought about by developments in information technology (Halton 1985).

Whilst Halton's suggestion of a new form of movement was made in the 1980s, the revolution within this country as it affected consultants began quietly much earlier during the period of the later-1950s and the 1960s; office mechanisation and improvements to administrative processes were by the post-war period fairly routine applications within consultancy circles. This position is confirmed by Bentley (1984) who suggested that the introduction of Organisation and Methods (O&M), coming to the fore in the 1950s and 1960s, was made possible through the new technology;

these included early computer technologies and other equipments that supported office mechanisation.

Initially in the period of the 1950s, before specialist IT consultancies had been formed and existing consultancies had created specialist divisions, the lead in providing advice to clients had been taken by the equipment manufacturers themselves. This was understandable because, unlike the consultancy skills that had been developed and improved upon within the operational setting, the use of computers within consultancy was different. Computer technology had been developed independently of consultancy and consultants needed specialist assistance to gain the necessary expertise and make best use of available technology; computer technology later brought about the introduction of a new breed of consultant, the IT consultant.

From the mid point of the 1950s the major consultancies operating at that time in Britain began to engage with computer technology. PA Consulting Group, recognising the importance of the emerging technology, adopted an approach that witnessed the Company taking positive steps in embracing this new specialist area. During 1957-1958 the value of embracing the application of information technology as both an aid to consulting and as a form of service was recognised by the Company, being reflected in the assessment carried out by it of the impact of IT on American companies at that time.[10] PA carried out its first specialist assignment in September 1958 and this was concerned with conducting a feasibility study for a client to determine the benefits associated with the deployment of the available technologies. In parallel with these developments in Britain, specialist staff of the Company in Australia carried out similar assignments at that time. Whilst these early assignments relating to the employment of computer technology were carried out as part of the general thrust of management consultancy, by the 1960s PA had experienced significant growth within this specialised field and, as a result, the Electronic Data Processing (EDP) Division was formed as a response to it (Hunt 1983). Initially, the Division was staffed by only three specialist consultants, rising to ten within its first year of operation, and by the end of the decade the Company had a professional staff of 80 specialist consultants. By the 1970s the EDP Division became the Management Sciences Group and consisted of three separate Divisions: a Computer Division, a Programming Division and a Management Sciences Division. In the 1980s the Group became PACTEL, with specialist groups operating throughout the world, and by 1983 the Group had three hundred professional staff within four geographical zones: Western Europe, Scandinavia, Pacific and North America (Hunt 1983).

In 1958 Urwick, Orr and Partners also began conducting feasibility studies for clients through the formation of new company, Urwick Diebold

(UD).[11] These principally involved identifying within the client's organisation those processes that easily lent themselves to transference to computer technology. Having completed that process, the next stage was to provide a specification of the new processes and conduct a cost comparison between the old and new methods.[12] Where computer technology had been deployed at that time it was largely concerned with credit control, wage calculations and personnel records where existing processes were previously based on punch card technologies and keyboard accounting systems (Bridgeman 1994). As the service matured into the early 1960s, and the deployment and usage of computers slowly became more commonplace, the Company found itself becoming increasingly involved in computer evaluations and the training of systems analysts and programmers.[13] There were three main spin-offs to this service for Urwick Orr:

- Training courses were developed and delivered at the Urwick Management Centre, thus expanding the portfolio of courses at the School;
- Expansion brought about the formation of a new company, Urwick Diebold Recruitment Services, specifically to act as a recruiting organisation for specialist IT staff for deployment to client companies;
- Services in software development were commenced, becoming an important aspect of the overall portfolio of services.

The latter spin-off resulted in the Company, in 1963, recruiting and establishing its own team of software engineers, a practice that was eventually mirrored by other major generalist consulting companies.

In the latter 1950s INBUCON, like the other major consultancies, began to involve itself in data processing. Growth in this area resulted in the Company forming a Computer Division, originating in the North West, where feasibility studies were being carried out for clients (Bocock 1968). Initially, the service was only taken up by the larger clients of the Company, but because of the increased interest expressed more generally it became necessary to develop expertise internally in order to best support rising demand (Wilson 1968). The Division later amalgamated with the Operational Research Division and, in 1964, a subsidiary company was formed, subsuming both Divisions into Management Sciences Limited. P-E, whilst slightly behind the other major consultancies of the day, formed a computer division in 1968 and by that time a significant proportion of the Company's consulting staff had some working knowledge of the practical use of information technology (PE 1984). The Division had extended its range of services to encompass systems analysis and programming by the beginning of the 1970s. Similarly, Harold Whitehead and Partners was involved in the use of computer technology to carry out assignments in relation to management science techniques. For the Whitehead company, management sciences consisted mainly of operational research techniques, including network analysis, linear programming, queuing theory, forecasting, mathematical modelling, decision theory and investment appraisal techniques. These were primarily to do with either problem solving or planning and control systems, and the use of computer technology was mainly concerned with the collection, processing and storage of data, either through client-owned technology or with hired, or shared, computer facilities on a time-share basis (Harold Whitehead and Partners 1968). An associate company, Lockyer and Partners, worked with the Company when assignments were carried out in this area.[14]

Unlike the other consulting companies at that time, Harold Whitehead and Partners did not specifically set up a specialised department or division to service the increasing demand for expertise in computer technology; other aspects of the service provided by the Company were concerned with feasibility studies and technology audits.

Feasibility Studies   Carried out to ensure that the use of technology supported the business needs and that its costs would produce a return on investment over time. Assuming such costs appeared acceptable, metrics were developed to monitor efficiency, company profitability and cost control.

Technology Audits   Today generally referred to as Benefits Management, technology audits were concerned with gaining maximum value from the use of technology.

Therefore, from the mid-1950s through to the end of the 1960s, the major British consultancies at the time were beginning to develop their links with information technology. It had become obvious to those companies that the use of IT was a specialised field in its own right, one requiring specific expertise that could not be developed in the traditional way through generalist consultancy services and, therefore, some consultancies developed associations with specialist firms, combining consultancy techniques with technical knowledge.

A number of definitive strands had been developed that made best use of collaborative arrangements and in-house expertise. The principal function related to the development of feasibility services to determine a client's fitness to embrace computer technology and the form it should take. Other strands included early forms of benefits analysis, specialist recruitment and some in-house programming services to develop bespoke applications for businesses. Information technology at that time tended to be used for the basic functions of business, for example financial transactions, office automation and some management science modelling services, it was a number of years before more advanced applications provided a wider range of benefits at a fraction of the cost of those in the period to the 1970s.

By the beginning of the 1970s this burgeoning aspect of consultancy work was beginning to witness a growth rate unparalleled in consultancy up to that point in time, albeit with limited application in the range of services. Electronic Data Processing (EDP), as it was generally known at the time, was carried out by a range of companies spanning the full spectrum of size from small (including sole practitioners) through to large consultancies. Unsurprisingly, with the new technology playing an important part in financial accounting, the accountancy based consulting firms in Britain were also well represented in the list of consultancies active in this field. The 'Register of Management Consultants and Advisory Services to Industry' (Smith 1972) recorded in excess of 200 firms supplying EDP services; of these, many were specialist information technology consultancies, as well as a range of educational and research institutions and the major consultancy companies.

Overall, the period of the mid-1950s to 1970 was the era when services in computer-based information technology made its first appearance and established itself as an important aspect of consultancy work. The end of the period marked a watershed in terms of the work of consultants because innovations in information technology, together with their greater involvement in the strategic aspects of business, was a turning point in the delivery of consultancy services. Chapter 6 pointed out that the mainstay of traditional consultancy work, improving productive performance, was beginning to give way to other services and information technology was becoming a distinctive aspect of the work of consultants, helping to change the general direction of consultant services. Other changes were also occurring on the shop floor with early experiments in robotics proving a success in terms of gaining greater productivity through investment in technology. During this period only limited applications were carried out, but from the 1970s onwards increasing usage of robotic technologies provided further opportunities for consultants seeking improvements to processes within production environments. Similarly, the use of computer aided engineering technologies became an important area for consultant involvement in the following years.

Information Technology in Business Prior to the Introduction of the Internet and the e-Business Revolution, 1970-1990

Whilst the 1970s may not have got off to a good start because of the downturn in consultancy services in the first few years (see Chapter 6), developments in Information Technology products provoked reciprocal changes to the range of services provided by management consultants. Whilst the majority of services provided in the early period revolved around conducting feasibility studies to determine the applicability of businesses to migrate to information technology solutions, the period also witnessed the appearance of a new breed of consultant specialising in the delivery of IT solutions. From the beginning of the 1970s, developments in information technology moved forward a pace with the introduction of the early personal computers and advances in software applications for specialist and general use.

This period, prior to the introduction of the Internet and e-business systems, was fast moving and witnessed consultants' involvement in IT expand beyond the imagination of the early pioneers in IT consultancy only a handful of years before. The demand for feasibility studies, brought about by the changing technology, increased through the passage of time and more businesses looked towards the computer to improve their business processes. In fact, feasibility studies were one of the mainstays of the IT service package offered by the major consultancies during the period of the 1970s and 1980s. What was beginning to emerge at that time was the relationship between IT services and strategic and operational services. For example, at the mid point in this period the Management Consultants Association (1980) identified a range of services provided by its member companies. From the perspective of strategy, whilst each of the services had a role to play, identifying the information needs, and the development of reporting and control systems clearly had a strategic orientation. Other services, largely to do with operations, included system analysis, design and installation, computer and data security, process control, operational research, and office automation and administration. Of the 25 member companies at that time, only seven did not explicitly describe their range of services as including information technology or electronic data processing as key elements.

What was beginning to occur during this period, as previous chapters have indicated in relation to other forms of service offerings, was that it was becoming increasing difficult to separate out IT from the range of services provided by consultants as well as becoming a distinctive area in its own right. Tisdall (1982) supported this view and suggested that the application of computer software was beginning to replace traditional methods of improving performance based on the delivery of efficiency techniques such as work-study. Looking forward into the 1980s and beyond, she suggested that the use of information technology would revolutionise business activity through acting as a facilitator for change in terms of integrating business operations. Such predictions, as it will be shown, have largely come true and the role of consultants in that change process was a pivotal instrument in improving overall business performance and processes within the enterprises they serviced.

During this phase of consultant involvement with information technology two main forms of consultancies emerged: traditional consultancies strengthened their involvement with the new technologies and new technology-based consultancies appeared in increasing numbers. Supplementing these, sole practitioners and smaller firms, providing specialised consultancy services either bridged the gap between technology and management consulting or concentrated on the delivery of technology solutions. The pattern, however, that emerged was that it was becoming increasingly difficult for consultants to continue providing services without some involvement in computer-based solutions and through the passage of time the partnership between consulting and technology strengthened. This is demonstrated by the orientation of services provided by the management consultants during this period.

The beginning of the 1970s witnessed the increasing involvement of consultants in the computerisation of routine processes. The previous section identified the different strategies employed by consultancies in embracing the challenges of the new technologies, technologies that were continually evolving. For most consultancies the challenge of the computer lay in identifying the benefits associated with the expense of investment. P-E, for example, provided services in conducting feasibility assessments associated with computerisation and also provided services in office mechanisation, based on more traditional technologies (PE undated). At the beginning of the 1970s the use of computers in business was mainly confined to routine office and business support processes including clerical tasks, data storage and statistical processes. The benefits, according to P-E, lay in the speed of processing, pre-programmable actions and data storage capacity, but the benefits had to be balanced against a number of factors, not the least of which was cost. For computers to produce benefits for clients then this invariably involved some form of change in processes and routines. Without such changes, computers merely automated existing processes with all their inherent faults.

Price Waterhouse carried out an analysis of the value of computers and at the beginning of the 1970s the Company identified a number of key areas of use; these included routine clerical tasks, data analysis, product design and the use of programming functions for conducting 'what if' scenarios, especially for making strategic decisions and in marketing (Jones 1995). As the 1970s progressed the Company found that the volume of work involving the use of computers increased as businesses sought independent advice of their value. By the beginning of the 1970s the relatively free reign enjoyed by consultancies in providing independent advice to clients on the use of computers within businesses was being challenged by those firms involved in the development of computer products. According to Cheadle (1995), firms such as John Hoskyns Associates were developing their own consultancy businesses, and by the turn of the decade were providing services to small and medium-sized companies.[15]

The 1970s was, therefore, a period when consultancy firms were generally defining their position with regard to deployment of services in information technology and technology firms were beginning to establish their own range of services of a consultancy nature. It was also a period when the scope of services were expanding to take account of advances in computer technology and in software applications. For example, INBUCON had by the end of the 1970s and the beginning of the 1980s expanded its range of services away from largely conducting feasibility studies to those that also included system design and implementation, computer strategy, system audits, project management, staff recruitment, and supplier selection (INBUCON undated). Supplier selection was carried out using an in-house developed system entitled 'Inbucon Systems Evaluation Technique'. This involved the evaluation of proposals in relation to hardware and software deployment, cost analysis and the management of formal tendering processes on behalf of the client, as well as providing recommendations on choice. In addition to these services, under the banner of 'Manufacturing and Design Technology', INBUCON Technology provided services to clients in other areas of technology. For example within computer aided engineering, the use of CAD and CAM programmes supported processes associated with production management. Services using CAD/CAM technologies included the development of strategies for use, system recommendations and the provision of training for engineers and operators. Other forms of technology were also associated with manufacturing management and automation, specifically high volume production lines, and these fell under the general label of 'Flexible Manufacturing Systems', or FMS. Within such systems, the use of robotic technologies, controlled through computer applications, provided an alternative to manual manufacturing methods; in the car manufacturing industry these functions included assembly tasks, welding and painting.

In addition to the direct application of technology, to provide greater assurance of the success of the application, softer services (the basic techniques of consultancy, for example consultation at all levels and the management of change) were and are a necessary prerequisite to support the change process. These softer services, the 'bread and butter' of consultancy from the perspective that the application of these separated out the management consulting companies from those purely supplying technology, as with all other forms of services tended to fall within either the areas of strategy or operations. From a strategic perspective, the provision of services associated with the identification of new markets, financial planning, future product development and design, as well as other forms of strategic services were applied in parallel with technological solutions in order to gain best value, or benefits, from the investment in technology. In terms of operations, process re-design, simplification and improvement were typical of the consultancy services provided to ensure both a smooth transition to technological change, and the harmonisation of old and new in order to optimise performance within the changing environment.

In general terms, the beginning of the 1980s provided an indication of the potential for growth in the broad areas associated with information technology into the future. Reviewing the performance of Peat, Marwick, Mitchell and Company in the 1980s, Wise (1982) reported that the growth in EDP consulting was in excess of 30 per cent on an annual basis. Whilst this is reference to growth within the Company internationally, it does reflect the growing importance of information technology at a more general level in terms of consultancy services. As an indication of the widespread use of IT in consultancy the 'Directory of Management Consultants in the UK 1983-84' identified a range of specialist areas and the firms associated with these within the publication (Management Consultancy Information Service 1983). Six specialist areas were referenced including identifying the firms providing those services; these included 'Management Information Systems' (in excess of 140 firms), 'Computer Feasibility Studies' (100 firms) and 'Computer Applications, Audit and Appraisal' (over 90 firms). The other service areas at that time were 'Information Retrieval Systems', 'Operations Research' and 'Word Processing'. In terms of the type of consultancies involved in providing these services, these included each of the major British generalist consultancies, accountancy company consultancy arms, international consultancies (principally those of American origin), software houses, and a range of small and medium-sized consultancies.

As the 1980s progressed the corporate supply of services in information technology broadened in response to changes in both the technology itself and the growing experience of management consultants within that whole environment. Generally speaking, the major consultancies at the time provided services in a range of areas associated with IT:

- *Strategy*   Including strategic studies and management information services in support of strategic objectives;
- *Systems Development and Evaluation*   Including hardware and software evaluation and selection, systems development and implementation (including infrastructure), system performance appraisals, and the application of micro and desktop equipments;
- *Support Services*   Including systems audit and security, project management, and training and development services;
- *Office Systems*   Including office automation, and clerical work measurement and improvement;
- *Manufacturing Systems*   Including computer aided engineering, robotics, and flexible manufacturing systems;
- *Communications Technology*   Including aspects with regard to both strategy and operations.

Because of the technical nature of much of the work carried out, a number of the consultancies adopted strategic alliances and partnerships with specialist companies. Typical of the range of services provided by the major management consultancies in the mid-1980s were those provided by Urwick Orr across its portfolio. These were categorised within the broad areas of 'Organisation and Management', 'Corporate Planning and Marketing', 'Human Resource Management' and 'Productivity Services'. Services in IT were both a fifth category within the portfolio and in support of aspects of each of the other main categories (Urwick, Orr and Partners Limited 1984b). For example, Urwick Orr developed a series of alliances based on specialisms in direct support of the Company's consultancy operations (Urwick, Orr and Partners c1985). These included BL Systems Limited with regard to manufacturing and business applications, BL Technology Limited for robotics, Delta CAE Limited for computer aided engineering, Design Audit Limited for equipment design and Corporate Business Systems Limited for office automation. Such strategic alliances and partnerships provided management consultancies with the technical expertise needed to support their operations in the absence of in-house facilities.

Overall, the two decades of the 1970s and 1980s witnessed an expansion of services in line with the progress made in the development of new technology. From a shaky start at the beginning of the 1970s, management consultancy at a general level grew steadily throughout the period. Table

9.1 provides a snapshot of the situation at the end of the period for the member companies of the Management Consultancies Association, revealing the growing importance of IT services to overall consultancy revenue.

Table 9.1   Comparison of Revenue of Services, 1989-1990

Services/Year	1989 £m (%)	1990 £m (%)	% change in revenue share
Information Technology and Systems	177 (31)	290 (41)	10
Financial and Administrative Systems	148 (26)	129 (18)	−8
Human Resources (including Selection and Interim Management)	77 (13)	84 (12)	−1
Production and Services Management (including technology, logistics, R&D and Quality Control)	68 (12)	73 (10)	−2
Corporate Strategy and Organisation Development	49 (8)	50 (7)	−1
Marketing and Corporate Communication	31 (5)	30 (4)	−1
Economic and Environmental Studies	27 (5)	36 (5)	0
Project Management	–	14 (2)	2
Total:	577 (100%)	706 (100%)	129 (22)

*   Percentages have been rounded-up and rounded-down.

Source: Management Consultancies Association (1990)

The revenue returns on the services supplied by the member companies of the Management Consultancies Association provides an important reminder of the growth in consultancy services generally, reflected in the rise of £129m or 22 per cent over the two years, and the significance of IT within them. All areas experienced growth in terms of revenue, with the exception of 'Financial and Administrative Systems', but services in information technology increased their share of the pot overall by ten per cent over the two year period. According to the Executive Director's statement within the report, this was a reflection of the importance of IT within all areas of consultancy work. This was a healthy position from which to enter into a new decade that witnessed change on a massive scale through the introduction of global network systems. These systems provided organisations and consultants with opportunities to exploit information technology even further through the development of e-business solutions that are supported through changes to relationship management, especially those relationships within organisations that include 'joined-up' solutions, between businesses (B2B), and between businesses and their customers (B2C).

e-Business and Beyond, 1990 to the Present

By the 1990s computer technology was smaller, more advanced, faster and more powerful, and more cost effective than it had been previously. There was widespread usage of IT and the early development of local and wide area networks (LANs and WANs) joined together business units in the sharing of information and processes.[16] The 1990s also witnessed the broadening of the World Wide Web away from the research and academic environments that spawned it into the business and personal computer sectors. The technologies associated with the Internet underpinned many of the developments concerned with the spread of IT and facilitated the arrival of e-business solutions in all its guises, embracing each and every aspect of management consultancy. It also spawned the development of a new business language based on terminology and acronyms peculiar to the use of information technology; a language that grows almost daily as new forms of technologies are developed in support of the wider application of electronic media for use in business and domestic markets.

Management consultancy has a significant orientation towards the delivery of services linked to information technology (Rassam 1998). Throughout the chapters covering the post-war period it has been strongly argued that IT is represented either directly or indirectly within each of the service areas associated with management consultancy, as well as being a distinctive area in its own right. Equally, it has been argued that it would be difficult, if not impossible, to identify consultancy work that was not linked in some way to IT, either as its focus or in some form of supporting role. This view is supported by Long (1998) who suggests that this has occurred partly through developments in IT and partly through businesses looking towards IT to provide some form of competitive advantage and, therefore, services related to IT fall within the domains of both strategy and operations in much the same way as other areas of consultancy activity tend to have a twin orientation.

The period of 1990 to the present day was dynamic in the sense that new forms of IT were being developed at a fast pace and management consulting services, in a bid to gain best value for clients, were continuously evolving in order to exploit these new technologies. The span of services today, the specialisms and the range of consultancies, and international and global markets all make for a complicated environment in which management consultants find themselves at the heart of service delivery. In order to untangle this complicated web and present a coherent picture this final section reviews two separate, but linked aspects of consultancy:

- Types of service providers.
- Types of services.

Through that review it will be possible to identify the use of technology and its deployment in markets throughout the world. Technology spans geographical boundaries and links together what in the past were disparate and separate functions.

Management consultancy has traditionally within the 20th century been made up of a corporate body consisting of sole practitioners, partnerships, co-operatives and consultancies of sizes ranging on a scale from small to large, with the general size of the major enterprises growing through the passage of time as the demand for management consulting services increased. Within that corporate body, especially with regard to consulting companies, management consulting was either the sole activity carried out or an important aspect of the overall business of the firm. Some consultants and consultancies operated solely in the domestic market whereas others had international interests, with the international aspect of consultancy more recently broadening out in support of a global marketplace. A number of consultants and consultancies are highly specialised, providing either a narrow range of services (some provide single-function services) or operating within niche markets; others are more generalist providing a greater range of services. Within those service areas, some operate at the strategic level and some are more concerned with operations, while others pitch their level of services to encompass the needs of the client regardless of level.

Within this mixed basket information technology further complicates the picture through its employment in all aspects of consultancy and at all levels, having increasingly become the case since the introduction of Internet technology in the 1990s. The use and employment of information technology, as has already been seen, resulted in the appearance of a new breed of consultants, today referred to as IT consultants. These specialists are found within consultancies and outside of them, the latter of which has produced a new mobile workforce operating on a time-limited contract basis. Because of the dynamics associated with information technology, a number of different types of consultancies are evident within the management consultancy environment:

Large Multinational Generalist Consultancies These provide a range of services that include the combination of IT services across their whole portfolio in concert with more traditional forms of consultancy. These firms tend to offer specialist e-business and IT services, organised within divisions that operate internationally (often globally), and supplement their in-house expertise with strategic alliances and partnerships on a short and long-term basis. Typical of these types of companies are PricewaterhouseCoopers, Accenture, McKinsey and A.T. Kearney.

Large Specialist IT Consultancies These provide a range of services with a distinctive e-business and IT orientation. Many link their bespoke in-house developed IT services with change management programmes designed to meet specific customer needs and gaining business benefits. These firms also operate on an international basis, but are less likely to rely on outside assistance for specialist support, although strategic alliances and partnering arrangements are becoming increasing common as a form of utilising economies of scale in those areas where the partners have dominance in specialisation. Typical of these companies are EDS, IBM, ICL and Logica, some have consultancy arms and others, like EDS with A.T. Kearney, have their own consulting companies within their group.

Narrow-Based Consultancies Usually the small and medium-sized firms, specialising in the deployment of IT solutions along a narrow range of services, combining a consultancy service with IT expertise, for example supply chain management, financial services, customer relationship management, etc.

Product-Based Consultancies Generally the smaller firms, specialising in one or a small number of services, usually including some form of training service in association with those services.

Sole Practitioners and Small Partnerships Specialising generally in a limited range of services or providing specific services in one specialist aspect of IT consultancy. This type of consultancy generally supports small and medium sized businesses, or larger consultancies in a contracting capacity.

Specialist Recruitment and Training Agencies A product of the rise in IT services, these provide specialist training and recruitment services to consultancies and other businesses.

The categorisation of consultancies above is broad-based and inevitably some consultancies will either fit outside each of the types or will be hybrid in nature, e.g. they will encompass aspects of two or more categories. The categorisation of consultancies with regard to services in IT will reflect the overall majority of organisations operating in Britain. However, this form of categorisation is not concerned with historical roots and in Britain history provides another way of modelling organisations and individuals involved in management consultancy and its use of information technology:

Generalist Management Consultancies These were formed specifically as a management consultancy to provide services in a range of areas. Most British generalist firms have either been subsumed into other consultancies or have become more specialised as the market has widened. Notable amongst these, and with a history that spans from the mid-point of the Second World War to the present, is the PA Consulting Group. The larger generalist consultancies tend to be specialism based in terms of organisation and employ IT specialists within each, as well as within those divisions that are technology-based.

Accountancy-Originated Consultancies In many cases with a tradition that spans into three centuries, these firms originated from professional accountancy companies that expanded their operations into consultancy. Amongst these are some of the major global firms that include Accenture, PricewaterhouseCoopers and Deloitte Consulting. These companies embraced information technology at an early stage in its development and they now have a strong tradition with regard to the supply of e-business solutions.

International Consultancies The majority of whom originated in the United States, these expanded outside of their country of origin in order to broaden their markets. In Britain the first instance of this phenomenon occurred in the 1920s with the arrival of the Bedaux company, although the main migratory wave occurred in the post-Second World War period with the arrival of firms such as McKinsey and Company, A.T. Kearney and Arthur D. Little, among a host of others. Many are organised on a global basis with specialist divisions, including global IT solutions, that span international markets.

IT Consultancies A phenomenon of the post-Second World War period with the development of computer-based technologies, developed specifically to provide IT-based services, many also providing advisory services in support of the deployment of IT. These consultancies, typified by IBM, moved into consultancy as an evolutionary process and now largely supply IT-based consulting services, although some have moved into other areas as a means of broadening their portfolios.

Niche Consultancies These tend to be the small and medium-sized firms that specialise in aspects of management consulting services. In terms of IT many specialise in specific aspects of the service and also provide consultants on a contracting basis to other firms in the specialisms required.

Independent Consultancies and Sole Practitioners Most of these are small and medium-sized firms, and sole practitioners. One or two may be generalist in nature, but the majority are specialists in the sense that they provide a narrow range of services.

Whatever form of classification is used, there is little doubt that the development of information technology has brought with it a significant level of growth for the management consulting community. This has become more evident in the period since 1990 with the development of e-business systems, providing electronic relationships between businesses and between those business and their customers.

In order to gain an insight into the value of IT to consultancy, Table 9.2 below indicates the revenue for services in relation to information technology for the member companies of the Management Consultancies Association for the period 1994-2000. What it indicates is that services in information technology are worth almost £1bn, commanding nearly two-fifths of total revenue for the member companies of the MCA at the end of the period. In terms of market share within Europe a similar pattern emerges with combined information technology services commanding 43.4 per cent of total consultancy revenue in 1999, with advance projections indicating that revenue share would increase to nearly 50 per cent in 2000 (FEACO 1999). Whilst FEACO classifies services in information technology services under three headings, 'IT Consulting' (23.2 per cent), 'IT Systems Development/Integration' (9.7 per cent) and 'Others' (10.5 per cent), this provides further evidence of the value of IT to management consultancy.

Table 9.2   Revenue of IT Services, 1994-2000

Year	IT Consultancy Revenue £m	IT Systems Development Revenue £m	IT Services Total Revenue £m	% of Total UK Consultancy Revenue
1994	258	213	471	55.3
1995	263	208	471	48.7
1996	280	186	468	42.5
1997	254	247	501	37.9
1998	341	407	748	44.3
1999	285	316	601	36.9
2000	465	469	934	38.8

* Total consultancy revenue does not include revenue for outsourcing services.

Sources: Management Consultancies Association (1996, 1998 and 2000)

But what are these services? The Management Consultancies Association classify them under two general headings, 'IT Consultancy' and 'IT Systems Development'. Within IT, as with other forms of consultancy services, each consultancy tends to adopt its own form of classification, largely based on its method of organisation and technical expertise. Previous chapters have indicated how consultancy services are categorised within some consulting companies and how information technology is both a distinct specialism in its own right as well as transcending each other service area. Even within specialisms associated with information technology there is no general classification, some consultancies separate out IT services and others include them within each type of service area within their portfolios. For those that separate out IT services specifically, a large number further distinguish between IT consultancy and e-business solutions, although other forms of nomenclature are often used, for example e-commerce. From an objective perspective, and ignoring individual service delivery, the classification adopted within this account will take into consideration both the major aspects of consultancy, 'strategy' and 'operations', and break down service delivery into a number of distinct branches. Within that breakdown, cognisance should be taken of the industry sector involved, as well as the generic and individual nature of the services. For example, consultancies will develop both standard services where the core of the function is largely generic and bespoke services where they are distinctly tailored to meet the needs of the individual clients. Within that framework, particular industries may have specific requirements that can be applied across the whole sector, for example within banking and insurance e-commerce solutions may dominate, whereas within manufacturing industry supply chain services are the central feature.

Taking each aspect of consultancy in turn, strategy can mean both business strategy and IT strategy at the same time; often they are described as one and the same thing. From the perspective of this account, information technology is viewed as a supporting aspect of the business and strategy is concerned with strategic deployment in support of the business objectives, even though those objectives could be re-aligned through the application of IT. In consulting terms, strategy consulting can be both to do with strategic development and organisation direction through a whole organisation approach, embracing issues in support of the development and application of objectives and aims. The role of IT within this area of consultancy is concerned with providing value and advantage to businesses in pursuance of their objectives. According to Long (1998) there are three main channels of involvement when a generic model of strategic IT services is applied: the development and deployment of IT solutions, and benefits realisation. The Generic Model is a way of viewing the deployment of IT services across the range of services provided by management consultants, specifically IT consultants, and the interrelationships between each aspect of the service. It is a high level view of the work of management consultants in a range of diverse environments that could each command its own model of delivery. In parallel with these, IT consultants play their part in reviewing and auditing current and future IT systems for their clients, and advising them on current and potential future developments applicable to their clients' business areas.

Long suggests that typically strategic IT consulting commences with advice and guidance on strategy and direction, followed by the development and implementation of one or a number of the three forms of IT services identified above. However, within this account it is intended to describe consultancy services within the two broad groupings adopted throughout this publication for the post-war period and attempt to categorise those services within each broad group. Examining strategic services initially, the following represents both the situation in the mid-1990s and the current situation at the turn of the century.[17]

IT Strategy

Today strategy services are an important aspect of management consulting within the vast number of portfolios of firms within Britain. The mid-1990s saw this form of service also as being important, although its spread throughout consultancies was less significant, being represented in approximately half of the member companies of the MCA. The range and depth of services provided by management consultancies differed greatly among individual firms and to a large extent were and are determined by the type of consultancy and its evolution over time. The supply of strategic IT services tends to parallel the delivery of strategy services in general, except where IT is the central focus of the firm. Typical of the type of services provided by consultancies is the development, planning and implementation of IS (Information Systems), and the development and implementation of IT and e-business strategies. The adoption of a high level approach to the implementation of strategic IT solutions elevates information technology as a crucial aspect of the corporate strategic decision-making process. As a consequence of their involvement in the strategic decision-making process within client firms, IT consultants offer a range of services in support of strategy development; these like other services vary between consultancies. Included within these are:

Risk Management Identifying, defining and managing the risk of adopting a specific course of action or employing a strategy involving a specific IT solution or package of measures. Through a thorough and definitive approach to the management of risks, success is a more likely outcome than failure. Risk management was an emerging aspect of consultancy services in the mid-1990s, but it is far more common today as a portfolio item. Potentially included within risk is the development of 'what if' type scenarios, both to assist with the management of risk and to offer choice of strategic decisions.

Strategic Outsourcing and Partnerships Identifying the need, defining the strategy, identifying the partner and service, and managing the change. The use of strategic partners and the development of outsourcing arrangements are methodologies that can be employed to minimise or spread the risk, as well as improving the level of service for a client where it has limited expertise and resources in the particular field. The potential outcomes of employing outsourcing strategies include a reduction in costs, improvements to service levels, greater flexibility and a reduction in the requirement for re-skilling the workforce. Often individual consultancies provide expertise in specific industry sectors or in the types of services (for example hardware deployment and supporting functions such as payroll) and are more likely to have preferred arrangements with a small number of partners. In some instances, consultancies are the strategic partners for clients, utilising their own in-house expertise to harness the benefits of outsourcing. This aspect of consultancy service in the mid-1990s was beginning to be an important part of the corporate business of consultancy, although not as widespread as it is today.

Benefits Management As part of the strategic decision-making process rather than as a post-deployment event, Benefits Management can be used to determine the value and negative aspects of the proposed change and inform on the direction and pace of that change. Benefits management can be used as both a strategic and an operational service. In terms of strategy, a benefits analysis can determine the value and effect of change at the higher level as a means of informing the strategic decision-making process. In terms of operations, benefits management can be used to focus on the individual change processes through gaining maximum value from investment in IT. It can be used for each application of IT as a separate event or in retrospect once change has taken place to re-align or improve processes and operations in order to gain that value. Benefits Management, used in this context as a generic term, is known by a whole range of titles referring to gaining maximum value from the use of IT. This has always been a core aspect of consultancy services in relation to investment in IT and at the strategic level is used to inform clients of the value of adopting specific approaches compared to a range of other solutions.

Management Information Systems The development of management information and intelligence services can be used for reviewing business performance in line with business objectives and aims. The development of reporting mechanisms at the strategic decision-making level determines the key indicators and performance measures of the client organisation. In line with strategic planning and development, the provision of services in relation to management information systems through automated data capture and warehousing techniques had become almost as important an aspect of IT consulting in the mid-1990s as they are today.

Strategic e-Business Solutions A cornerstone of consultancy services today, e-business solutions was emerging in the mid-1990s as a distinct specialism within management consultancy. These tended to be strategy specific then, for example strategies in relation to supply chain management, or in support of specific aspects of the business such as enterprise resource planning. Today, however, they are common aspects of consultancy assignments across the whole range, specifically those that deal with relationships between businesses (B2B) or between businesses and customers (B2C). Often, as alluded to above, e-business solutions are distinctly specialised within consultancies, representing a specific form of service within individual portfolios.

The range of services described above are only a selection of those generally provided by management consultancies in support of the strategic objective. Strategic support services, by their very nature, are also those that can be found within the operational offerings of management consulting companies portfolios dependent upon the setting employed within the client firm. The main thrust of IT services, however, are those that are targeted at either specific aspects of information technology or within other service areas in support of their strategic and operational delivery.

IT Operations

As with all other consultancy services, IT operations consulting varies greatly among consultancies and, as indicated above, some strategic services also have a role to play within operations when pitched at the appropriate level within the client firm. Adopting the perspective that strategic services are provided to senior management and in the high-level decision-making processes within an organisation as a means of assisting the client in developing its strategy and direction, operations is to do with all other aspects of the business. IT operations, whether they are concerned with systems development or IT consulting, using the MCA's categorisation, are to do with providing solutions at the operational level of the firm, whether systems specific, department specific or in support of key strategic objectives. As a means of identifying the different aspects of operations, a useful way of categorising the work of management and IT consultants is to group together like services under generic headings. Whilst this cannot possibly identify all services supplied in this field, it will have the effect of providing an indication of the work being carried out.

Feasibility Studies and Surveys An aspect of IT consulting from the very beginning when consultants first became involved with computer-based technologies, the term 'feasibility' was still evident within some portfolios in the mid-1990s, although it has lost its significance as a descriptive label today. Feasibility studies, based on either client specifications or through an analysis of the business needs, may come in many guises. For example, often the term 'requirements specification' is used to mean the same thing, subsuming client specification and business analysis within a single approach. Feasibility studies can be a reference to a whole range of services, often based on the specialist capabilities of the consultancy. These include network solutions, use of Internet technologies, software applications and bespoke development by third parties, hardware delivery, and database applications.

Systems and Software Development Many consultancies today offer services in systems and application development designed to meet specific client needs. These can encompass solutions based on bespoke development, off the shelf packages or any combination of the two. They can also include network, hardware and software solutions in any combination. They can reach across the organisation or be department or application specific. In the mid-1990s services in this area included systems design and implementation, architecture development, systems integration, application development and network communications. Today the range is almost endless, with new technologies and applications being developed with regular frequency, either for specific business processes or to cover a range of common functions. Equally, development is carried out in support of strategic objectives or to help drive future change. Ranking highly among initiatives in support of development are those related to e-business solutions, IT architecture (including Internet technologies and networking), and the integration of existing and new technologies.

IT Project Management In recognition of the differences inherent within information technology solutions when compared with, say, project management based on physical structures, IT project management is a distinct field of activity. The management of IT projects by consultants is an important aspect at all stages of the delivery of solutions where change is brought about by information technology in its range of guises. IT project management has been an important aspect of consultancy services throughout the 1990s and remains so to the present day. Most consultancies provide services in this area and some distinctly specialise in all its aspects, including the training of client personnel.

Support Services Almost a catch-all aspect of IT consulting, support services in terms of this account is concerned with those aspects of consultancy that cannot easily be subsumed in their entirety within the other areas; these are a diverse range of services many of which are specific to individual consultancies. In the mid-1990s these included systems security, systems support, and IT recruitment and training. Often the title IT consulting was used to describe many aspects of the support function. Today each of these areas remain equally important, with IT training and recruiting expanding faster than many other areas of consultancy services. Systems audit and systems security, in response to change and the globalisation of markets has also become increasingly important as supporting services.

Specialist IT Consulting Services Throughout management consultancy's corporate portfolio, a whole range of specialist services has emerged that cover a single or small number of highly specialised aspects of IT consulting. These are largely provided by individual consultants or the smaller enterprises that have developed an expertise in a narrow range of fields. These are difficult to categorise because there are so many that could be included, but a common feature of a number of these is that they combine consultancy with training or coaching to allow the application to be continued after the assignment has been completed. In some instances, highly specialised software applications lie at the heart of these services where a technique or a process is the primary objective of its use.

Outsourcing Table 8.3 in Chapter 8 highlights the importance of this aspect of consultancy work. There are principally two main thrusts to this form of service: consultant services in the development and implementation of outsourcing strategies and applications, and the provision of outsourcing services by the management consultancies acting as the supplier. Outsourcing can cover a range of services and functions, largely specialised within consultancies where the supply of in-house services is the dominant feature. These tend to occur where the development of in-house expertise would be too expensive for the client to gain advantage or where greater economies of scale could be acquired elsewhere. Outsourcing is, therefore, an approach to business where greater benefits and the reduction of risk can be obtained through passing on operational responsibility for a function to a third-party supplier.

Strategic Alliances and Partnerships These are an important aspect of consultancy work in an environment where the dynamics of change and the breadth of service delivery force consultancies to seek arrangements in those areas where they themselves do not command specific expertise or scale of available service. Often arrangements are reciprocated when the partner requires expertise in those areas where the consultancy holds the dominant position. In the mid-1990s strategic alliances were less well known as a practical solution, although one or two of the major consultancies began to forge partnerships in order to provide a wider range of services. Today, alliance partnerships are relatively commonplace, providing consultancies with the ability to deliver solutions that require the application of complex technologies and processes that otherwise would be beyond the capabilities of individual firms.

Computer Aided Engineering CAD/CAM remained a small but important aspect of consultancy work throughout the 1990s. The use of computer technology in the design and development stage improved the speed and efficiency of the development of products, and a small number of consultancies provided services in assisting clients in the use of the technology.

Production Management Historically an important aspect of consultancy work, production management deserves special mention through the utilisation of technologies to improve aspects of the production process and the creation of supply chain environments for leveraging wide ranging improvements to the production process across a range of geographical and business sectors. Chapter 6 specifically covered this aspect of consultancy work, but to leave it out of information technology would generate a void within the overall range of services provided throughout the 1990s, specifically the period from the mid-1990s to the present day.

This high level review of the involvement of information technology in management consultancy cannot do justice to the detail overall within this service area. In quantitative and remunerative terms, and in the way in which IT spans all aspects of management consulting, services in information technology are the most important of all aspects of management consulting today, a trend that will continue into the future.

One final point, by way of a health warning, is that while the importance of information technology to management consulting is difficult to overstate in corporate terms, individual services can go out of vogue. Over the recent past, the phenomenon of the dot.com companies that appeared with much hype have been going through an extremely shaky period with many returning high losses and a significant number going out of business altogether. Specifically within this context, dot.com companies is a reference to Internet-based company operations in a range of services, highly automated, with minimal back office support; typically, there would be very little actual capital value associated with these operations. There has been a whole range of explanations of why this has occurred from lack of business acumen through to unrealistic market opportunities. Recently, an article in *IT Consultant* entitled 'Perishing Pure Plays' suggested that the future of specialised e-consultancies associated with the dot.com companies is looking uncertain.[18] The reason given in the article is that many of these consultancies have entirely specialised in this field, using technology to drive change without paying full regard to the use of established business practices. In other words, failing to use consultancy techniques in addition to employing technology. Because of this, the article suggests that companies are turning towards more traditional consultancies that have an e-business portfolio in order to combine the skills associated with business improvement in concert with the potential gains of technological development.

Notes

1. The term 'information technology' is used to describe the use of computers in all instances throughout this text unless otherwise stated.
2. For example, typical of the technology in use within British banks in the inter-war period were accounting machines that supported data handling and the production of customer statements. This had the effect of driving change through the standardisation of procedures and operations in an expanding and increasingly competitive environment (Wardley 2000).
3. The term 'analogue' is used to describe a method of modelling to examine specific problems. Typical functions for analogue machines were weather predicting, tide formulations and, for military and scientific purposes, code breaking and trajectory analysis in weapons production.
4. Digital simply means that the computer relies on numbers in order to make calculations (0 for on and 1 for off). Colossus, however, was not public knowledge at the time and, whilst it is now recognised as the first digital computer, it was only during the mid-1970s that it became known (Brech 2002c).
5. In 1954 LEO Computers Limited was formed and the LEO progressed through three generations of manufacture. The LEO was installed in a range of businesses and government departments throughout its lifetime. These included, apart from J. Lyons, the Ford Motor Company, W.D. and H.O. Wills Limited, Ministry of Pensions, H.M. Customs and Excise, and Shell-Mex and BP Limited. The last machine was de-commissioned in the 1980s.
6. It was reported at a meeting of the Industrial Management Research Organisation in September 1954 that eleven office machine and electrical engineering companies were active in the development of computer technology in Britain (Brech 2002c).
7. Stored programmes based on a computer language (for example Fortran and Cobal), resident within the computer's memory, rather than a binary code, made it much easier to instruct the technology to carry out a series of functions.
8. Whilst research in computer-aided engineering was underway in the 1950s and early programmes were introduced in the 1960s, it was not until the advent of the desktop computer and improvements to software applications that affordability and access provided widespread use of Computer Aided Design (CAD) and Computer Aided Manufacturing (CAM). Assignments involving the use of CAD/CAM were carried out by management consultants progressively as the technology improved and the benefits increased.
9. As a general definition throughout this publication, e-business is a reference to the conduct of business using some form of electronic media, usually Internet-based technologies in the wider sense, but also network and wireless enabled technologies.
10. The United States was selected because it was believed that it was a more mature environment for the deployment of the new technology at that time (Hunt 1983).
11. Urwick Diebold was a joint venture between Urwick Orr and an American computer specialist John Diebold. This partnership survived until 1970 when ties were severed.

The reason given for the break up of the partnership was that John Diebold himself was becoming too generalist in his approach to computing, thus failing to provide the focus that Urwick Orr believed was appropriate within its own environment. A new Company was formed within the Group, which was given the title of Urwick Dynamics, taking over the role previously filled by Urwick Diebold and the use of its acronym UD.

12. The Company had a less than vigorous start because, although some within business circles were predicting that computers were the way forward, many within businesses could not identify the benefits of the new technology. Those that did primarily adopted the technology to establish their positions at the forefront of their fields, and these tended to be the more progressive and larger organisations within Britain. However, information technology was in its early stages of development concerning general business employment and the use of computers up to that point, and even beyond, had not always proven cost effective, in fact the reverse was generally true.

13. There are numerous accounts of the expansion in use of computing equipment at that time, but Price Waterhouse provides a practical example of real-time growth. In 1963 it was estimated that of its clients, 63 of them were utilising computer equipment. By 1967 this figure had risen to 275, more than four times the 1963 figure (Price Waterhouse 1967).

14. Lockyer and Partners used some part-time consultants who were recruited from graduate business schools.

15. John Hoskyns Associates developed modular computer software programmes that were, at that time, concerned with financial systems and those associated with inventory control (Cheadle 1995). One software application that the Company developed was an early version of today's enterprise management systems, specifically for smaller companies. The software was developed as a suite of applications so that clients could decide which particular aspect(s) they would use.

16. The use of server technology, joining together a network of desktop units, was beginning to replace the massively cumbersome main frame computer systems that dominated IT environments in the past.

17. References for the mid-1990s are taken from the Management Consultancies Association (1995) 'Directory of Member Firms and their Services to Clients 1995/96'. The current situation is confirmed from the portfolios of a range of consultancies of all sizes and types operating within Britain in 2001.

18. *IT Consultant*, May 2001, pp.15-20.

CHAPTER 10

The International and Global Aspects of Management Consultancy

British management consultancy today is headed by a group of global and international management consulting companies. Beneath these in terms of size is a whole range of small and medium sized companies, many of which have a presence abroad, and sole practitioners and small partnerships. Some of the latter operate only within Britain and others venture abroad exploiting opportunities whenever they arise. Among this mix of enterprises are other organisations and individuals that do not fit within this basic model, but that is the nature of consultancy, the firms within it are as diverse as the range of services they provide. One would be forgiven for thinking that the structure of management consultancy has always been the same, certainly in recent memory, say the last 10 years or so, but consultancy in Britain has evolved slowly to assume its present organisational form. A wider historical examination of management consultancy provides a picture of an environment that has moved through three distinct phases of development: domestic, international and global.

This final short chapter in the series of five reviewing distinct aspects of the post-war scenario in Britain examines management consultancy from a geographical perspective in terms of operations. It is concerned with the spread of consultancy abroad by British firms and the migration into Britain by overseas consultancies in an increasingly global industry. Before such an examination is possible two things are necessary to provide an understanding of what is meant by phases of development and what may have caused them. Firstly, phases of development, and their evolutionary processes, can be understood through defining what is meant by the terms domestic, international and global operations.

Domestic Phase The activities of management consultancies within Britain in which operations were wholly or largely carried out in client companies where solutions were applied that had little or no impact abroad, or where assignments in international client companies were specific to their British operations. This includes the work of some international consultancies that set up specific country-centred operations in Britain, and where their direct management of operations occurred in this country (for example see Chapter 3 and the Bedaux company). This phase in Britain was largely a product of the period to 1945.

International Phase The activities of British management consultancies and overseas firms operating in Britain where the control of international operations was carried out from the centre in their country of origin. This is regardless of whether or not specific country names were given to the subsidiaries operating overseas. These operations tended to be country-specific in the areas in which they were applied, with little or no co-ordination in terms of a global marketplace or operational environment. This phase was largely a product of the period between 1945 and 1990, although international operations by British consultancies and overseas firms without a global orientation continue to occur to the present.

Global Phase The activities of management consultancies, regardless of country of origin, that have a global orientation either in terms of specific services or of operations more generally. This phase of development recognises the blurring of international boundaries and the partial loss of identity of country of origin of individual consultancies. This phase is supported by advances in technology that do not recognise geographical boundaries, for example Internet technologies, and the operations of client companies that are globally positioned. This phase is largely a product of the post-1990 period.

The introduction of this chapter indicated that phases of development are largely concerned with the wider movements in consultancy and cannot represent the activities of all enterprises within the management consultancy environment worldwide. These are trends in terms of development of the major consultancies operating both in Britain and elsewhere within the world within the specific time frame identified as applicable to Britain.

These changes came about through two separate, but linked, forces that have had the effect of eroding national boundaries so that there is the appearance of a global marketplace in terms of service delivery: technology that recognises no national boundaries and the business environment that has increasingly exploited international markets. The first of these, technology, was well documented in Chapter 9, specifically in terms of network technologies that include the Internet and e-mail systems that link together geographically dispersed organisations and partnerships through an electronic communications medium that bridges national boundaries. Chapters 6 and 9 also pointed towards specific forms of services, exemplified through the concept and operation of supply chain management that link companies in a range of countries and environments into an interdependent whole through applying an integrated approach to production by exploiting communications and common aims. These partnerships not only included production and service companies, but also strategic alliances between groups of consultancies, and consultancies and other forms of service providers. Once again it is the exploitation of technology that made this possible through leveraging the strengths of individual partners in specific business areas or technological application.

In parallel with technological development an evolving business environment has also moved through phases of organisational change. Each of the previous chapters has described the background scenario as it affected the specific subject in hand and it is possible to pick out from them the evolutionary nature of business that have also included domestic, international and global orientation. Domestic companies, servicing domestic markets, whether local, regional or national, have been present throughout the time frame associated with this history. Strategies that have included consolidation, mergers, diversification and alliances in product ranges and locations have provided the necessary structure for companies to become internationally positioned. However, there is a difference between a multinational company and a global one, with global organisations being a phenomenon of more recent times.

There is probably no one definition that is accepted by all of what marks out the difference between a multinational company and a global or transnational organisation. Some definitions centre on the branding of products, where common brands are present throughout the world, thus the national identities of origin are partially lost through its common brand name throughout the world. Some other definitions look towards markets that are bonded by a common currency, for example the dollar, that are traded globally with equal recognition, regardless of national setting. Others have argued that there cannot be a truly global company even though some may trade with apparent ease across national borders. That is because it is difficult, if not impossible, to lose the national identity of the company of origin and that consideration has to be made for the different cultures present in each of its areas of operation. At the same time, the term global would indicate that the whole world was open in terms of a single market, but there still remain barriers to trade in some countries where overseas companies are not viewed as entirely welcome. Regardless of definition and the present possibility of creating a truly global organisation that satisfies the conditions and constraints of all definitions, recent research projects have indicated that the world is becoming a smaller place in terms of trade in goods and services, presenting the possibility of moving towards a more global model of business organisation.

The Management Consultancies Association created in 1997 a 'Think Tank' for the purpose of conducting research to pool the collective knowledge of consultants, businesses and government. The second in a series of five reports, entitled 'Book 2: Globalisation and the Knowledge Society – The New Drivers for the Business and the Workforce', suggests that multi-national businesses are being transformed from consisting of self-contained business units throughout the world to a single company operating in a single market that is global. The report goes on to identify a number of factors that have helped shape an emerging global model of business (Management Consultancies Association 1999b).[1] Amongst these factors are strategic issues, technological issues, barriers and facilitators of trade, and social and economic factors.

Whilst the report was written from the perspective of the United Kingdom, it develops a model of change that is itself trans-national and it is within the environment described within the report that the global phase of consultancy can be positioned. Within that environment consultancy itself could be considered both a driver for change and a follower as the global strategies of companies are developed and supported by individual consultancies within their portfolios of services. That is the end point in this chapter and before reaching that both the domestic and international models need to be discussed in order to identify the evolution of management consultancy.

The Domestic Phase

The Domestic Phase, by and large, covers the period since the beginning of management consultancy until the end of the Second World War. It is concerned with delivery of consultancy services by British companies and sole practitioners on the British mainland, and by one or two American firms that set up operations in this country as autonomous units to exploit the opportunities afforded in Britain at that time.[2] For many consulting enterprises, mainly the smaller firms and sole practitioners, Britain remains their operational environment, providing all the opportunities necessary at present to sustain their existence and growth. However, this situation occurred by accident rather than design during the period to 1945.

Prior to 1926 sole practitioners and small partnerships operated on the British mainland in the specific environments appropriate to their skills and narrow portfolio of services. The arrival of the Bedaux company in 1923 and the setting up of a permanent office in 1926 was the first attempt by a non-British consulting company to internationalise its operations in Britain. It quickly became apparent that the employment of services developed elsewhere at that time, without taking into account the peculiarities of the British industrial environment, met with resistance from both client personnel and senior managers and employees of the British operation (see Chapters 3 and 4). This attempt to internationalise consultancy operations in Britain failed and the Bedaux company eventually established itself as an autonomous British company. Even the attempt by another American company at about the same time, Stevenson, Jordan and Harrison, failed to materialise in terms of a major international presence on British soil. Britain was dominated throughout this history to 1945 by consultancies that operated as British domestic firms.

The British mainland, therefore, formed the basis for operations by domestic firms with one or two exceptions throughout this period. For example, Associated Industrial Consultants (AIC) had been conducting assignments in Northern Ireland since about 1935. These were relatively small-scale assignments and did not in any way reflect a growing trend at that time in terms of widening the Company's area of operations. Eventually, an office was opened in Belfast to strategically position AIC in both Northern Ireland and Eire, but advantage was not taken of this until after the War (Ferguson 1999). Production Engineering had always maintained close links with Canada through its association with Woods Gordon and by 1939 had conducted an assignment at a Newfoundland paper mill (Wayne 1959). However, assignments in the period prior to the War were opportunistic and whilst there may have been ambitions to expand operations outside of Britain by individual companies, these were unrealised. The Second World War witnessed some international work (see Chapter 5) but this was in support of the war effort and not part of any expansionist policies. In any event, the War prevented movements outside of the United Kingdom.

The whole of the first part of this historical account to 1945 has provided examples of the domestic operations of the management consultancy companies operating in Britain. Individual consultancies were expanding in the UK and, whilst plans may have been developed to grow elsewhere, concentrated their efforts on the British domestic scene through the development of a growing portfolio of services. For the major consultancies 1945 and the cessation of hostilities opened up new opportunities for growth in wider markets abroad, and the post-1945 period was one in which the development of international business was an important feature of consultancy operations.

The International Phase

The International Phase commenced in the post war period in Britain and is reflected by two parallel but opposite movements. British consultancies looked towards overseas markets, initially mainly those with a colonial history, to expand their operations abroad and foreign consultancies came to Britain as part of their international expansionist policies. Therefore, these are two aspects of a similar trend resulting in the internationalisation of management consultancy.

In terms of time in the British case expansion overseas from Britain was the first movement in this international phase of consultancy operations. With regard to overseas firms, internationalisation was a phenomenon of earlier periods, although not in Britain (Kipping 1996; McKenna 1995).

Consultancy Overseas

In the immediate aftermath of war the concept of international operations was being developed by the major British domestic consultancies. Initially these were viewed as being geographical extensions to the services supplied in Britain with a strong orientation towards improvements to productivity using techniques that had been developed at home. The general strategy employed by British consultancies at first was the employment of consultants from Britain on assignment abroad. Eventually as the demand for services spread within countries and in geographical areas overseas, local offices and subsidiary and associate companies were formed employing local consultants. Growth in terms of the portfolio of services abroad paralleled similar growth patterns in Britain.

In the five years following the end of the Second World War a number of the major consultancies began to make inroads into international markets. Closer to home, making use of its Belfast office, Associated Industrial Consultants ventured into Eire and conducted assignments for clients such as Waterford Ironfounders Limited and for Bord Na Mona, a government peat organisation. As the number of assignments increased a further office was established in Dublin to co-ordinate activities south of the border. Whilst until 1943 assignments carried out in Northern Ireland were relatively small-scale, an important assignment for Newforge Limited (later to become Robert Wilson and Sons Limited), a company engaged in war supply production, resulted in considerable savings in terms of overhead costs. Newforge provided references for AIC and this led to quite a number of further assignments on both sides of the Irish border; by 1965 over 460 assignments had been carried out in Ireland by the Company (Brownlow 1972). In 1947 the Company appointed a director with responsibilities for Africa, New Zealand and Australia. Although the first work in Australia and New Zealand was not carried out until the mid to late-1950s, in 1948 the first assignment in Africa was carried out for the East African Railways and Harbours Administration in Kenya. This was largely a training assignment in operational and administrative tasks, although the provision of advice in relation to new business ventures also formed a key part of the overall assignment. The Johannesburg office remained the administrative hub of the African operation until 1959 when subsidiary offices were opened up in other countries. Having earlier severed its links with its parent company (see Chapter 3 and 4), AIC found itself competing with consultants from the Bedaux Company for Africa Limited, a subsidiary of the International Bedaux Company Incorporated.

Closer to home, by 1947 Production Engineering had been engaged in providing services in France, typically improving the processes associated with mineral water production. This heralded the commencement of one of its key objectives of expansion abroad (Wayne 1959) and in 1950 Production Engineering (South Africa) (Pty) Limited was formed as an associate company.[3] In the early years the work of this associate company in South Africa centred on the gold mining industry with prestigious clients such as Ashanti Goldfields Corporation Limited. Subsequently, mining and quarrying became one of Production Engineering's specialist fields with the formation of Mining Services (PE) Limited being a later edition to its associate infrastructure (Wayne 1959). Personnel Administration, looking even further afield, commenced its international operations in 1948. A visit by the Chairman, Ernest Butten, to Australia in the March of that year resulted in a series of assignments being sold. The first assignment was carried out for British Tube Mills by three British consultants, specifically travelling to Australia to complete the task, producing an increase in output by 30 per cent and operative productivity rose by 40 per cent (Bowman 1983). Later in 1948 ten local consultants were employed, two of these consultants travelled to Britain by flying boat (a journey of eight days) to complete their consultancy training (Bowman 1983). By 1958 the consultant force consisted of 60 professional personnel and 10 years later over 100 consultants were operating in Australia. By the early 1980s PA (as it was then known) boasted the 'largest comprehensive' consultancy company in Australia (Bowman 1983).

After this initial period of internationalisation British consultancies expanded their operations to all four corners of the globe. Initially these centred on the European market and former colonial countries. Unlike the majority of other major consultancies operating internationally by the 1950s, Harold Whitehead and Partners, with an international reputation that had been established at its formation (see Chapter 4), retained its British company title whenever operating overseas. Recognising the uniqueness of the culture of individual countries, services were tailored to take account of the peculiarities of the situation. The main thrust of service delivery lay in the direction of improving efficiency within companies engaged in both the public and private sectors of the various countries. Services within these sectors included 'production' (productivity services), 'distribution and selling', and 'organisation and control'. It was an assignment in organisation and staff recruitment that won the company the Queens Award for Industry for Export Services in 1974. Harold Whitehead and Partners was the first consultancy to gain this prestigious award and throughout a large part of the post-war period the Company gained a large portion of its revenue from its international operations.

The 1950s were an important period for British consultancies in establishing their international operations and it heralded the way forward for greater expansion throughout the remainder of the twentieth century. The first overseas assignment for Urwick, Orr and Partners Limited occurred in Singapore at the beginning of the 1950s hailing the commencement of the Company's international business. The purpose of the assignment was to review the structure and work of the Singapore Civil Service in readiness for independence from Britain. The initial survey took three months to complete, and the full assignment involved three consultants over a three-year period.[4] In 1952 the Company expanded into Canada and the first assignment involved work in a high alloy steel foundry business near Toronto where the existing premises were being extended. The work involved improving production methods, and the establishment of labour and materials cost control procedures. Further work followed in the mining industry and this became the mainstay of the Canadian operation for the next 39 years (Thompson 1994). In 1955 the Company in Canada amalgamated with McDonald Currie (a Canadian accountancy practice) and subsequently became known as 'Urwick Currie'. The international work of the company spread throughout the world in the ensuing years with Urwick Orr becoming recognised as an international management consulting organisation.

Similarly, AIC expanded into Canada in the 1950s with the establishment of Associated Industrial Consultants (Canada 1952) Limited. However, the Company found that the North American continent had a well-established consultancy industry and, therefore, AIC concentrated on assignments in relation to management accounting, preventative maintenance of equipment and maintenance scheduling. These were areas of consulting that had not been well supported by American and Canadian consultancies. By the mid-1950s Production Engineering of London Pty Limited was formed to conduct assignments in Australia, operationally commencing in 1956 in a fiercely competitive environment. The first assignment conducted there was with the Australian Mercantile Land and Finance Company that was largely concerned with wool production (Howell undated). This assignment centred on wool merchandising, specifically at sheep packing and despatching stations. As the decade progressed British consultancies were competing amongst themselves in a range of geographical areas throughout the world. Typical of these was Australasia where consultants from the major consultancies had established their international operations. One of the last to develop a presence there was AIC which carried out its first assignment in 1957. The Company's first assignment unusually occurred in New Zealand; the other major consultancies initially centred their operations in Australia. This assignment was concerned with improving throughput in a new industry producing 'phormium', a locally grown fibrous substance used to replace imported 'jute'. By 1965, 300 assignments had been carried out in New Zealand, including work in support of local authorities, the utilities, forestry operations, and a whole range of industries and commercial undertakings. In Australia the first assignment occurred in 1959 for a subsidiary of a British engineering company. Owing to the geographical spread of work in this type of industry, it was largely discontinued. Assignments were carried out in a diverse range of fields, including administration in schools, hospitals, executive selection, costings for prescription charges and, later, computer feasibility studies. This latter form of assignment expanded into Singapore, Malaya and Hong Kong. By 1965 the work of AIC abroad accounted for 15 per cent of the total company income (Brownlow 1972).

By the 1960s international work became one of the mainstays of British consultancy operations. The practice of sending British consultants on overseas assignments was largely discontinued as international offices were established by the companies to administer and control their geographically dispersed operations. As the major accounting companies firmly established their own consulting businesses, they also expanded their operations abroad. The principal difference between these and the generalist consultancies was that accounting companies had already established international business markets throughout the world and had an infrastructure in place that was well used to supporting international operations. The principle of expansion abroad had already been established with accountancy, thus enabling consultancy to follow a tried and tested path.

In terms of organisation the distinguishing feature of this whole period was the dispersed nature of international consultancy operations. Semi-autonomous operating units developed their own consultancy operations, including specialist service delivery, reporting to the parent in terms of performance and strategic direction. The services supplied overseas paralleled those in Britain, the major difference occurred in the industry sectors supported as overseas operations provided the opportunity of moving into different industry sectors and in the size and scale of some of the early projects. For example new industry sectors included the gold fields of Africa and in the oil industries of the Middle East, and size and scale was reflected in some of the major engineering projects overseas that the consultants were asked to support, many of which ran into billions of pounds in the 1950s and 1960s, unparalleled within Britain at that time.

With regard to importance, the international side of consultancy operations is emphasised by the growing revenue streams associated with overseas operations. Table 10.1 highlights the revenue gains of the member companies of the Management Consultancies Association for the period 1960-1990.

Table 10.1 Domestic and International Revenue, 1960-1990

Year	Domestic Revenue (£m)	Overseas Revenue (£m)	Overseas Revenue as a Percentage (%) of Total Revenue Earned
1960	4.9	1.1	18.3
1970	22.5	6.8	23.2
1980	43.9	17.9	28.9
1983	70.1	24.1	25.6
1985	142.2	26.3	15.6
1986	201.1	27.1	11.9
1987	265.0	29.4	10.0
1988	350.0	33.3	8.7
1989	576.7	76.2	11.7
1990	706.3	103.8	12.8

Source: Management Consultancies Association (1990)

In terms of revenue generation, each of the recorded years witnessed an increase in monetary terms. However, as a percentage of overall revenue, international revenue growth was not consistent and the early gains of the first twenty years were followed by a downturn and levelling off for the remainder of the 1980s. A simple explanation could be that the massive growth in the United Kingdom simply could not be matched by a similar growth in overseas revenue. However, some of it may have been due to the reorientation of services on the home front, reflected in the falling off of work in productivity techniques, with overseas assignments trailing behind the curve, playing catch-up.

Overall, the exportation of British management consultancy appears to have been subjected to a number of unique experiences:

- Initially, isolated opportunistic work was conducted employing British consultants on one-off assignments. Many of these were for British companies expanding their operations overseas, with a strong orientation towards operations in former colonial countries.
- As the volume of work increased within geographical areas, permanent offices and associate companies were formed, with strategic direction and control being maintained from the centre. Local consultants replaced travelling British personnel as an air of permanence prevailed in distinct geographical locations.
- Variety and scale expanded the consultant experience as new industries were supported and larger projects were conducted outside of the United Kingdom.
- Service delivery eventually matched that provided in the United Kingdom as semi-autonomous units paralleled the operations within the UK.

While all this was going on overseas a parallel movement occurred with overseas consultancies setting up operations in Britain as part of their international strategies. Initially, as it will be seen, these consultancies exploited opportunities in service delivery areas that were not fully exploited, for one reason or another, by the British firms.

Consultancy from Overseas

The opposite but parallel effect of the internationalisation of British consultancies was the impact of overseas consultancies entering Britain in pursuit of their own internationalisation strategies. This is exemplified through the arrival of consultants from McKinsey and Company in 1959 and the establishment of an office in London. Whilst McKinsey was not the first American consultancy to establish itself in Britain, it had a significant impact in terms of the internationalisation of management consultancy as it affected Britain. The Company started up on a relatively small scale in Britain with a handful of consultants that even in the late 1960s numbered only approximately eighty overall; small in comparison with the size of some of the established British firms (Tisdall 1982). There were three principal reasons why McKinsey's presence was immediately felt: the Company worked for high profile clients in the private and public domains, it attracted considerable publicity because of its high profile clients and it provided services involving strategic direction (see Chapter 8). Similar to its British counterparts when they expanded overseas, McKinsey used consultants from its home country until it fully established itself in Britain.[5] McKinsey was not alone and in the ensuing years a number of other consultancies also established a presence in Britain; among these were Arthur D. Little and Booz-Allen and Hamilton. Each of these were providing services in board room-type management from experience gained in the United States, whereas British consultancies had not had such a long history in providing these forms of services.[6] Therefore, initially American consultancies filled a requirement that was not being fully serviced by the British firms.

The Americans were not alone, consultancies from other countries settled in Britain during the post-war period, some of these consultancies are today members of the Management Consultancies Association. A parallel movement was also occurring as some of the major international accounting companies, many of whom had an Anglo-American history, having already established a presence worldwide, expanded their consultancy arms on an international footing. According to Kipping (1996) these firms from the late 1970s onwards partly established their presence through the development of services based on information technology, a growing aspect of management consultancy (see Chapter 9). As footholds were gained in Britain, the range of services provided by overseas consultancies began to expand to reflect those provided by the British domestic firms. At the same time the number of overseas consultancies increased through the passage of time, either through setting up a presence in Britain or through buying-out British firms.[7] Therefore, there was a merging of the type of services provided and this had the effect of partially masking the origins of individual firms. Nevertheless, what marked out the international phase of consultancy from the other phases was the general trend of the major overseas consultancies, in much the same way as the British firms, to organise themselves opportunistically, almost piecemeal, as semi-autonomous national groupings with strategy and direction largely coming from the centre.

All of this in terms of consultancy began to change with the advent of technologies that spanned national boundaries, the partial erosion of trading barriers across the world, the globalisation of business ventures and, amongst a host of other movements, the merging of tastes and product ranges on a more global scale.

The Global Phase

This is the current phase of consultancy operations and for the sake of identifying a point in time when this occurred, the last decade of the twentieth century has been identified as the appropriate starting point; although, no doubt, within individual consultancies an earlier date could be selected. The Global Phase, like the other two phases, is marked out by developments in the major consulting companies operating in Britain. It can in no way provide an explanation of all that is going on within management consultancy as the overall environment is far too complex and diverse to accommodate such a simplistic explanation of evolution.

Management consultancy is both a driver and follower of change. The globalisation of industries and markets have acted as a facilitator of change, made possible through improvements to network technologies (communications), converging tastes, common currencies, regional trading blocs and the freeing up of many barriers to trade. In response to these, management consultancies have organised themselves and developed services that support change as well as driving it. Consultants are at the forefront of change and facilitators of the change process overall. Whilst many commentators have argued that it may never be totally possible to have a true global economy, at least in the foreseeable future, that does not prevent consultancies from striving towards developing a global organisation that treats the world as a single market. There are a number of visible aspects of change that provide knowledge of this emerging global model of consultancy, these include strategy, the development of common services and growth, and at the heart of these is technology. Each will be examined in turn to provide an account of an emerging transnational global marketplace for consultancy services.

Strategy

Strategy, in this account, is concerned with organisation and direction, and the effects of these on the emerging global model of consultancy. It could be argued that many consultancies had the desire during the International Phase to position themselves and compete on a global scale.[8] What prevented this occurring was the way in which consultancies conducted semi-autonomous operations on a national scale within those countries where they had a presence and developed tactics to accommodate the national situation. Organisation and direction in terms of globalisation employs a different range of strategies that views the organisation as a whole, operating in terms of a team approach. The global organisation is controlled from the centre, employing a common approach throughout its empire. Some commentators have suggested that the first stage in this form of approach could be described as a 'satellite', or 'hub and spoke' system (Hall 1998). Once this particular methodology becomes too unwieldy, a further stage is the development of a global network. Whatever approach is employed by individual consultancies, many of them group their organisations in line with the major trading blocs, or geographical areas to exploit common approaches to trade.

Global strategies are not, however, just about hierarchy and control, they can also be to do with developing global partnerships, leveraging the strength of partners based on core competences, global positioning and economies of scale. By and large, global strategies are about developing common approaches and processes across the whole organisation, and adjusting those to more comfortably fit the location where consultants are operating. In other words, it is about a common theme supporting a culturally diverse global market. At the same time, whilst the organisation may wish to provide the impression that it is local in terms of the way it operates, at the centre it may give off a different signal. For example, PricewaterhouseCoopers web site is addressed www.pwcglobal.com, indicating both its position in the market and its common service base internationally. Likewise KPMG offers a range of services that it describes as 'global services', giving a similar impression to that of PwC; this aspect is covered in more detail under 'common services' following. Positioning in this way is partly in response to client businesses that organise themselves across national boundaries and partly to do with developing common services. Strategies of these kinds are enabled and supported through technologies that recognise no national boundaries in terms of communications and which can be positioned anywhere in the world to support specific client needs.

In order to support a global infrastructure consultancies make best use of information from external sources or their own internal research organisations. Again, many of these give the overt impression of supporting a global organisation. For example, the McKinsey Global Institute, founded in 1990, was set up to conduct research on themes that affect a global economy.[9] Many of the major international and global consultancies conduct or commission research in topics that affect the global economy, both for their clients and their own use, and in many instances wider public consumption. In parallel with a strategic approach to organisation, services have been developed that are underpinned by a common core. For the purpose of this history, these are described as common services and have been developed to span national boundaries. Again, at the heart of these, information technology plays a major role.

Common Services

As a general description, common services are those that are based on a generic approach for application anywhere in the world, possibly with subtle changes to their delivery and content to align them to take account of local cultural and economic factors. These services have been developed from experience gained in operating in a wide range of countries and across the whole range of industry and commerce, as well as serving governments and public institutions. Many global services have been developed in parallel with business practices, for example in the creation and support of supply chains across industries and continents, or through the employment of common technology such as Internet-based solutions. Consultancies that describe themselves as global organisations provide common global services; some firms offer specific global service types and others describe their whole range as being global.

Some forms of service, however, lend themselves to being global through their orientation within the business process. For example, in relation to global clients, services in strategy consulting would support the ambitions of international firms and supply chain management solutions position themselves wherever the chain is in operation. Other services, for example the development of international marketing solutions for clients that are globally positioned with products that are or would strive to be globally distributed, or financial services that are heavily dependent nowadays on Internet technology that can deployed anywhere to support an international customer base are typical examples of these. Each of the major consultancies provide services of this nature through either a global solutions group based on a single form of service or through its distributed network of country consultancies working from a common methodology. In some instances, hybrid configurations are applied that make use of centralised expertise in direct support of a distributed network of geographical offices.

Common services are about common solutions, employing the lessons learnt from a wide range of assignments throughout the world and through the employment of common technology. Individual consultancies have developed their own strategies based on their own experiences and aspirations, the theme that runs through each is their desire to reach out across borders and grow their businesses in what is increasingly becoming a global consultancy environment.

Growth

The final aspect of globalisation, growth, indicates the level to which consulting companies rely on revenue from overseas. In the British experience the revenue returns of the Management Consultancies Association provide an example of the volume of revenue generated from overseas work. Table 10.2 indicates the revenue streams of the member companies of the MCA for the period 1994 to 2000, which demonstrates that, as a percentage of the whole, overseas revenue for the whole period remains within a band with 15.1 per cent at one end to 26.2 at the other. However, an examination of year-on-year revenue growth presents a different picture, one that indicates dramatic fluctuations from one year to the next.

Table 10.2 Domestic and International Revenue, 1994-2000

Year	Domestic Revenue (£m)	Percentage (%) Change on Previous Year's Domestic Revenue	Overseas Revenue (£m)	Overseas Revenue as a Percentage (%) of Total Revenue Earned	Percentage (%) Change on Previous Year's Overseas Revenue
1994	852	–	158	15.6	–
1995	968	13.6	172	15.1	8.9
1996	1101	13.7	236	17.7	37.2
1997	1319	19.8	281	17.6	19.1
1998	1619	22.7	474	22.6	68.7
1999	1627	0.5	578	26.2	21.9
2000	2413	48.3	514	17.6	−11.1

* Less revenue earned through outsourcing.

Sources: Management Consultancies Association (1996, 1998 and 2000)

Domestic revenue, on the other hand, is more consistent in terms of growth. Therefore, the collective revenues of the MCA provide a fluctuating picture of growth of overseas revenue, with domestic income demonstrating greater stability.

Growth within individual companies provides a different picture again. Apart from individual firms opening new offices throughout the world, the leading global consultancies are generally reporting increases in global revenue. For example, PricewaterhouseCoopers have reported 14 per cent increase for the fiscal year 2000, Computer Sciences Corporation global commercial revenue increased by 12 per cent and Andersen reported increases across all its global areas (except Latin America where revenue remained static).[10] Apart from revenue growth, the leading global consultancies demonstrate their worldwide presence through the spread of their services throughout the world. An examination of each in turn would indicate a presence in most, if not all, the continents of the world, with individual consultancies having a significant presence in specific areas of the world.

Whilst globalisation may not be totally complete in terms of both business and consulting, the global model is strengthening with the major consultancies leading the way in breaking down barriers in all four corners of the world. The three aspects of globalisation examined in this historical account (strategy, common services and growth) would indicate that a global model of consultancy is one that the leading players are striving towards. There are barriers, including cultural and identity differences, but information technology, common products and increasingly liberal regimes in terms of trade are all facilitators for the globalisation of consultancy services.

Notes

1. There are five reports in the series: 'Book 1: The Development of the Internet and the Growth of e-Commerce', 'Book 2: Globalisation and the Knowledge Society – The New Drivers for Business and the Workforce', 'Book 3: Business, Government and the New Citizen', 'Book 4: Business and the Environment', and 'Book 5: Technology and the New Workforce'.
2. Whilst in terms of the Bedaux company it was always the intention that the British operation would be part of a wider international business, the events described in Chapters 3 and 4 witnessed the breakaway from the parent to the establishment of an autonomous British unit.
3. During these first few years after the Second World War Production Engineering found itself providing services to a range of diverse clients on a one-off basis throughout the world, typical of these was seaweed cultivation in the Falkland Islands.
4. The assignment attracted publicity for the Company which, in turn, led to further work. The international operation of the Company in the ensuing years spread to Malaysia, Fiji, the West Indies, Brazil and Cyprus. According to Withers (1994) earnings from its overseas work became more significant than that in the United Kingdom.
5. According to Kipping (1996), McKinsey used its British base to establish its presence in Europe and subsequently opened up offices in Dusseldorf and Paris (in 1964 and 1965 respectively).
6. Often reported within this history, the prevailing ethos that management was an inbred quality prevented the earlier development of high-level management services by the major British consultancies.
7. Typical of this form of strategy was that employed by A.T. Kearney when it bought out Harold Norcross and Partners in 1974 as a means of establishing its presence in Britain.

8. The International Phase in Britain started much later than in some other countries, for example in the United States a number of American consultancies internationalised their operations at the beginning of the twentieth century (see Chapters 2 and 3).
9. The outputs of the research projects are published in the McKinsey Quarterly and in hard copy, and reports are available for public consumption. The McKinsey Quarterly can be found at http://www.mckinseyquarterly.com.
10. PricewaterhouseCoopers Annual Report at http://www.pwcglobal.com, Computer Sciences Corporation 2001 Annual Report at http://www.csc.com and Andersen 2000 Annual Report at http://www.arthurandersen.com.

CHAPTER 11

A Summary and Review of Management Consultancy

The history of management consultancy in Britain has been a relatively long and complicated affair, situated in three centuries and through two world wars. During the course of that evolutionary process management consultancy has never stood still, factors outside of it and individuals within it have forced change on a massive scale over the 130 years or so of its history. The British experience has been unique as this history has demonstrated, although the consultancy environment of today would belie that statement as increasingly consulting services are being delivered within a global environment by a group of leading consultancies with a presence in every continent of the world.

This final chapter breaks the tradition in terms of structure of the remainder of this historical account and provides a condensed history of management consultancy in Britain. Its purpose is to provide a pocket history of management consulting, bringing the various threads together through an approach that divides the whole period into a series of time frames. These individual snapshots collectively make up the history and provide a general view of the evolution of British management consultancy. This is a supplement to and not a replacement for the remainder of this account, and provides an outline description of evolutionary trends of the British management consultancy as an executive summary to the main text.

Throughout the history of management consulting in Britain a number of strong themes have been identified as being important. These include the evolution of management thought and business practices, the prevailing ethos within businesses, government intervention and macroeconomic forces, more recently the development of computer-based information technology, and the parallel stream of management and business education and training for which the consultants have played an important role throughout their history. These themes are strongly represented throughout the text of this history although their importance may appear less prominent in a condensed account of this nature. They should not be forgotten, as in many instances they were both barriers and drivers of change.

1869-1900

In the period of the mid to late-nineteenth century the financial aspects of businesses had taken on a greater prominence in an environment when British industry found itself competing with other industrial nations for its share of world and domestic markets. Traditional forms of accountancy provided only a retrospective review of the business and as an operational function could not give accurate information of the present or help predict the future. Cost management techniques, more precisely cost recording, review and control, were employed within some firms at the time, but these tended to be in-house developed schemes. In the late-1860s there appeared in Britain a small group of individuals providing consultancy services in cost management. The earliest recorded instance of these involved a chartered accountant named Montague Whitmore who provided services in costing and management accounting that would have provided his clients with timely financial information and other information on the deployment and usage of all forms of resources within the production process.

Whitmore was a full-time consultant, but other accountants also provided financial services outside of accountancy, many making best use of the quiet periods within their own profession. Typical of these was Edwin Waterhouse, a founder of the firm of Price Waterhouse. The prevailing ethos within businesses at that time, and for many years in the future, was that management was an inbred quality and not an activity that could be taught. Therefore, the offer of outside assistance would have been refused, except where improvements could be made to operational processes. This may explain why the early management consultants were accountants by profession as they would have been the exception to this unwritten rule, being already accepted as outside agents. It would also explain why services provided by this ,handful of early management consultants were concerned with the financial aspects of business.

In the last few years of the century another consulting pioneer, Alexander Hamilton Church, an engineer by background, also provided services in costing, linking these to production planning and control. Church became a prolific writer, although most of his work in this area occurred following his emigration to the United States in 1905. Importantly, he developed the concept of production centres and the machine hour rate as a method of apportioning costs within the production environment. Therefore, whilst Church's services were linking the production process with financial application, this early phase of consultancy was dominated by a small handful of pioneers that developed services in relation to the financial aspects of manufacturing.

1900-1925

The turn of the century did not immediately bring with it any significant change to the way in which consulting was carried out. One early consultant, Percy Martin, through an emphasis on the relationship between manufacturing planning, and estimating and costing, developed an early form of standard costing. By this time a pattern had begun to emerge in that an important activity of the consultants was the publication and public notification of their ideas. This was achieved through articles written by them appearing in the technical press, the presentation of papers at professional venues and the publication of books.

This period was also marked by the appearance of a number of engineers that had developed their own form of services in production management, more precisely production efficiency. One engineer during this period, H.W. Allingham, is credited with having provided assistance in implementing the only serious application of scientific management in Britain at the firm of Hans Renold during the period 1911-1914. One important contribution during the First World War was a book written by E.T. Elbourne, 'Factory Administration and Accounts', who later became a consultant. The importance of the book related to both its content and wide distribution. The content provided in-depth information on works management, organisation and methods, and wide-ranging circulation occurred because of the encouragement given by senior officials in the Ministry of Munitions. The Ministry was being supplied at the time by a large number of contracting firms employing varying, but generally inefficient production methods and the book was viewed as a means of improving and standardising these.

During the War and beyond, the work of Herbert Newton Casson, not a consultant but a publisher, writer and purveyor of advice in production methods raised the profile of efficiency through his various activities. His work was no doubt an important source of information for the practising consultants of the day. In the years after the War, two other areas of consultancy were developed by individual consultants broadening the range of services on offer to potential clients. These areas were salesmanship, sales promotion and publicity, exemplified through the work of Wallace Attwood, and the use of financial and operational information in the management decision-making process, pioneered by T.G. Rose. The latter form of service was initially developed for medium-sized manufacturing enterprises, although the consulting companies formed in Britain during the 1920s and 1930s later copied his ideas.

One final aspect of this period was the arrival in Britain of management consultants from the United States in 1923 to carry out an extension of an assignment for an American multinational. The work of these consultants from Charles E. Bedaux and Company did, as it later turned out, partially inspire the founder of the Company to set up a permanent operation on British soil. Throughout this whole period, however, it is highly unlikely that at any one time more than 20 freelance consultants were operational in Britain, and then only in the latter years.

1926-1933

The mid-1920s was a significant turning point in the history of management consulting in Britain, irreversibly signalling the end of a service that was provided solely by a group of freelance practitioners. Charles E. Bedaux and Company set up offices in London and brought with it a standard approach to production efficiency and personnel reward payments. This standard approach, with some modifications in terminology and application, became the benchmark for consulting services in production efficiency for the next half century in Britain, changing only with the application of information technology in the 1980s and beyond. At the heart of the system lay eight principles of application and the development of consultant and client personnel training. It was, regardless of its appearance as a systematic and objective approach, controversial in application and outcome, which resulted in changes to practices within individual firms, industrial action across a broad front and the subject of many debates. It also inspired others to do better through the creation of other consulting companies led by former Bedaux consultants in direct competition with their ex-employer. For all that, Bedaux raised the profile of consultancy through its notoriety.

At the same time that Bedaux was raising the profile of consultancy the Company also drove it underground when forceful reactions to its application forced individual consultants to adopt clandestine techniques to hide their association with the Company. In parallel with Bedaux's arrival and slightly later in terms of time (1929), a wholly-owned British consultancy was formed, Harold Whitehead and Staff, to deliver services in salesmanship (specifically training), sales management and marketing in contravention to the general direction of consultancy at that time. The founder, Harold Whitehead, although of British antecedence and birth had considerable experience as a business academic and freelance consultant in the United States in the period prior to his return to Britain. Knowledge of his work followed him back to this country and an approach by the Chairman of the British Commercial Gas Association persuaded Whitehead to set up a consultancy business. At the turn of the decade, another American company laid down roots in Britain. Stevenson, Jordan and Harrison provided services in labour and production cost planning, principally within the textile industries, but never grew to any significant size or importance.

The latter 1920s and early 1930s was a period in Britain when management consultancy was largely confined to the shop floor, or in the operational aspects of sales and marketing. Some freelance consultants were providing other forms of service, but these were largely piecemeal and ad hoc. The Bedaux company widened its portfolio of services to include factory and workshop layout, and workflow management, while at the same time maintaining its approach to operator training and personnel development. Whitehead's salesmanship training service was expanding and the production of case studies and tutorial notes became his modus operandi. Diversifications in service orientation occurred in the first couple of years of the 1930s with the Company conducting a market research assignment within the retail trades. This is the first identified instance of contract staff being employed by a consultancy for a specific task. The other diversification resulted from an approach by Pitman Publishing for Harold Whitehead and Staff to develop a correspondence course in salesmanship.

The period was further marked through developments in consultant training within the Bedaux company. Previously new recruits to the Company were given on-the-job training in the company of an experienced consultant. This was obviously subjective and the content was totally dependent upon the type of assignments being conducted at that time. In 1930 the Company issued a training manual for the first time in Britain and consultant training followed a more structured approach. There was a series of phases to the training requiring the trainee to gain experience in specific skills, and each phase was concluded by an examination to prove the fitness of the individual continuing with both his training and consultancy career within the Company.

1934-1939

1934 was another watershed year for management consultancy because it heralded the formation of two new consultancies in direct response to the negatives associated with the Bedaux service. Those companies, Production Engineering Limited and Urwick, Orr and Partners Limited, were both partly founded by disillusioned ex-Bedaux consultants, aiming to provide a better and more comprehensive service than their ex-employer. The Bedaux company was forced to change its name in 1936 to British Bedaux Limited and was floated on the Stock Exchange to distance itself from its American origins and weaken the hold on the British arm by its founder whose personal activities were beginning to embarrass the management of the British operation.

The period of 1934-1939 was one in which management consultancy's portfolio of services widened to break away from its concentration on work-study and payment reward services for the production-centred consultancies and the introduction of the notion of professional services. In terms of the development of professional services, this was a positive step forward to eradicate the negatives associated with the industrial action that had been sparked off by Bedaux in the late-1920s and early-1930s. In support of this movement, and parallel to it, the new consultancies formed in 1934 actively sought the full co-operation of the unions and organised labour as part of the consultancy process.

In terms of service delivery, a whole range of new services was added to the corporate portfolio by the mid-1930s. Within production, factory and workshop layout, workflow management, and standard costing as a tool for monitoring variations were all new additions. In parallel with these, specifically within Urwick Orr, clerical management, accounting, administration and organisation broadened the portfolio even further. All of these were developed for delivery within operational areas of firms in keeping with the prevailing ethos within businesses that did not encourage external involvement in the high-level management functions. Nevertheless, consultancy had established itself as a service that produced significant improvements to operational performance through definitive measurable results.

In the last few years of the decade, apart from a further broadening of services in general, two evolutionary movements set in train patterns within consultancy that would continue well after the conclusion of the Second World War. The first of these was the adoption of a common service package between the major consultancies as Whitehead moved into production and others, notably Urwick Orr, moved into marketing and sales. The second movement was concerned with the embryonic beginnings of strategy services as a distinct new area of involvement, albeit not known by that name at the time. These services were the Urwick Orr 'Management Audit' and the Whitehead 'Higher Control' service, both based on pioneering work carried out previously by T.G. Rose.

By the end of this period, four firms and an unknown number of sole practitioners dominated management consultancy. In terms of consultant numbers, there were probably about 150 active consultants operating in Britain in 1939. One further change occurred in 1938, again relating to a name change for the Bedaux company, when British Bedaux Limited became Associated Industrial Consultants. This was in response to Charles Bedaux's open association with fascist leaders and organisations in Continental Europe at a time when there were worsening relations with Germany. As war approached, the attention of management consultancies turned towards those firms engaged in production in support of the Armed Services and the majority of work in other areas fell away.

1939-1945

The immediacy of war brought with it uncertainty in terms of the future of management consultancy in Britain, specifically the future of many of the individual consultants. That uncertainty ended when management consulting was declared a 'Reserved Occupation' and when a number of consultants that were on the reserve lists of the three services were called up for active duty. Initially the main thrust of consultancy services was converting firms from peacetime to wartime production, and initiating programmes of training for operatives replacing the experienced labour force that had been called up into the three services.

During the six years of war, management consultants from each of the major consultancies found themselves involved in activities in many new areas of consultancy that were developed expeditiously within the prevailing circumstances. There were two main thrusts throughout the whole period that brought consultants into contact with a diverse range of clients. The first of these, direct war supply production, witnessed consultants for the first time working at an industry level and having a direct impact on output across a range of firms. Also with regard to production, in 1943 another consulting company was formed by a disaffected Bedaux employee, Personnel Administration, initially to provide services in relation to operator training using a new method developed by one of the founders of this company. That method, Process Analysis Method of Training, or PAMT, was put to good effect during the latter wartime years and in the period of resettlement at the conclusion of hostilities.

The second main thrust of consultant involvement during the war years was the assistance provided to Government Departments. Whilst the Whitehead company had worked with Government Departments in the pre-war period, the period of the Second World War witnessed involvement on a broad scale unprecedented up to that point in time. Each of the main companies provided services in this area, unfortunately because of the nature of a lot of the work much of it went unnoticed at that time.

Internally within consultancy, a significant feature of the period was the development of centralised consultancy training away from the workplace. A three-week course in work-study and base rate analysis was developed by a consultant from Urwick Orr who decided to set up on his own in the second year of the War (1941). Whilst the scale and appointment of the training venue was insignificant when compared with today's standards, at the time this was an important step forward for consultancy training because it set the principle of training in the basic skills away from the work environment. At the end of the War management consultants found themselves reversing some of the changes made by them in the early stages through providing services in enabling firms to revert to peacetime production. Many of those firms changed back to producing the goods and services for which they were established prior to the War.

1945-1960

The main thrust of Government in terms of the economy in the post-war period was reconstruction. A number of Government initiatives in the next twenty or so years were directed at improving productivity, unsurprisingly therefore management consultants continued to provide services on an increasing scale towards that orientation with recognised effect. Whilst productivity services were the mainstay of consultancy work during this period, a number of other aspects were also important. Firstly, British consultancy became increasingly dominated by four major firms: Associated Industrial Consultants (AIC), Production Engineering (PE), Urwick Orr (UOP) and Personnel Administration (PA), collectively becoming known as the 'Big Four'. A number of smaller firms were created during the period and Whitehead maintained its important position as a middle order firm.

Throughout this period a number of main strands to the business of management consulting began to appear as definitive aspects of service delivery: marketing and sales, human resource management, financial services, strategy, and production. Each aspect contained individual services that for the first time could comfortably be fitted into either strategy or operations. The period also witnessed the embryonic beginnings of services in information technology, although feasibility studies and computer bureau services were the mainstays during this period. Significantly, the late-1940s and 1950s was the period when the major consulting companies opened up their own management training schools for consultants and client personnel alike. Initially courses were developed that had an orientation towards operational techniques and functions, but through the process of time, general management subjects and specialisms began to take on importance within the curricula of the schools. At that time, the consultant input into business and management training was an important contribution overall when compared with all else that was occurring. In 1956 the Management Consultants Associations (later renamed Consultancies) was formed as the trade body for the industry, initially with four members.

Increasingly throughout the whole of this period a wider movement within consultancy was the internationalisation of services as the major British domestic firms expanded their services overseas. Some assignments were one-off and opportunistic using travelling British consultants, but increasingly local offices were established as the hub for geographical operations, with semi-autonomous firms created that came under the control of the centre. In parallel with this movement overseas, and in the opposite direction, the period was also marked out by the migration of overseas consultancies into Britain. This movement is exemplified by the operations of McKinsey and Company that set up offices in London in 1959 to provide services at the higher management level. Whilst the McKinsey operation was relatively small-scale at first, it was perceived as a threat by the British firms largely because of the publicity it attracted and its high profile clients.

1960-1970

In the first couple of years of the 1960s an important research project carried out by Professor J. Johnston identified the value of management consulting services in terms of improvements to productivity in those firms where assignments had been carried out. Whilst the Johnston study attracted very little publicity outside of consultancy, it indicated that if sufficient consultants were employed within Britain then, there would be a significant improvement in productivity levels within the economy overall. Johnston looked to the future and suggested that the long-term value of consultants would, however, not be found in services that produced short-term gains but in other areas, notably services that may produce immeasurable results but had a positive long-term impact in those firms where they were applied.

Among other aspects of consultancy, Johnston was probably identifying the benefit to firms of the strategy services that were beginning to feature as an area of consultancy service. This form of service was exemplified at the time by the work of McKinsey and Company that delivered services in relation to company re-organisations that resulted in a multi-divisional structure. High profile clients such as the Post Office, the BBC, Royal Dutch Shell and British Rail produced publicity at the time for the work of management consultants. The major British firms were also developing their own boardroom type services in competition with their American rivals and these are exemplified by the newly created MbO service of Urwick Orr. Whilst MbO was initially an operational service, its principles permitted the strategic orientation of their application through utilising the business drivers to effect a coherent and positive thrust to business activity within the firm.

The end of the 1950s and the 1960s witnessed the broadening of IT services within management consultancy. A number of the major British consultancies created specialised divisions or entered into partnerships with leading firms in the field; in effect this period heralded the appearance of specialist consultants who are today referred to as IT consultants. These consultants combined the skills of business consultancy with specialised knowledge. A number of new spin-offs to the service included software development, specialist training and recruiting services, although technology audits, feasibility studies and computer bureau services were still strongly represented within the corporate portfolio.

The dominance of the four major consultancies in Britain, the 'Big Four', was challenged during the latter half of this period when in 1966 the consultancy arms of a group of accounting companies joined the MCA. This signalled the death knell of the position of the traditional consultancies at the top of the industry, although it was not until the next decade that the challenge was fully effective. Also during this decade the Institute of Management Consultants was formed as a body in 1962 to represent individual consultants in response to a weakness in the professional structure of the industry that until then had only been represented by a trade body for the major consulting firms.

1970-1980

The 1970s got off to a bad start when two waves of external pressure forced management consultancies to review their organisations and rationalise their consultant strengths. The first wave came from a world recession and the introduction of industrial relations legislation by the then Conservative Government that had the effect of removing wage controls, which resulted in a series of industrial disputes. The negative impact on company profits brought about by stagnant industrial output and a rising wage bill forced companies to reappraise their investment opportunities. The expected increase in demand for consultancy services of between 15 and 20 per cent did not materialise, instead a fall of 10 per cent in demand was echoed by a 25 per cent reduction in overall consultant strength in Britain. At the end of 1973 before management consultancy had fully recovered from its earlier setback, the war in the Middle East resulted in the price of oil quadrupling on the world market and this brought with it the second wave of pressure. Once again management consultancy felt the effects of macroeconomic forces through erosion in demand for their services that was reflected in a further 25 per cent reduction in corporate British consultant numbers.

These macroeconomic effects brought home to management consultancy the knowledge of its vulnerability to wider influences, a phenomenon never before experienced by consultants in Britain. In terms of the corporate structure of consultancy, these external factors had a further effect when the numbers of sole practitioners and small partnerships rose as a direct consequence of some of the redundant consultants and industrial managers setting up on their own account. The organisation of Britain's consultancy industry had irreversibly changed to reflect a structure that was made up of a number of large consultancies, some developed from the offshoots of accountancy firms and specialist IT companies, some from the established British domestic firms, and others that had originated overseas. Underpinning all of these was a growing number of smaller firms, partnerships and sole practitioners.

Recovery following the downturn in consultancy services in the first few years of the decade was initially slow, but the corporate portfolio continued to broaden as new services were added through the policies of individual firms and the arrival of new entrants into management consultancy. By the end of the decade, the corporate portfolio could be clearly partitioned into two broad service areas, operations and strategy. Noticeable, however, was the reduction in the number of assignments conducted using efficiency techniques based on work-study and an increase in production services that covered aspects of the business at an organisational level. Within information technology there was the appearance of embryonic services in the areas of computer aided engineering, consisting of Computer Aided Design (CAD) and Computer Aided Manufacturing (CAM), and the application of robotic technology within manufacturing. Overall corporate recovery continued throughout the latter years of the 1970s and by the turn of the decade expansion had once again put management consultancy on a positive footing to enter into the 1980s.

1980-1990

By 1980 there were seven major service areas associated with the corporate delivery of management consultancy services: 'Organisation Development and Policy Formulation', 'Marketing, Sales and Distribution', 'Production Management', 'Finance and Administration', 'Personnel Management and Selection', 'Economic and Environmental Studies', and 'Management Information Systems and Electronic Data Processing' (EDP). This range of services had been established slowly over the preceding 35 years in the majority of cases, with services in production management and finance having a longer antecedence.

The 1980s were also marked by the implementation of consultancy services across the world in support of Japanese inspired management practices that involved the use of flexible production systems that were underpinned by quality processes. Within Britain total quality management (TQM) and flexible manufacturing processes, for example just-in-time systems, inventory control and lean production methodologies, were typical of these. Some of these systems were greeted with enthusiasm by trade unionists because they had the benefit of opening up lines of communication between the employer and the employed. By the mid-1980s the concept of the value chain was being adopted as an effective method of improving output across client organisations, this concept later leading into the supply chain that became a phenomenon of the 1990s. The value chain was means through which companies could examine the disparate activities of the organisation with a view to identifying those elements that could provide competitive advantage. It was a strategic tool that brought together a distinctive chain of activities within a firm that represented its key processes.

This was a period in which services in information technology became the driving force for growth within management consulting, heralding the beginning of that point in time when it would become difficult to separate out IT from consultancy and consultancy from IT. In other areas of consultancy growth was the norm rather than the exception, but none of these areas could match information technology as the leading growth area. Finally, the end of the 1980s was marked by developments in network technologies, Local Area and Wide Area Networks (LANs and WANs). These technologies acted as the stimulus for moving away from main frame computers to distributed systems, based on servers, which provided the capability of sharing information and processes across linked communities. It was also in the latter part of this period that the global communications system that came to be known as the World Wide Web was developed, and this heralded the commencement of services that used Internet technologies as the drivers for change.

1990-2001

Two main features, the development of e-business services and the globalisation of management consultancy, mark this final period in the history of management consultancy in Britain. In parallel with these developments, other features of the period include the introduction of Business Process Reengineering (BPR), the development of strategic partnerships and the outsourcing of services.

Services in Business Process Reengineering first commenced in Britain under that title in the early part of the decade, although changes to business processes has been a hallmark of consultancy services from the early days. Because of the radical nature of the change demanded through initiating full-blown BRP, often process simplification or process improvement lay at the heart of service delivery. BPR remains an important activity within the corporate portfolio through to the present day. The development of strategic partnerships between consulting companies, and between consulting companies and other service providers was again not a new phenomenon. In the 1990s it became increasingly important as a strategic action because of the complexities involved in the delivery of consulting services in an environment where information technology plays a leading role. Strategic partnerships are a means of leveraging the advantages gained through association with dominant partners in specific delivery areas. This has meant that consulting assignments have become broader and more complex. Linked to this notion of leveraging advantage, outsourcing arrangements through providing support services directly or arranging strategic partnerships for clients with other firms have provided a significant revenue stream for many consultancies in Britain. However, the main features of this final period are those of e-business services and the globalisation of management consultancy.

The development of the World Wide Web and Internet technologies underpinned many of the developments concerned with the spread of IT and facilitated the arrival of e-business solutions in all its guises, embracing each and every aspect of management consultancy today. Because of the dynamics of the situation, management consulting services were continually expanding in a bid to gain best value for clients. Out of this environment was spawned the concept of supply chain management, a method of facilitating wide ranging improvements to the production process across a range of geographical and business sectors, and a host of other electronic services that provide joined up solutions, for example B2B (business-to-business) and B2C (business-to-customer).

In parallel with these developments in technology, and as a driver in the process of change, management consultancy has re-positioned itself to become a global service industry amongst the major players. This phase of consultancy, preceded by the domestic and international phases, is concerned with the global orientation of specific services or operations more generally. Globalisation is associated with the blurring of international boundaries and the partial loss of identity of the country of origin of individual consultancies. Within the business environment generally, management consultancy has become both a driver and follower of change. The globalisation of industries and markets has acted as a facilitator of change, made possible through improvements to network technologies (communications), converging tastes, common currencies, regional trading blocs and the freeing up of many barriers to trade. In response to this management consultancies have organised themselves and developed services that support change as well as driving it, and this is the structure of consultancy in 2001.

Bibliography

Part A: Published Sources

Babbage. C. (1832), *On the Economy of Machinery and Manufacturers*, Charles Knight, London.

Barnett. C. (1986), *The Audit of War: The Illusion & Reality of Britain as a Great Nation*, Macmillan, London.

Bedaux. C.E. (1917), *Industrial Management: The Bedaux Efficiency Course for Industrial Application*, The Bedaux Industrial Institute, Cleveland, Ohio.

Bentley. T.J. (1984), *The Management Services Handbook*, Holt, Rinehart and Winston, London.

Boakes. N. (1999), 'What is a Management Consultant?', in Institute of Management Consultants, *The Inside Careers Guide to Management Consultants 2000*, Cambridge Market Intelligence Limited, London.

Brech. E.F.L. (1953), *The Principles and Practice of Management*, Longman Group Limited, London.

Brech. E.F.L. (2002), *The Evolution of Modern Management*, Thoemmes Press, Bristol:
Volume One (2002a), *Profession in Management and the Gestation of Britain's Central Institute in that Area, Covering 1902-1976*.
Volume Two (2002b), *Productivity in Perspective, 1914-1974*.
Volume Three (2002c), *Evolution in Clerical, Office and Administrative Management, 1891-1974*.
Volume Four (2002d), *A Century of Management-related Literature, 1832-1939*.
Volume Five (2002e), *Education, Training and Development for and in Management in Britain, 1852-1979*.

British Institute of Management (1975), *Yearbook of Management Education 1975-76*, Gower, Aldershot.

Broadberry. S.N. (1997), *The Productivity Race: British Manufacturing in International Perspective, 1850-1990*, Cambridge University Press, Cambridge.

Brown. G. (1977), *Sabotage: A Study in Industrial Conflict*, Bertram Russell Peace Foundation for Spokesman Books, Nottingham.

Campbell-Kelly. M. and Aspray. W. (1996), *Computer: A History of the Information Machine*, BasicBooks, New York.

Channon. D.F. (1973), *The Strategy and Structure of British Enterprise*, The Macmillan Press, London.

Chatfield. M. (1977), *A History of Accounting Thought*, Robert E. Krieger Publishing Company, New York.

Cheadle. N. (1995), 'The History and Growth of the Profession', in Institute of Management Consultants, *Management Consultants 1996*, Cambridge Market Intelligence Limited, London.

Child. J. (1969), *British Management Thought: A Critical Analysis*, George Allen and Unwin Limited, London.

Christy. J. (1984), *The Price of Power: A Biography of Charles Eugene Bedaux*, Doubleday Canada Limited, Toronto.

Church. A.H. (1910), *Production Factors*, The Engineering Magazine Company, New York.

Church. A.H. (1914), *The Science and Practice of Management*, The Engineering Magazine Company, New York.

Curr. J. (1970), *Coal Viewer and Engine Builder's Practical Companion*, Frank Cass and Company Limited, London.

Drucker. P. (1989), *The Practice of Management*, paperback edition, Heinemann Professional Publishing Limited, Oxford.

Elbourne. E.T. (1914), *Factory Administration and Accounts*, Longmans and Company, London.

Feinstein. C.H. (1976), *Statistical Tables of National Income, Expenditure and Output of the U.K. 1855-1965*, Cambridge University Press, Cambridge.

Garcke. E. and Fells. J.M. (1887), *Factory Accounts: Their Principles and Practice*, Crosby Lockwood and Son, London.

Habgood. W. (1994), *Chartered Accountants in England and Wales: A Guide to Historical Records*, Manchester University Press, Manchester.

Hall. J. (1998) 'Consulting Internationally', in P. Sadler (ed) *Management Consultancy: A Handbook of Best Practice*, Kogan Page Limited, London.

Halton. J. (1985), 'The Anatomy of Computing', in T. Forester, *The Information Technology Revolution*, Basil Blackwell Limited, Oxford.

Hammer. M. and Champy. J. (1993), *Reengineering the Corporation*, Nicholas Brealey, London.

Handy. C. (1988), 'Great Britain', in Handy. C., Gordon. C., Gow. I. and Randlesome. C. *Making Managers*, Pitman Publishing, London.

Handy. C., Gordon. C., Gow. I. and Randlesome. C. (1988), *Making Managers*, Pitman Publishing, London.

Hannah. L. (1976), *The Rise of the Corporate Economy*, London, Methuen and Company, London.

Hardwick. C.M. (undated), *Time Study in Treason: Charles E. Bedaux Patriot or Collaborator*, Peter Horsnell, Chelmsford.

Harold Whitehead and Staff (1932a), *Report on a National Survey of Retail Selling Practices*, Harold Whitehead and Staff, London.

Harold Whitehead and Staff (1932b), *A Course of Training in Retail Salesmanship*, Harold Whitehead and Staff, London:

Volume I, *Selling from the Customer's Point of View*.

Volume II, *Guiding the Selection*.

Volume III, *Convincing the Customer of Value*.

Volume IV, *Making the Most of Your Goods*.

Volume V, *Overcoming Difficulties*.

Volume VI, *Creative Selling*.

Harold Whitehead and Staff (1932c), *A Course in Telephone Salesmanship*, Harold Whitehead and Staff, London.

Harold Whitehead and Staff (1944), *Post-War Planning and Anglo American Economic Relations: A Report on Practice and Opinion in British Industry 1944*, Shaw and Sons limited, London.

Hiscox. W.J. (1921), *Factory Administration in Practice: Organization and Administration from the Factory Standpoint*, Sir Isaac Pitman and Sons, London.

Hiscox. W.J. (1923), *Workshop Routine*, Sir Isaac Pitman and Sons, London.

Hiscox. W.J. (1924), *Factory Layout, Planning and Progress*, Sir Isaac Pitman and Sons, London.

Hiscox. W.J. (1926), *Engineering Factory Supplies: The Purchase, Receipt, Storage and Distribution of Factory Materials*, Sir Isaac Pitman and Sons, London.

Holmes. A.R. and Green. E. (1986), *Midland: 150 Years of Banking Business*, Batsford, London.

Horn. C.A. (1983), *Essays in the Development of Modern Management*, Beacon Publications, Oxford.

Huntswood Associates (1999), *The Directory of Management Consultants in the UK, 1999-2000*, Management Information Publishing Limited, London.

Hutton. G. (1953), *We Too Can Prosper: The Promise of Productivity*, George Allen and Unwin, London.

Hyman. S. (1970), *Associations and Consultants: External Aid to Management*, George Allen and Unwin, London.

Imai. M. (1986) *Kaizen: The Key to Japan's Competitive Success*, McGraw-Hill Publishing Company, New York.

Institute of Management Consultancy (1996), *Consulting 1996/7: The Official Yearbook of the Institute of Management Consultants*, A.P. Information Services, London.

Jeremy. D.J. (1998), *A Business History of Britain, 1900-1990's*, Oxford University Press, Oxford.

Jones. E. (1988), *The Memoirs of Edwin Waterhouse: A Founder of Price Waterhouse*, B.T. Batsford Limited, London.

Jones. E. (1995), *True and Fair: A History of Price Waterhouse*, Hamish Hamilton, London.

Keeble. S.P. (1992), *The Ability to Manage: A Study of British Management, 1890-1990*, Manchester University Press, Manchester.

Kettle. R. (1957), *Deloitte & Co. 1845-1956*, Oxford University Press, Oxford.

Kreis. S. (1992), 'The Diffusion of Scientific Management: The Bedaux Company in America and Britain, 1926-1945', in Nelson. D. *A Mental Revolution: Scientific Management Since Taylor*, Ohio State University Press, Columbus, Ohio.

Kubr. M. (1977), *Management Consulting: A Guide to the Profession*, International Labour Office, Geneva.

Latham. F.W. and Sanders. G.S. (1980), *Urwick Orr on Management*, William Heinemann Limited, London.

Lewis. J.S. (1896), *Commercial Organisation of Factories*, E. and F.N. Spon, London.

Littler. C.R. (1982), *The Development of the Labour Process in Capitalist Societies: A Comparative Study of the Transformation of Work Organization in Britain, Japan and the USA*, Heinemann Educational Books Limited, London.

Long. K. (1998), 'The Impact of IT on Consultancy Practice', in Sadler. P. (ed), *Management Consultancy: A Handbook of Best Practice*, Kogan Page Limited, London.

Lytle. C.W. (1929), *Wage Incentive Methods*, Ronald Press, London.

Management Charter Initiative (1991), *Management Standards Implementation Pack*, Management Charter Initiative, London.

Management Consultancy Information Service (1983), *Directory of Management Consultants in the UK 1983-84*, Alan Armstrong and Associates Limited, London.

McKillop. M. and McKillop. A.D. (1917), *Efficiency Methods: An Introduction to Scientific Management*, George Routledge and Sons, London.

Millerson. G. (1964), *The Qualifying Associations: A Study in Professionalization*, Routledge and Kegan Paul, London.

More. C. (1989), *The Industrial Age: The Economy and Society in Britain 1750-1985*, Longman, London.

Mosson. T.M. (1965), *Management Education in Five European Countries*, Business Publications Limited, London.

Mulligan. J. and Barber. P. (1998), 'The Client-Consultant Relationship', in Sadler. P. (ed) *Management Consultancy: A Handbook for Best Practice*, Kogan Page Limited, London.

Obolensky. N. (1998a), 'Implementation', in Sadler. P. (ed), *Management Consultancy: A Handbook for Best Practice*, Kogan Page Limited, London.

Obolensky. N. (1998b), 'Strategy Formulation Models', in Sadler. P. (ed), *Management Consultancy: A Handbook of Best Practice*, Kogan Page Limited, London.

PE (1984), *Fifty Years of Professional Enterprise: The Story of P-E*, S. Straker and Sons Limited, London.

272 THE RISE OF MANAGEMENT CONSULTING IN BRITAIN

Pollard. S. (1965), *The Genesis of Modern Management: A Study of the Industrial Revolution in Great Britain*, Edward Arnold (Publishers) Limited, London.

Porter. M. (1985), *Competitive Advantage: Creating and Sustaining Superior Performance*, The Free Press, New York.

Preen. H. (1907), *Reorganisation and Costings*, Simpkin, Marshall and Company, London.

Preen. H. (1908), *Falling Sales, Yet Increased Profits*, Simpkin Marshall and Company, London.

Rassam. C. (1998), 'The Management Consultancy Industry', in Sadler. P. (ed) *Management Consultancy: A Handbook of Best Practice*, Kogan Page Limited, London.

Roll. E. (1930), *An Early Experiment in Industrial Organisation: Being a History of the Firm of Boulton & Watt, 1775-1805*, Longmans and Company, London.

Rose. T.G. (1930), *Business Charts*, Sir Isaac Pitman and Sons, London.

Rose. T.G. (1932), *The Management Audit*, Gee and Company, London.

Rose. T.G. (1934), *Higher Control*, Sir Isaac Pitman and Sons, London.

Rose. T.G. (1954), *A History of the Institute of Industrial Administration 1919-1951*, The Institute of Industrial Administration, London.

Sadler. P. (1998) 'Consultancy in a Changing World' in Sadler. P. (ed) *Management Consultancy: A Handbook of Best Practice*, Kogan Page Limited, London.

Seymour. W.D. (1968), *Skills Analysis Training: A Handbook for Managers, Supervisors and Instructors*, Sir Isaac Pitman and Sons Limited, London.

Shaw. A. (1952), *The Purpose and Practice of Motion Study*, Harlequin Press, Manchester.

Sheldon. O. (1924), *The Philosophy of Management*, Sir Isaac Pitman and Sons, London.

Simmons. J.R.M. (1962), *LEO and the Managers*, Macdonald and Company (Publishers) Limited, London.

Smith. D. and Pickworth. P.C.N. (1914), *Engineers' Costs and Economical Workshop Production*, London.

Smith. F. (1878), *Workshop Management: A Manual for Masters and Men*, London.

Smith. R.J. (1972), *The Register of Management Consults and Advisory Service to Industry*, Gower Press Limited, Epping.

Stannard. J.W. (1911), *Factory Organisation and Management*, Harmsworth Business Library.

Storrs. C. (1954), *General and Industrial Management*, Sir Isaac Pitman and Sons Limited, London.

Tatham. L. (1964), *The Efficiency Experts: An Impartial Survey of Management Consulting*, Business Publications Limited. London.

Tisdall. P. (1982), *Agents of Change: The Development and Practice of Management Consultancy*, Heinemann, London.

Townsend. R. (1970), *Up the Organization: How to Stop the Corporation Stifling People and Strangling Profits*, Michael Joseph Limited, London.

Urwick. L. (1928), *Organising a Sales Office*, Gollancz, London.

Urwick. L. (1929), *The Meaning of Rationalisation*, Nisbet and Company Limited, London.
Urwick. L. (1933), *Management of Tomorrow*, Nisbet and Company Limited, London.
Urwick. L. (1956), *The Golden Book of Management: A Historical Record of the Life and Work of Seventy Pioneers*, Newman Neame, London
Urwick. L. and Brech. E.F.L. (1946), *The Making of Scientific Management*, Management Publications Trust Limited, London:
Volume I (1946a), *Thirteen Pioneers*.
Volume II (1946b), *Management in British Industry*.
Volume III (1946c), *The Hawthorne Investigations*.
Urwick, Orr and Partners Limited (1957), 'L. Urwick: A Bibliography', The Sheneval Press Limited, London.
Vangermeersch. R. (1988), *Alexander Hamilton Church: A Man of Ideas for All Seasons*, Garland Publishing, New York.
Whitehead. H. (1918a), *The Business Career of Peter Flint*, Page Company, Boston, Massachusetts.
Whitehead. H. (1918b), *Dawson Black: Retail Merchant*, Page Company, Boston, Massachusetts.
Whitehead. H. (1922), *How to Run a Shop*, G.G. Harrop and Company, London.
Whitehead. H. (1923), *The Business of Selling*, American Book Company, New York.
Whitehead. H. (1932), *B.C.G.A Course in Domestic Gas Salesmanship*, Harold Whitehead, London, in six volumes.
Whitehead. H. (1937), *The Administration of Marketing and Selling*, Sir Isaac Pitman and Sons, London.
Willsmore. A.W. (1932), *Business Budgets and Budgetary Control*, Pitman, London.
Wilson. J.F. (1992) *The Manchester Experiment: A History of Manchester Business School 1965-1990*, Paul Chapman Publishing Limited, London.
Wilson. J.F. (1995), *British Business History, 1720-1994*, Manchester University Press, Manchester.
Wise. T.A. (1982), *Peat, Marwick, Mitchell & Co.: 85 Years*, Peat, Marwick, Mitchell and Company.
Wren. D.A. (1994), *The Evolution of Management Thought*, John Wiley and Sons Incorporated, New York.

Part B: Journal, Magazine and Newspaper Articles

Bostock. F. and Jones. G. (1994), 'Foreign Multinationals in British Manufacturing, 1850-1962', *Business History*, Vol 36, Part 1.
Bowman. P. (1983), 'Geographical Expansion', *Password*, 40th Anniversary Issue of the house journal of PA.

Bridgman. P. (1994), 'UD's Role in UOP's Practice', in *Keeping In Touch*, 60th Anniversary Edition, Journal of the UOP Keeping in Touch Association, No 58.

Butterworth. J.F. (1920), 'Motion Study in Offices', *Engineering and Industrial Management*, 12 February.

Church. A.H. (1900), 'The Meaning of Commercial Organization', *The Engineering Magazine*, Vol 20.

Church. A.H. (1901), 'The Proper Distribution of Establishment Charges', *The Engineering Magazine*, Vols 21 and 22, a series of six articles.

Coopey. R. (1999), 'Management and the Introduction of Computing in British Industry, 1945-1970', *Contemporary British History*, Vol 13, No 3.

Downs. L.L. (1990), 'Industrial Decline, Rationalization and Equal Pay: The Bedaux Strike at Rover Automobile Company', *Social History*, Vol 15, No 1.

Egolf. J.R. (1985), 'The Limits of Shop Floor Struggle: Workers Vs. The Bedaux System at Willapa Harbor Lumber Mills 1933-35', *Labor History*, Vol 26, Part 2.

Ferguson. M. (2001), 'Models of Management Education and Training: The Consultancy Approach', *The Journal of Industrial History*, Vol 4, No 1.

Flanner. J. (1945a), 'Annals of Collaboration: Equivalism I', *New Yorker*, 22 September.

Flanner. J. (1945b), 'Annals of Collaboration: Equivalism II', *New Yorker*, 6 October.

Flanner. J. (1945c), 'Annals of Collaboration: Equivalism III', *New Yorker*, 13 October.

Hunt. H. (1983), 'Computers and Telecommunications: PACTEL's Progress', *Password*, 40th Anniversary Issue of the house journal of PA.

Jelinek. M. (1980), 'Towards Systematic Management: Alexander Hamilton Church', *Business History Review*. Vol 54, Spring.

Johnston. J. (1963), 'The Productivity of Management Consultants', *Journal of the Royal Statistical Society*, Vol 126, Part 2.

Kipping. M. (1996) 'The U.S. Influence on the Evolution of Management Consultancies in Britain, France, and Germany Since 1945', *Business and Economic History*, Vol 25, No 1.

Kipping. M. (1997), 'Consultancies, Institutions and the Diffusion of Taylorism in Britain, Germany and France, 1920s to 1950s', *Business History*, Vol 39, No 4.

Lawson. F.M. (1920), 'The Influence of Exposed Records on Output', *Engineering and Industrial Management*, 11 November.

Litterer. J.A. (1961), 'Alexander Hamilton Church and the Development of Modern Management', *Business History Review*, Vol 35, Winter.

Mathews. D. (1998), 'The Business Doctors: Accountants in British Management from the Nineteenth Century to the Present Day', *Business History*, Vol 40, No 3.

McKenna. C.D. (1995), 'The Origins of Modern Management Consulting', *Business and Economic History*, Vol 24, No 1.

Northcott. C.H. (1932), 'The Bedaux System: A Critical Appraisal', *Unity* (the house journal of the National Industrial Alliance), May.

Sanders. G. (1994), 'The Urwick Management Centre', *Keeping In Touch*, 60th Anniversary Edition, Journal of the UOP Keeping in Touch Association, No 58.

Sellie. C.N. (1982), 'Group and Individual Incentive Plans: A Comparison of their Benefits, Drawbacks', *Industrial Engineering*, November.

Standring. P.K. (1934), 'The Bedaux System', *Industry Illustrated* (the house journal of the British Works Management Association, British Industrial Purchasing Officer's Association and the Office Management Association), May/June issue.

Thompson. W. (1994), 'Urwick, Orr & Partners Limited – Canada', in *Keeping In Touch*, 60th Anniversary Edition, Journal of the UOP Keeping in Touch Association, No 58.

Wardley. P. (1999), 'The Emergence of Big Business: The Largest Corporate Employers of Labour in the United Kingdom, Germany and the United States c.1907', *Business History*, Vol. 41, No 4.

Wardley. P. (2000) 'The Commercial Banking Industry and its Part in the Emergence and Consolidation of the Corporate Economy in Britain before 1940', *The Journal of Industrial History*, Vol 3, No 2.

Wheatley. M. (2001) 'E-Manufacturing Techniques Ensure that the Production Line Rolls On and On and On and On ...', *Management Consultancy*, March.

Wise. T.A. (1960), 'The Auditors Have Arrived', *Fortune*, November.

Withers. R.A. (1994), 'Urwick Orr & Partners' First Overseas Assignment', in *Keeping In Touch*, 60th Anniversary Edition, Journal of the UOP Keeping in Touch Association, No 58.

Part C: Consultancy Sources

Associated Industrial Consultants (1963), *Labour Cost Control and Incentive Schemes*, Associated Industrial Consultants, London.

Blackstone. S.E. (1980), *Notes Set Down by S.E. Blackstone to Mark the 25th Anniversary of the Foundation of Production Engineering Ltd., on 21st April 1934*, internal P-E historical account of the Company's history.

Blandford. O. (1947), *Typical Results Achieved in Small Companies*, paper read to the 4th Annual Staff Meeting, PA Consulting Group, London, 3 May.

Bocock. C.W. (1968), *History*, INBUCON internal historical paper, 10 June.

Carney. C.J. (undated), *A History of Charles E. Bedaux Company Ltd., Period 1926-1936*, internal unpublished INBUCON historical account on the early period of the Company's history.

Charles. E. Bedaux Limited (1934), *Training Course for Field Engineers*, Charles. E. Bedaux Limited, London.

Chanter. A.J. (1945), *Talks on the P.A. Method of Training*, paper read at the second annual reunion of Personnel Administration, 4 May.

Cullen. R.C. and Buttery. M.H.C. (undated), *Marketing Aid: Management By Objectives*, Urwick, Orr and Partners Limited information document.

Dowson. A. (1969), *Changes in the Competition*, annual conference paper, Urwick, Orr and Partners Limited, London, 12 April.

FEACO (1984), *A Study of the Management Consulting Profession 1960-84*, Federation Europeenne des Associations de Conseil en Organisation conference papers, Helsinki, 14-15 June.

FEACO (1999), *Survey of the European Management Consultancy Market*, Federation Europeenne des Associations de Conseil en Organisation, Brussels.

Fogg. A. (1980), *PA's Early History*, internal unpublished PA Consulting Group historical account of the Company's history.

Harold Whitehead and Staff (undated), *Harold Whitehead and Staff: Business Consultants*, services information brochure.

Harold Whitehead and Partners (1947), *Management Consultancy*, Company information booklet.

Harold Whitehead and Partners (1968), *Annual Report*, London.

Howell. B.J. (undated), *Notes in contribution to 'Fifty Years of Professional Enterprise: The Story of P-E'*, internal unpublished P-E historical account of the Company's history.

INBUCON (undated), *Consultancy Services*, service information brochure, circa late 1970s/early 1980s.

INBUCON (c1986), *Corporate Strategy and Business Development*, service information brochure.

Lamond. A.W.H. (1948), *An Outline of the Standard Costing Technique*, paper read at the 5th Annual Reunion of Personnel Administration, 1 May.

Management Consultants Association (1978), *Statistical Information for 1978*, internal Management Consultants Association report, London.

Management Consultants Association (1980), *Directory of Member Firms and their Services to Clients*, Management Consultants Association, London.

Management Consultancies Association (1990), *President's Statement and Annual Report*, Management Consultancies Association, London.

Management Consultancies Association (1995), *Directory of Member Firms and their Services to Clients 1995/96*, Management Consultancies Association, London.

Management Consultancies Association (1996), *President's Statement and Annual Report*, Management Consultancies Association, London.

Management Consultancies Association (1998), *President's Statement and Annual Report*, Management Consultancies Association, London.

Management Consultancies Association (1999a), *President's Statement and Annual Report*, Management Consultancies Association, London.

Management Consultancies Association (1999b), *Book 2: Globalisation and the Knowledge Society – The New Drivers for the Business and the Workforce*, Management Consultancies Association, London.

Management Consultancies Association (2000), *President's Statement and Annual Report*, Management Consultancies Association, London.

Mead. F.R. (1926), *Engineers Reports: British Goodrich Rubber Company Ltd.*, a series produced for both the client and the British Bedaux Company archives.

PA (undated), *P.A. (Process Analysis) Method of Training: Summary for the Managing Director*, information leaflet.

PE (undated), *Consulting Services Offered by the Production-Engineering Group*, services information brochure.

PE (1953), *Production-Engineering Ltd*, internal report on the distribution of the Company, including services, locations and industries.

P-E Inbucon (1988), *A Major New Force in Consulting*, services information brochure.

Pleming. N. (1927), *Engineers Reports: J. Lyons and Company Ltd.*, a series produced for both the client and the British Bedaux Company archives.

Pleming. N. (1968), *Charles E. Bedaux Ltd*, internal unpublished INBUCON historical account on the early period of the Company's history.

Price Waterhouse (1967), *Partners' Newsletter No 6*, 10 November.

Raymond. J. (1981), *The Early Days of Production Engineering Ltd.: As Seen Through the Eyes of its First Non-Director Employee*, internal unpublished P-E historical account on the early period of the Company's history.

Thompson. R.S. (1961), *Proposals for the Formation of a Marketing Research Unit*, internal Urwick, Orr and Partners Limited report.

Urwick, Orr and Partners Limited (undated), *Urwick Management Centre: Induction Notes for New Staff*, new staff induction note.

Urwick, Orr and Partners Limited (1935), *Minutes of the First Annual Conference of the Operating Staff of the Company*, London, 11 May.

Urwick, Orr and Partners Limited (1936), *Minutes of Staff Conference of the Company*, London, 16 May.

Urwick, Orr and Partners Limited (1951), *Consulting Specialists in Organisation and Management*, services information brochure.

Urwick, Orr and Partners Limited (1962), *Development Manual*, London.

Urwick, Orr and Partners Limited (1978), *A Brief History of Urwick Orr & Partners Limited*, new staff induction note number UG/I2/6.

Urwick, Orr and Partners Limited (1984a), *Urwick Group Assignments Using Management By Objectives*, internal report of the Reports Section of Urwick Orr Management Intelligence Services.

Urwick, Orr and Partners Limited (1984b), *Urwick Dynamics Limited: A Profile*, services information brochure.

Urwick, Orr and Partners Limited (c1985), *Urwick Orr and Technology*, services information booklet.

Wayne. F. (1959), *The History of P.E.: Notes Set Down by Francis Wayne to Mark the 25th Anniversary of the Foundation of Production Engineering Ltd., on 21st April 1934*, internal P-E historical account of the Company's history.

Wilson. A.D. (1968), *History of INBUCON*, internal INBUCON historical account of the Company's history.

Part D: Unpublished Sources

Brownlow. M. (1972), *A History of Inbucon*, unpublished historical account of the British Bedaux company.

Ferguson. M. (1996a), *Charles Eugene Bedaux, 1886-1944: The Man Whom Time Forgot*, Open University occasional paper.

Ferguson. M. (1996b), *Management by Objectives: A Case Study*, Open University occasional paper.

Ferguson. M. (1999), *The Origin, Gestation and Evolution of Management Consultancy within Britain: The Principles, Practices and Techniques of a New Professional Grouping*, unpublished PhD thesis, School of Management, Open University Business School.

Kreis. S. (1987), *Toward the Discovery of a Science of Labor: The Bedaux System and British Scientific Management, 1923-1945*, University of Missouri-Columbia occasional paper.

Part E: Official Publications

Committee on Industrial Productivity (1949), *First Report on the Committee on Industrial Productivity*, HMSO, London.

National Economic Development Office (1967), *The Making of Managers*, HMSO, London.

Part F: Other Sources

Cotton Board (1948), *Report on Labour Redeployment in the Musgrave Mill Cardroom Bolton*, internal Cotton Board report, March.

Cotton Spinners and Manufacturers Association (1949), *Official Handbook of the Agreed Conditions of Introduction, Rates of Payment and Methods of Calculation for the C.M.C. Wage Weaving System*, Cotton Spinners and Manufacturers Association, Manchester, 13 December.

Faraday. J.E. (1961) *The Story of Work Study in Imperial Chemical Industries*, internal ICI historical account of the spread of work-study and training.

Federation of British Industries (1961), *Stocktaking on Management Education*, conference papers, 27 April, London.

Rowe. D.M. (1959), *Biographical account of the life and work of Lyndall Fownes Urwick*, typewritten note held in the Urwick Archives at the Henley Management Centre.

Trades Union Congress (1932), *The T.U.C. Examines the Bedaux System of Payment by Results*, internal TUC report to the findings of an inquiry into Bedaux methods.

Tress. R.C. (1961), *The University Approach to Management Development*, in Federation of British Industries, *Stocktaking in Management Education*, conference papers, 27 April.

Urwick. L. (1961a), *The Part Played By The Management Consultant*, in Federation of British Industries (1961), *Stocktaking on Management Education*, conference papers, 27 April.

Urwick. L. (1961b), *Analysis of American Experience in Education for Management*, background paper at the Federation of British Industries, *Stocktaking on Management Education*, conference papers, 27 April.

Index

For Product Safety Concerns and Information please contact our EU
representative GPSR@taylorandfrancis.com
Taylor & Francis Verlag GmbH, Kaufingerstraße 24, 80331 München, Germany

www.ingramcontent.com/pod-product-compliance
Ingram Content Group UK Ltd.
Pitfield, Milton Keynes, MK11 3LW, UK
UKHW021013180425
457613UK00020B/923